ABOUT THE EDITOR

Bill Fawcett is the author and editor of more than a dozen books, including *You Did What?*, *It Seemed Like a Good Idea . . .* , *How to Lose a Battle*, and *You Said What?* He is also the author and editor of three historical mystery series and two oral histories of the U.S. Navy SEALs. He lives in Illinois.

How to Lose the Civil War

How to Lose

~ the ~

Civil War

Edited by

Bill Fawcett

HARPER

NEW YORK • LONDON • TORONTO • SYDNEY

HARPER

HarperCollins books may be purchased for educational, business, or sales promotional use. For information please write: Special Markets Department, Harper-Collins Publishers, 10 East 53rd Street, New York, NY 10022.

FIRST EDITION

Designed by Rosa Chae

Library of Congress Cataloging-in-Publication Data is available upon request.

ISBN 978-0-06-180727-5

11 12 13 14 15   OV/RRD   10 9 8 7 6 5 4 3 2 1

In memory of Brian Thomsen, scholar and editor.

contents

No Rebels in D.C.

1861: The Confederacy's Failure to Capture the Union Capital

—

John Helfers

One of the main goals of both sides in the Civil War (actually, it's a main goal in just about any war throughout history) was to capture the enemy's capital. This was particularly acute for the South. General Robert E. Lee knew that the shortages the Confederacy faced in men and equipment, especially versus the massive population and manufacturing advantages of the Union, could be nullified if he could just take Washington, D.C. This would also have the added benefit of contracting the overall war. However, since Lincoln and his cabinet also realized this, they were prepared to take whatever measures necessary to ensure that it didn't happen.

Once the blinders came off after the First Battle of Bull Run (where the Union forces were soundly defeated) in 1861, and the Union realized it was in for a protracted fight, attention was given to the practically defenseless city of Washington, D.C. Under the command of General George B. McClellan and General John Gross Barnard, the chief engineer of the Army of the Potomac, the next eighteen months were devoted to building an incredible chain of forts and earthworks around the city. By the end of the year, nine miles of defensive perimeter encircled Washington, studded with 480 artillery pieces, including everything from twenty-four- and thirty-two-pound howitzers, twenty-four-pound siege guns, Parrott guns (a combination cast- and wrought-iron muzzle-loading cannon prone to breakage), and lighter-caliber artillery mounted on field carriages.

By the end of 1862, Washington was a heavily armed and protected fortress city. Fifty-three forts and twenty-two artillery batteries ringed the city proper, from the Potomac to the shoreline opposite Alexandria, Virginia. Barnard didn't leave the Virginia side empty, but constructed more forts there as well.

And still Barnard and his engineers built more. By spring of 1864, Washington was pretty much impregnable. Its defenses consisted of an interconnected string of sixty-eight forts over thirty-seven miles, along with almost one hundred artillery batteries and blockhouses (a small, single-building fort), all connected by a twenty-mile network of rifle pits and trenches. Built to contain an estimated 23,000 men, the Union's only real problem was keeping the formidable line of defenses manned, particularly toward the end of the war. Regardless of troop level, if the traditional ratio of four attackers for every defender held true, then the Confederacy would have needed to send an army of at least 60,000 to 100,000 men against the city to have a hope of conquering it. Lee could barely field the lowest number of troops, and he never approached six figures, coming the closest in 1862 with 72,500 men at Fredericksburg.

But what about earlier in the war, when the Union capital wasn't so well fortified? One theory claims that Brigadier-General P.G.T. Beauregard should have followed up his victory against the Union at the First Battle of Bull Run and pursued the Union soldiers to Washington. This would have been an ill-advised decision from the start; no matter how gallant it sounds, the truth is that the pursuit of a defeated foe by the victorious one is the stuff of legends. Any victorious army in the nineteenth century had to rest its soldiers, resupply, and tend to its own wounded after a battle, and was never in any shape to chase after a retreating enemy. Officers killed or wounded in battle meant that units were left leaderless, and a pursuit requires a lot of organization of the remaining forces. General Joseph E. Johnston did try to cut off retreating Union troops on his right flank, but the effort ended in failure, with Brigadier Generals Milledge L. Bonham and James Longstreet arguing with each other about how best to proceed, as their brigades were supposed to be pursuing the enemy together. In the confusion, the Federal soldiers slipped away.

And even if Beauregard had been able to bring men up to pursue, they would have run into General Irvin McDowell's three reserve brigades, which would have been ready for any assault the tired Confederates could have mustered. And even if they had somehow managed to defeat those men, they next would have come up against Washington, D.C., itself, manned by the 17,000 soldiers who had just left the field, now behind what was even then daunting defensive fortifications. Simply put, the chances of the Confederacy seizing Washington after Bull Run were nil.

The other great what-if that is always examined is whether Lee could have taken Washington if his forces had been victorious at Gettysburg. Even barring the reasons stated above regarding casualties and exhaustion (Gettysburg was three days of long, hard fighting, and the 28,000 casualties the 75,000-man Confederate Army took ensured that it couldn't keep going), Lee could not have resumed his invasion no matter how the battle turned out—because on July 4, 1863, it rained. Not just a summer shower or cloudburst, but what became a days-long downpour that would have mired the Army of Virginia in knee-deep mud, bogged down artillery, and killed men and horses. Even if Lee had decisively crushed General George Gordon Meade in battle, there simply would have been no way he could have continued north.

There was one more try made for the city before the war would end. In 1864, Lee sent Lieutenant General Jubal Early north with 10,000 men to stop General David Hunter, who was running amok in northern Virginia. Upon hearing that Early was looking for him, Hunter retreated into West Virginia, leaving the path to the capital wide open. Early pushed across the Potomac into Maryland in early July, advancing to the suburb of Silver Spring before meeting any real resistance.

The commander of Washington's defenses, Major General Christopher C. Augur, lacked both men and artillery—most of which had been called up to the front lines—and could only muster 9,600 men, most of which were Veteran Reserve Corps or Ohio militia who had never seen combat. Added to this was the District militia as well as detachments of government clerks, most of whom had barely touched a rifle.

On July 11, both sides met in skirmishes that were observed by President Lincoln himself. Early tested the defenses while weighing the risks of trying to penetrate the perimeter. The chance to bloody the Union's nose and revive the morale of the South versus failing to do so, or even worse, getting cut off by Hunter's army, had great appeal. Taking the Union capital might just have given the Confederacy its quick victory. Unfortunately, Early deliberated too long. Grant had ordered troops sent north several days earlier, and by the 11th, VI Corps, led by General Horatio G. Wright, had disembarked to reinforce the Washington line. After testing the opposition once again (and finding it considerably more firm this time), Early ordered a withdrawal, saying to his aide, "Major, we haven't taken Washington, but we've scared Abe Lincoln like hell." This wasn't quite the case, as the president was so engrossed in watching the battle from Fort Stevens that the commanding officer had to invoke his authority as a front-line officer and order Lincoln off the observation parapet.

Early's strike into Maryland would be the last chance the Confederacy had to raise the Stars and Bars over the Union capitol. Even if he had succeeded, it would have been more of a propaganda exercise than a true victory, as even if Early had managed to take the city, he wouldn't have had the men to hold it for long. Whatever effect it may have had might have lasted long enough to force the North to the negotiating table, but even that is doubtful. With Sherman about to take Atlanta and Grant still pursuing Lee in the east, the Union, still on top in terms of men and equipment, most likely would have continued its war of attrition.

In the end, the idea of the Confederacy conquering the Union capital was never to be. Even when they were close enough to see it, the Rebels never had enough men or equipment to wage the overwhelming battle necessary to take the city, and not only take it, but hold it for any length of time afterward. Lee could never muster enough men to accomplish this goal without being whittled away by the Union, and by the time General Early's men were at the outskirts of the city, it was already too late. By 1864, the fate of the Confederacy was just about sealed, leaving the what-ifs about the southern conquest of the nation's capital to be just another cherished dream.

King Cotton's Tarnished Crown

1861: The Confederate States

Frieda A. Murray

"What would happen if no cotton was furnished for three years? . . . England would topple headlong and carry the whole civilized world with her. No, you dare not make war on cotton! No power on earth dares make war upon it. Cotton is King." From Senator James Henry Hammond of South Carolina's speech before the United States Senate, March 4, 1858.

The South Carolinian's bombast had some ballast under it. By the end of the 1850s cotton from the southern states accounted for 57 percent of American exports, 20 percent of the raw material for American textiles, and 70 percent of the raw material of the British textile industry. Also, the international textile industry had contributed to the creation of many financial institutions on both sides of the Atlantic.

Cotton also boosted northern wealth in other ways. It was shipped overseas in Yankee or British bottoms, mostly from northern ports. Northern, especially New York, banks provided loans for land and slaves, and northern factors provided credit, insurance, and shipping for the planters. The finished goods returned for raw cotton were manufactured in the North or overseas, not in the cotton-growing areas.

The 1850s were boom years for cotton. Its price doubled from the beginning to the end of the decade, and the land devoted to cotton, sugar, and tobacco increased to the point that food production in this agricultural region actually declined. Southern planters were convinced that these times would never end.

The panic of 1857 added to their confidence. It started when the New York branch of the Ohio Life Insurance and Trust Company, a major financial institution, collapsed due to massive embezzlement. Shortly after this, the following mangled public confidence:

- British investors decided to remove funds from American banks, raising questions about their overall soundness.
- Grain prices fell.
- Manufactured goods piled up in warehouses, leading to massive layoffs.
- Overbuilding led to widespread railroad failures.
- Land speculation programs collapsed with the railroads, ruining thousands of investors.

(Sound familiar?)

While the North and West were still dealing with the effects of this depression as late as 1861, the South was not hit nearly as hard. Grain prices fell, but cotton prices rose. In the 1840s, some southerners had worried about their region's dependence on outsiders for banking, transport, and manufacturing. By 1858 a planter from Alabama was proclaiming, "That the North does our trading and manufacturing mostly is true, and we are willing that they should. Ours is an agricultural people, and God grant that we may continue so."

The Confederate cabinet was composed of men who firmly believed in the power of cotton. Withholding it was their only plan to secure foreign recognition and assistance. When the navy blockaded the southern ports, Richmond called it a "paper blockade" and fully expected the British navy to appear and disperse it. They were shocked when Whitehall agreed to respect it.

To avoid the appearance of provocation, Richmond did not formally embargo the shipping of cotton. But many planters voluntarily kept the 1861 crop off the market, even those with some way of shipping it.

And thereby they played right into Federal hands. The late 1850s had produced bumper cotton crops. The planters had sent so much abroad before hostilities started that the British mills had close to a year's supply on hand, at a time when the market for textiles was getting a bit glutted. Some mill owners, and certainly the Liverpool speculators, saw the war as a breathing space, a chance to pare down their excess. The British even had enough to send some back across the Atlantic to the New England mills.

Of course, in the spring of 1861, a lot of people on all sides thought the war would be short, even if they were hedging about the outcome. By the spring of 1862, the cotton famine predicted by the Confederacy had indeed emerged. Seventy-five percent of the Lancashire mill workers were out of work or on reduced hours. This caused a great deal of concern in Whitehall, which was augmented by McClellan's antics in Virginia's peninsula. Should any, or all, of the European powers intervene and get the cotton shipments restarted? Parliament debated through the end of the session, and the cabinet continued the debate, reconsidering every time word came across the ocean, through the better part of 1862.

But by then the blockade and the capture of New Orleans were definitely keeping cotton on this side of the Atlantic. You can't call a blockade ineffective if goods don't move.

Liverpool, which was pro-Confederate, played both sides. The speculators cleaned up on the high prices they got for stored cotton, and the Confederate commerce raiders came from Liverpool shipyards.

Another factor: western European harvests were poor in the early 1860s. Governments importing grain and meat from the North were not inclined to bite the hand that was feeding them. Moreover, the North imported a fair amount of war matériel at the beginning of the conflict—and paid for it. You don't trade a customer who pays in cash for one that pays in futures.

Besides, in spite of the tariffs that some Lost Causeniks claim to this day were the true reason for the war, Britain exported a great deal to the United States, and there were a lot more customers in the North than in the South. The Richmond cabinet did not consider that Great Britain valued the Union as a customer and sometime ally, and did not wish, at the outset, to meddle in what they considered to be an internal squabble. And France would not aid the Confederacy, except as a backup to Britain.

In the end, the British developed other sources of cotton: Brazil, Egypt, and India. Since the southern infrastructure was a long time rebuilding, and the land was not only war-wrecked but worn-out from overplanting, this worked out well for the international textile industry. Even today India is the second-largest cotton producer in the world (China is the largest), and Egyptian cotton is the finest on this planet.

Also, during the war, the British wool and linen industries prospered.

Still, the Richmond cabinet correctly predicted that the loss of southern cotton would severely cripple the European textile industry. What went wrong?

First off, Whitehall was concerned about more than the textile industry. Britain had just finished fighting two wars, and needed to rebuild its army after the Crimea and restructure India as an imperial colony. They did not want to intervene in a nasty but presumably short squabble at the end of a long supply line.

As the war continued, so did talk of European mediation. But every time it started to get serious (especially in the summer of 1862, but also in the fall of 1863 and the summer of 1864) the North came up with just enough advantage that it stayed talk.

Also, while it had not been seriously tested, Whitehall preferred the Monroe Doctrine to stand. One of the last things they wanted to do was give the appearance of abrogating it themselves, or actually fighting the Union. Among other things, the nascent Canadian union could have been seriously destabilized, even to the point of civil war.

Then there was slavery. Make that SLAVERY. How much sympathy existed for the slaves themselves is a good question. Prior to the hostilities, noted author Charles Grenville wrote, "Any war will be almost sure to interfere with the cotton crops, and . . . this is what we care about. With all our virulent abuse of slavery and slave-owners, and our continual self-laudation on that subject, we are just as anxious for, and just as interested in, the prosperity of the slavery interests . . . as the Carolinian and Georgian planters themselves." But it was a point of British pride, in the Lancashire mills as well as in Whitehall, to condemn the institution. Nor would the French government support it, not openly, anyway.

One thing that the Richmond cabinet would not have considered in 1861, and may not even have known, was that Britain and France had an arms race going, building ironclads. As the British government had no desire to find a new model ironclad hovering off any of their ports, they were still less inclined to send their warships to break the blockade. Napoleon III was the sort you had to keep your eye on.

Reliance on King Cotton backfired in yet another way. Most of those classified as planters concentrated on cash rather than food crops. The small farmers grew food, but seldom more than was needed for their families. With the planters reluctant to convert to food crops, the small farmers in the army, the blockade, and the poor harvest of 1862, there were serious food shortages in the South by 1863. Confederate President Jefferson Davis tried to get the planters to grow more food, and many of them did, but too little, too late, and by harvest in 1863 the Federal army was interfering with the transport system as well.

And even during the fighting, cotton paid for itself—if you could sell it. A flourishing trade in cotton for gold or salt or shoes grew up, especially after Nashville, New Orleans, and Memphis fell into Union hands. Such trade was supposed to be regulated, but smugglers are smugglers. Still, while this trade filled the pockets of many unscrupulous individuals, it was no real help to the Confederacy.

Much of this is hindsight, of course. But was the risk of depending on King Cotton for victory well calculated?

There is as much consensus as can be found on anything connected with the American Civil War that the Union superiority in men, matériel, and transport facilities was a major contributor to its victory. This was especially true starting in 1863. Had the war ended in 1862 this superiority, which developed as the war continued, would not have made the difference that it did. So the Confederacy was depending on a short war and a negotiated peace.

In that case, Europe's lack of southern cotton would have been an inconvenience, not the predicted disaster. So withholding the cotton in the expectation of a short war looked like blackmail, not diplomacy.

There also appears to have been a blindness to any other factors that might have influenced the European powers. The Confederate cabinet could not have foreseen the poor harvests that made northern food an eagerly sought commodity, but they might have considered that it could take more than a threatened embargo to move war-weary European countries to intervene in what was expected to be a short conflict. This comes back to the expectation that the fighting wouldn't last long. But the major reason it wasn't expected to last long was the threat of European intervention. So it seems there was circular thinking there.

The South was not prepared for a long war. Neither was the North, at first, but they were better able to gear up.

It has been speculated that if the Confederacy had been able to ship the 1861 crop overseas and store it, it could have been used to purchase supplies in 1862 and later. But that countered the point of withholding it in the first place, required planning for a long conflict, and would have left the British less inclined to break the blockade since the cotton would be on their side of the Atlantic.

The Confederate cabinet did not expect the British to call their bluff. When Whitehall did, they had no alternate plans except military victory, which was not impossible.

It is not wise to go to war with a single strategy and expect everything to go according to plan. The Confederacy did, and ended up at Appomattox.

We Don't Need No Stinkin' Feds!

1861: The Slave States

—

Paul A. Thomsen

In 1861, the southern states took a bold step in declaring their independence from the United States. Like their American Revolutionary War ancestors, they were independent-minded, rooted in an agrarian tradition of slave economics, and distrusting of the often heavy-handed policies of higher authorities. They wanted supreme state sovereignty, weak presidents, and the continued endurance of slavery as a southern institution. Fearing for their safety, eleven southern states formed a new nation, called the Confederate States of America (CSA). By modifying the United States Constitution to their new southern designs, these new Rebels also hoped to protect and coordinate their potential prosperity without jeopardizing the member states' level of individuality. Yet in drafting their breakaway constitution, the southerners made a tragic mistake. By attempting to preserve state sovereignty at all costs, the CSA limited their leadership's ability to fight the Civil War effectively.

The failed CSA government had deep roots. Throughout the early republican era, several southerners felt the executive branch was too large and too powerful. When industrialization took hold and cities arose in the North, many more feared the loss of the southern slave power's grip on the House of Representatives. Moreover, well into the nineteenth century, southerner leaders such as John C. Calhoun frequently complained about the abusive taxes on southern exports, the political challenges to slavery, and alleged northern corruptive influences in Federal governance. In the 1830s, Jacksonian-era discussions over tariffs had rapidly devolved into posturing, name calling, charges of tyranny, and threats. In the late 1840s, the situation became still more heated in the antislavery/proslavery debates over the acquisition of vast territories won in the Mexican War and the modernizing of the West. Year after year, the South, however, saw few northerners willing to provide a redress of their grievances.

By the presidential election of 1860, most southerners had concluded that separation remained the only viable alternative to stagnation and the apparent impending delegitimization of their livelihood, their culture, and their representation in Federal governance. Following the tradition of their American Revolutionary War forefathers, the southern states moved to legitimize their new independence through the assembling of state conventions to vote on secession. In 1860, South Carolina, long considered the most radical southern state, was the first state to hold a convention and secede. Next, the states of the Deep South (Georgia, Florida, Louisiana, Alabama, and Mississippi) followed suit. Finally, in mid-1861, the remaining five less solidly slave states (Texas, Virginia, Arkansas, North Carolina, and Tennessee) joined their brethren. With fears of attack from the North and a desire for mutually beneficial ties, in February 1861 the seceded southern states finally agreed to a loose confederated alliance called the Confederate States of America.

In March 1861, the new Confederate States of America created a permanent constitutional structure and expanded governance. Under their new constitution, each state was considered to be "acting in its sovereign and independent character." The states, therefore, held the supreme authority over southern Federal action. The constitution also specifically allowed cabinet members to hold seats in the Confederate Congress simultaneously. In theory, these cabinet members in congress were supposed to assist the president in influencing and being influenced by the legislative tide. Likewise, to offset the powers delegated to congress, the new constitution stipulated that the president, elected to office by congress for a single term of six years, was granted the ability to edit approved bills by line-item veto. As a check against potential abuses from both branches, the framers also followed the U.S. constitutional tradition of a judiciary and incorporated the Bill of Rights into the main body of the new social contract. Finally, the Confederate founders cemented slavery both as an immutable component of the economy and as a factor in calculating populace and congressional representation.

For the southerners, the Confederate constitution seemed like a good idea at the time, but their powerful desire to maintain an independent statist posture created a fundamental conflict between theory and the practical ability of a wartime government. In fact, most of the Confederacy's problems originated in three major areas: the practical application of state supremacy in congress, the consequentially limited purview of presidential power, and the corresponding political quagmire of defense policies.

First, in attempting to apply the lessons of the recent past to their present situation, the southern founders created the Confederate Congress to ensure the supremacy and voting equality of each southern state. But their focus on the state discouraged member states from engaging in the life blood of politics: compromise. In fact, by law, congressmen were not allowed to promote businesses for fear of being considered corrupt and impeached. Instead, constitutional law encouraged individual congressmen to restrict their deal making solely to the precise wishes of their constituents. Moreover, as a collective body, a clear two-thirds majority was needed to pass congressional legislation. Consequently, in 1862, the Confederate Congress actively resisted the prospect of taxation and state-based tariffs regardless of wartime need and were forbidden to compromise or engage in deal making to resolve the situation. As a result, Confederate congressmen were forced either to beg their constituents for "gifts" of money and war supplies or to print reams of currency to keep the South in business at the cost of a devalued currency.

Second, the president of the Confederacy, Jefferson Davis, was likewise caught between the proverbial rock and hard place. While the primary duty of the presidency was to execute congressionally sanctioned laws, the inability of congress to meet war needs compelled Davis to court a fine constitutional line in the service of the Confederacy. At times, he played diplomat to the southern states in the hope that his rebel presidential prestige might coax some southern support for the war effort. On other occasions, Jefferson Davis was forced to abandon all hope of influencing congress with shrewdly chosen appointees in favor of a less wholesome approach. Due to congress's inability to provide a sustainable revenue stream of supplies and goods, Davis, for example, relegated a candidate's personal abilities a distant second priority to a cabinet member's state's socioeconomic prowess as a near prerequisite for cabinet membership.

The Confederacy's diffusion of the president's ability to defend the South was another problem. Unable to now trust his cabinet to advise and effectively administer their departments, Davis by 1863 was forced to shift much of the war's management from the congressionally created military offices into the southern executive mansion. By 1864, Davis was also regularly forced to subvert political will and the Confederate legal system to meet the practicalities of keeping experienced men and supplies on the front lines. He returned court-martialed veterans and deserters to combat status. He shepherded southern war production industries and, likewise, bypassed congress to deal directly with state governors over urgent interstate issues. As a result, by 1865, the Confederate circumstances had created in Jefferson Davis what most had initially feared in Lincoln—a one-man government.

Third, while the confederated alliance was initially created to protect the southern states, the Confederate version made little provision for the creation of a formal defense structure. The slow peacetime growth of a personally armed militia force into a small volunteer professional army over decades had worked reasonably well for the United States, but, as in other areas, the Confederacy had no time to grow. They needed an instant military with a military structure to vet a command staff, the ability to equip a force, and a plan to defeat a well-resourced military power like the Union Army—and they needed one yesterday.

Again facing limited options, the Confederacy adopted a loose militia structure and a locally raised and almost independently managed collection of armies to challenge the North. In the 1861 Battle of Fort Sumter, several ragtag bands of southern volunteers served as the first line of defense. Later, at First Bull Run, a slightly more organized collection of Confederate militia forces was barely able to deploy effectively its personal weapons and a limited cache of liberated Federal weapons to beat back the first Union action on southern land. As a result, more seasoned officers, such as P.G.T. Beauregard and Thomas "Stonewall" Jackson, were forced to compensate for their army's many shortcomings against a superior foe with tactical surprises, battlefield flexibility, and steadfast resolve. In fact, their only assets were southern morale, a mass of civilian volunteers, and a dedicated cadre of experienced command-level officers.

Again, the southern government's efforts at war making were also mired in bureaucratic problems. In February 1862, the Confederate Congress finally responded to the needs of the military for formal validation and a formal operating system. In the CSA congress's twenty-first legislated act, it sanctioned the creation of a munitions department. There were, however, only a small number of seized Union cannons in their possession, and states often refused to remove them from their homeland defense. In their twenty-sixth act, the congress united the states' militias under a single war department. The department, however, was mired in heavy bureaucracy and political infighting, leaving some of the most capable officers, such as Robert E. Lee, behind desks and causing the fielding of less capable officers. In its fifty-second legislated act, congress finally recognized the creation of both the Confederate Army and Navy. Yet, as most states ran their own defenses and local heroes largely fielded their own armies, the recognition added little to the Confederacy's defense. As a result, Davis spent most of his time plugging holes in a heavily leaking, congressionally mandated system.

The creation of a confederate constitution based on individual powers of states and limited governance was nice in theory, but on paper and in wartime, the legislative act became an enemy greater than the adversary that had prompted its creation. The uncompromising Confederate Congress effectively robbed the rebel nation of structure and vitality. Similarly, while their usurper president did manage to offset the legislature's initial shortfalls, Jefferson Davis's own acts effectively forfeited the state-run and corruption-free independent government the southern founders had designed. Only the sheer willpower of the Confederate soldiers and sailors enabled the South's poor national defense structure to stave off the effects of entropy, which seemed to destroy everything else within the Confederate States of America.

By 1865, not even the dream of a southern slave Confederacy could long hold the rebel states together. The Confederate economy was bankrupt. Their laws went unenforced. The surviving unoccupied states had reverted entirely to autonomous rule and only grim determination kept the army together. Where state sovereignty and fiery spirits of individualism had once propelled the South into revolutionary action, the governmental system and constitutional framework they had created now made the southern dream of freedom impossible and their defeat inevitable.

The Imperfect Art of the Ironclad

1861–1862: North vs. South vs. Ignorance

———

Roland J. Green

T he *Monitor* and the *Merrimac* (or *Virginia*, the name under which she actually fought) weren't the first ironclads. They were only the first to meet each other in combat.

The nineteenth-century ironclad came to be as a response to the shell-firing gun. These weapons shattered wooden hulls and then set the wreckage on fire. The British and the French sent self-propelled floating batteries with wrought-iron plates bolted to heavy wooden timbers to the Crimea to face Russian forts; they stood up tolerably well.

By 1861, Britain and France both had seagoing ironclads in commission, with more under construction. Both sides knew of these developments when the American Civil War began in 1861.

The Confederacy's naval situation might have looked hopeless, at first. More than 90 percent of the American iron, shipbuilding, and steam engine output lay in the North. The South had only one first-class foundry, the Tredegar Iron Works in Richmond, Virginia. Even their railroad net was inadequate for hauling heavy ship components all over the Confederacy.

They also had two assets. One was Secretary of the Navy Stephen Mallory, knowledgeable and shrewd. Knowing that the Confederacy could not hope to build a conventional navy to rival the Union's, he proposed a navy of harbor and river ironclads to keep ports and rivers open. With cotton exports, the Confederacy would pay for building commerce raiders and seagoing ironclads abroad—particularly in Britain, expected to be sympathetic to the Confederacy.

The other Confederate asset was gained by capturing the Gosport Navy Yard (now Norfolk Naval Shipyard) in Virginia. With it came a thousand heavy guns, and the sunken hull of the steam frigate *Merrimac*. Without these, the Confederacy would have lost the ironclad race before the starting gun was fired.

The North had more than its industrial superiority to bring to one of the first industrial armaments races. It had an equally capable secretary of the navy in Gideon Welles, ably assisted by the innovative and experienced Gustavus V. Fox, both prodded forward by the rock-stubborn genius of John Ericsson.

The Confederacy set about building an armored casemate (a slope-sided superstructure box) on the hull of the *Merrimac*, while laying down four more casemate ships from scratch, two in New Orleans and two in Memphis. They also commissioned the first Civil War ironclad to see action and the only ironclad privateer in naval history. CSS *Manassas* was a converted tugboat with a thin armored shell, and in October 1861 gave the Union blockaders at the mouth of the Mississippi quite a fright while disabling her engines in the process.

Almost tied with the *Manassas* was a squadron of Union river gunboats, the "Pook turtles" (for their designer). They were essentially steam river scows with armored bows, pilothouses, and paddle wheels—and also respectable gun batteries. They were slow, hard to maneuver, and hardly invulnerable, but the Confederacy had nothing like them—and could never have had them in service in less than six months from a standing start as Samuel Pook and his builders did.

Meanwhile, on the coasts both sides were hammering and bolting away at their ironclad contenders. The Union had the novel turreted *Monitor* well under way, as well as a seagoing armored frigate, the *New Ironsides*. Slow, clumsy, and drawing too much water to work close to Confederate ports, she was still the most powerful ironclad either side commissioned during the war.

The Confederacy was also doing all that could be done with hard work in spite of problems with the supply of timber and iron, not just for armor but for things like bolts and boilers. They also discovered that one of their creations in New Orleans needed a longer propeller shaft than anybody in the Confederacy could forge.

The builders tried the expedient of bolting two shorter shafts together—but hadn't finished that job by April 24, 1862. That night, Union Admiral David G. Farragut steamed past the forts below New Orleans, routed its river fleet (*Manassas* included), and kicked open the southern door to the Confederate heartland. Both New Orleans ironclads were scuttled, without ever moving under their own power.

The Union riverine fleet, meanwhile, was kicking in doors farther north. They had such numerical superiority that they would hardly have needed ironclads, but they had the turtles and an increasing number of riverboats hastily covered with boilerplate or heavy timbers. These were some of the most grotesque warships ever built, but they were floating gun platforms when the Union needed them.

Imperfect as they were, the Union gunboats were strategically decisive in 1862. They opened not only the upper Mississippi, but the Cumberland and Tennessee rivers. The "internal lines of communication," which European observers thought would give the Confederacy a decisive advantage, rapidly fell into Union hands. It was Union troops and supplies that moved along the rivers—and even that gifted cavalryman Nathan Bedford Forrest couldn't burn a river.

But what about that famous first duel between ironclads? It certainly grabbed headlines then and historians since, but what else?

Not much, actually, except for giving the Union Navy its worst day of the war. On April 8, 1862, *Virginia* came down the Elizabeth River, with two tugs helping her to steer. (She took half an hour to turn around, and drew too much water to leave the main channel without running hard aground.)

Once in Hampton Roads, she ambled toward the anchored Union blockaders. Just as well they were anchored—*Virginia* still had *Merrimac*'s original engines, condemned before the war and not improved by being submerged for several months. But her top speed of about five knots was enough to let her ram the sailing sloop *Cumberland* and burn the sailing frigate *Congress*. She did not escape without casualties, including losing her ram and smokestack and having her captain and two guns disabled. But the honors of the day were hers.

When she came back the next morning, however, to destroy the grounded Union steam frigate *Minnesota*, the Union champion had entered the ring. *Monitor* had made a storm-plagued voyage south from New York, nearly sinking twice and proving that her low freeboard made her only marginally a seagoing vessel.

As a gun platform, however, she proved herself in a four-hour duel with her heftier opponent. Both ships were handicapped—*Virginia* by her deep draft, slow speed, and lack of armor-piercing shot for her rifled guns, *Monitor* by the need to protect *Minnesota* and the inability of her eleven-inch Dahlgren smoothbores to penetrate *Virginia*'s casemate armor with a standard full charge. It still might have been all over when *Virginia* ran aground, but she struggled off before *Moni-*

tor up a position that let her beat the Confederate's casemate in with repeated hits in the same place.

The second day's fighting was almost a draw—but any edge went to the Union. And both ships had passed their baptism of fire, even though it was the equivalent of sending a modern warship into combat on her shakedown cruise.

Both ships had also demonstrated how much Americans did not know about building ironclads, and neither survived to the end of the year. *Virginia* drew too much water to go up to Richmond when the Union Army advanced on the city and had to be scuttled. *Monitor* was sailing south to join the blockade of Charleston when she ran into a storm. This time the armored raft of her upper hull began separating from the wooden lower hull. Leaks started and finally overwhelmed the pumps. *Monitor* went down with sixteen of her crew.

On the Mississippi, 1862 ended with the brief career of a refugee from Memphis, the *Arkansas*. Cobbled up to battleworthiness in an improvised yard on the Yazoo River, she ran through the Union fleet blockading Vicksburg. Then her engines gave out (beginning to sound familiar?) and her crew scuttled her.

On the plus side, a Confederate torpedo (what we would call a mine) sank the turtle gunboat *Cairo*. This misfortune was about to become familiar to Union sailors.

In 1863 the Union was commissioning ironclads by the squadron, the Confederates by one and twos. This is not to say that in the rush to keep up the numbers, the Union avoided all major flubs. Converted into a super-monitor, the steam frigate *Roanoke* proved so top-heavy that she had to spend her career defending Union harbors against raids that never came. And the *Cascio*-class river monitors were so overweight that they couldn't safely navigate a duck pond, let alone a river, and in the end they were all scrapped (along with their designers' careers).

The Confederates had challenged an industrial power to a high-tech armaments race, but the only question for the rest of the war was how badly they would lose. They got some help from new arsenals established at Selma, Alabama, and Columbiana, Georgia, including the excellent Brooke rifle, but no ships in time to prevent the Union river fleet from running the batteries of Vicksburg and letting Grant's army cross the river for the final act of the Vicksburg campaign, which made the river Union property.

Nor did the plan to buy state-of-the-art ironclads abroad bear much fruit. Commerce raiders, yes—Confederate agents in Britain procured the *Alabama*, the *Florida*, and the *Shenandoah*. But the "Laird rams" (two formidable seagoing turret ships under construction in Liverpool) left such a paper trail that it was easy for Union diplomats to trace it and pressure the British not to let them sail. (Since this was after Gettysburg, the British did not need too much pressuring.)

From the James River south, the Confederates kept trying. The three ironclads of the James River squadron lasted until the fall of Richmond, when they were scuttled. Savannah's pride and joy, the *Atlanta*, ran aground on her first sortie and became the first armored target for a monitor with the new fifteen-inch Dahlgren gun. She surrendered after four devastating hits.

Charleston deployed *Chicora* and *Palmetto State*, which effectively raided the Union blockading squadron early in 1863. When the Union sent a whole squadron of monitors into the harbor to try to batter the forts into submission, the ironclads remained in reserve. The forts could fire ten shots to the monitors' one, and while the monitors could not be hurt much, neither could they hurt land targets. Charleston and its ironclad squadron fell to the Union in 1865.

Mobile, Alabama, had for its defense the Selma-built *Tennessee*, probably the most formidable warship of the Confederacy. She had six-inch armor and heavy rifled guns; but unfortunately she also had surplus riverboat engines, steering chains that led over the stern and so were completely exposed to enemy gunfire, and gunport shutters hinged at the top, ready to slam shut if damaged.

Admiral Farragut took precautions against her. When he steamed into Mobile Bay on August 5, 1864, he had four monitors with him. One, the *Tecumseh*, struck a mine and sank with most of her crew, leading to Farragut's damning the torpedoes. *Tennessee* then came out to challenge Farragut, one ship against eighteen, and the Union fleet battered her into submission over the next three hours, with the three surviving monitors doing most of the damage.

Ton for ton, the most combat-effective Confederate ironclad was the *Albemarle*. The smallest of the casemate ironclads, she was built in a cornfield on a river flowing into her namesake sound, and armored with railroad iron. (One wonders how many rails went to outfit ironclads that would have been better used keeping the Confederacy's ramshackle railroad net from collapsing completely.)

In her first battle, she sank a Union gunboat and helped recapture Plymouth, North Carolina. In her second battle, she gave better than she got—but before she could be repaired for a third try, the Union sent a steam launch with a spar torpedo upriver and sank her at her moorings.

The last Confederate ironclad afloat was the only foreign-built one to fly the Confederate flag. The *Stonewall* was a small French-built ram, barely seaworthy enough to cross the Atlantic to Cuba, where her captain learned that the war was over. He sold her to the Spanish, who sold her to the Japanese, and so the last ironclad of the Confederacy became the first to fly the Rising Sun.

The last of the Union's Civil War ironclads, the *Canonicus*, served until 1908. The success (however qualified) of the monitors helped win the war, but also gave the U.S. Navy a fixation on the type, which delayed by nearly a generation the construction of modern seagoing warships.

The Confederacy's ironclad fixation was more serious. Fighting an essentially defensive war, the Confederacy needed many more mines and spar-torpedo boats, since it was not short of barrels, tar, and gunpowder, nor hopelessly short of locomotive boilers to drive the torpedo boats.

If Farragut had come upriver to New Orleans to find all the defending vessels from *Manassas* on down ready to ram two-hundred-pound charges of powder into his ships, and a minefield in front of the forts, he might have enjoyed less success—and the Confederacy might have had time to complete its ironclads. Or at Mobile Bay, victory might have been too costly to ease Union war weariness if the torpedoes had been strewn a little too thickly to be safely damned and torpedo boats had been ready to sneak out at night.

The Confederacy could not have won a war on the water. But it might have fought a more effective delaying action under it with some of the resources devoted to the ironclads.

Buy American: Colonel Ripley and the English Enfield Rifles

1861: Washington, D.C., United States

William R. Forstchen

Colonel James Ripley, West Point class of 1813, might very well have been responsible for prolonging the bloody four-year American Civil War, a conflict that might have ended in a matter of months. Sixty-seven years old when he assumed control of the Ordnance Department of the U.S. Army in 1861, Ripley was disdainful of any new innovations proposed for arming the burgeoning armies of the North. Among Civil War buffs he is well-known as the man who used every bureaucratic means possible to block the introduction of breech-loading weapons for the infantry, especially the rapid-firing Spencer rifle, which he claimed would only encourage men to "waste ammunition which is expensive."

His greatest folly, however, was not a sin of commission, but rather of omission. It cost the lives of tens of thousands of soldiers on both sides, and without a doubt prolonged the war.

⸺

The story actually begins in 1852, when England sponsored the first of the modern world's fairs at the newly constructed Crystal Palace. The American display was opened with nothing more than boxes of machine parts; volunteers were taken from the audience, and within a matter of minutes guided through the assembling of these parts into a fully functional Colt revolver, a masterpiece of precision interchangeable manufacturing. So revolutionary was this demonstration that the British Parliament assigned a commission to travel to America to unlock the secrets of this new technology, and one of their first stops was at the Springfield (Massachusetts) Armory, which at this point was just gearing up for the mass production of the new 1855 model Springfield .58 rifled musket. Awed by this precision capability, the British government purchased a full working factory. Within three years the British began manufacturing their own rifled musket, the .577-caliber Enfield, which was in all ways nearly identical to the American Springfield except for slight modifications in the hammer and a three-thousandths-of-an-inch difference in caliber.

The advent of hostilities in America caught the Federal army completely flatfooted (though some would later claim that Jefferson Davis, secretary of war under President James Buchanan, had in fact deliberately sabotaged key decisions for preparation while still in office). The army was less than 20,000 strong, but far more important, the stockpile of modern weapons that should have existed was in fact nonexistent. The model 1855 Springfields that were on hand numbered only in the tens of thousands, of which many were in southern armories. Weapons dating all the way back to the Revolution in various state armories were all that were available.

Three days after the Confederates fired on Fort Sumter, Lincoln called for 75,000 volunteers, and by the end of the summer further calls went out for an additional half a million men. The biggest problem facing the Union was not getting volunteers—in fact, men were being turned away—but rather how to arm, and this question landed on Colonel Ripley's desk.

First off, Ripley announced that he saw no problem with smoothbore weapons. They had worked well enough for the army he had fought with in 1812, but if everyone insisted on rifled weapons, the rifled muzzleloader would be good enough to serve. There was one little wrinkle, though: it would take a year or more for the Springfield Armory and various subcontractors to manufacture the needed weapons. Any suggestion that the Union Army turn to private arms makers for the development or manufacture of high-tech repeating weapons was rejected out of hand.

Faced with this dilemma, a staff officer serving under Ripley presented a very simple solution to the crisis: go to England and purchase the needed Enfields from the British, who were offering the weapons at rock-bottom prices on a cash-and-carry basis since by this stage the British were already considering going over to breech-loading weapons. With such a solution, the Union Army could be fully armed within a couple of months.

Colonel James Ripley, however, went through the roof when he was approached with the idea. After all, he had once fought the British, and the mere thought of now running to them for weapons was an idea beneath contempt. Second, Ripley openly stated his opinion that the war would be over with by the end of the summer and the purchase of several hundred thousand rifles would thus prove to be a total waste since the armies would already be demobilizing by the time the new weapons arrived. And finally he presented the most telling argument of all: that this was an American war and he intended to buy American. Anything less would be unpatriotic!

The staffer retreated from this tirade, mulled things over, and then returned several days later with a far more convincing argument that he knew would win the old man over: intelligence sources were reporting that Confederate agents were already in England negotiating to buy up every Enfield in stock and were also contracting for additional production runs.

Ripley again hit the roof but not in panic. His response was that first of all, if the Confederates wanted to buy the damned English guns that was their business and not his. Moreover, he again asserted that the war would be over before the guns would even come into play and that American soldiers would go to battle armed with American-made guns. The staffer persisted, finally arguing that for the good of the cause, if need be the Federal government should outbid the Confederates and thereby prevent them from acquiring the stockpile. The comment was even passed that if Ripley was still so resistant to the acquisition of the Enfields, then at the very least the guns should be purchased and, if need be, dumped into the ocean in order to prevent the Confederate states from using them.

The staffer was dismissed and ordered never to bring up the subject again.

THREE MONTHS LATER, AT MANASSAS, MORE THAN 35,000 UNION troops went into battle, primarily armed with aging smoothbores. Their final assault up Henry Hill came within mere yards of carrying the day and breaking the back of Confederate resistance. That final gallant charge, however, was shredded by the concentrated volleys of Stonewall Jackson's men, armed primarily with newly issued Enfield rifles that could kill at four hundred yards and were murderous at a hundred yards or less, a range at which the smoothbores of the Union were all but useless.

Finally buckling to pressure from the administration, Ripley broke down and started to order Enfields, but by then it was too late: the initial stockpile was already in the South. One of the ironies of the war was that the British continued to manufacture Enfields, with both Union and Confederate purchasing agents waiting at the end of the assembly line. In desperation Ripley turned to the Prussians, who were more than eager to sell off their own muzzleloaders since the Prussian army had already converted to bolt-action breechloaders. These muzzleloaders, and additional arms purchased from the Belgians, were almost all condemned by the European armies as more dangerous to the man behind the gun rather the target in front of it. As to the far more advanced breechloaders such as the Sharps and Burnside rifles, or the highly advanced Spencers, many Union regiments simply stepped around the bureaucracy by purchasing the weapons with their own funds, accepting with a cold, simple logic that their very lives on the battlefield depended on superior firepower and they were willing to take money out of the twelve dollars a month pay to purchase it, along with the "expensive" ammunition Ripley kept complaining about.

One of the great mythologies of the American Civil War is that throughout the war the Confederate armies labored under the burden of inferior equipment. This was definitely not true in the first year of the war, thanks to Colonel Ripley. Right up until the summer of 1862, Union troops, especially in the western theater of operations, fought primarily with smoothbores, while the vast majority of Confederate troops were armed with English-manufactured Enfields. Without the Enfields, the southern cause might very well have collapsed on the battlefields of 1861 and early 1862. If they had been forced to confront a Union Army outfitted with breechloaders and been denied access to the Enfield as well, without a doubt there never would have been a Second Manassas, an Antietam, a Gettysburg, and the bloody killing match of the Wilderness Campaign.

Ripley's army lost most of their first battles; they were outgunned and outranged by the very rifles he could have bought. He fought change so that the Gatling gun and repeating rifles barely appeared. Above all, more than any other person his decisions may have prolonged the American Civil War for years. As for Ripley, who was finally pushed out of office in 1863, it is doubtful if he ever considered that there was an alternative or a need to apologize. To his way of thinking, not buying British rifles was a good idea.

Christmas in April

March–April 1861: Fort Sumter, Charleston, South Carolina

Paul A. Thomsen

For a collection of rebel states, in early 1861, the new Confederate States of America seemed to be sitting on top of the world. While the northern states were consumed by partisan bickering over how best to wield Federal power to carve up the west, southerners were united in their opposition to the supremacy of Federal governance. They acted with eminent decorum in withdrawing from the Union. They were even prepared to defend themselves. War was neither inevitable nor required. In fact, were it not for their byzantine system of leadership, their awkward negotiating policies, and a few overzealous Rebels in South Carolina, the Confederacy might well have changed the entire landscape of the Civil War. Instead, in April 1861, elements within the Confederacy chose to throw caution to the wind. They assumed an aggressive military posture and fired on a tiny Union fort. In that one act, the South lost the sympathy of many potential northern and western allies in favor of starting a shooting war against a militarily superior and, now, united foe.

The delicate relationship between the urban (industrialized) North and the largely agrarian (slave-based) South had shaped much of eighteenth- and nineteenth-century American history. While northern businesses grew rich from Federal-sponsored infrastructural improvements, the rural South, suffering heavy taxes, gained little. When southern farmers expanded westward in search of prosperity, the North agitated against the increasing influence of the slave power in the U.S. Congress. The quarreling escalated from cold silence to pushing, shoving, and the threatened shattering of the American union over slavery and the newly acquired western territories in the 1860 national election. When they received word of Abraham Lincoln's 1860 victory, the southern states felt they had no choice but to secede from the Union.

Instantly, the move divided the North. Many northern businesses were reliant on southern cotton. Proslavery settlers in western states started causing political and criminal trouble for regional Republicans. States' rightists argued the government was growing too fast and encroaching too deeply on the rights of individuals. Republicans, who saw the South as a backward region caught in a bygone era, even threatened the fragmentation of their own party over how to punish the rebel South.

In March 1861, Abraham Lincoln attempted to quell national disunity and entreated the already seceded southern states to return to the national table:

"Think, if you can, of a single instance in which a plainly written provision of the Constitution has ever been denied. If by the mere force of numbers a majority should deprive a minority of any clearly written constitutional right, it might in a moral point of view justify revolution. . . . But such is not our case. . . .

"We are not enemies, but friends. We must not be enemies. Though passion may have strained it must not break our bonds of affection. The mystic chords of memory, stretching from every battle-field and patriot grave to every living heart and hearthstone all over this broad land, will yet swell the chorus of the Union, when again touched, as surely they will be, by the better angels of our nature."

RATHER THAN STANCH THE BLEEDING WOUND, LINCOLN'S SPEECH fell on deaf ears. Republicans in Congress questioned the president's apparent softness. American military officers responded by pledging their loyalty to the South. Similarly, members of Lincoln's own cabinet, William Seward and Salmon Chase, attempted to convince the newly elected president that he was not capable of leading the nation in this time of crisis. Yet all was not lost. Although Lincoln quickly realized that only time would cool southern tempers, the president was able to buy some time for his party by cunningly manipulating his cabinet members and his own party. Still, if the South didn't soon make a mistake to change the game, Lincoln feared the Union might very well implode.

Initially, the South remained steadfast and wise, but over time, vulnerabilities began to surface in the secessionist game plan. Jefferson Davis, both a reluctant secessionist and an initial refuser of the Confederate presidency, attempted to ease northern feelings by attempting to foster a rapprochement with the North. As his first presidential act, Davis formulated a peace delegation to craft a peaceful conclusion to crisis. These motions of amelioration, however, amounted to little after the Federal government refused to legitimize the Rebel government by engaging in direct intercourse. In response, Davis accepted the rerouting of negotiations through the southern state governors. Yet this new diplomatic method was time-consuming and invited a number of additional (and largely undesirable) voices to join the negotiations, including the governor of South Carolina, Francis Pickens, and Confederate Army General P.G.T. Beauregard, who were working to evict the Union from the port city of Charleston. Still, as long as all orders came from the southern president and both parties remained patient, Davis felt certain a peaceful separation from the North could be achieved.

Sadly, Davis overlooked the other forces at work. By April 1861, thousands of southern militiamen were laying siege to Federal military bases throughout the South. Not wishing to be responsible for starting a war and unable to resupply, the Union fort commanders of landlocked installations surrendered their base to the Rebels when their provisions were depleted. In response, the soldiers were largely treated generously by the southerners, who allowed the forces now perceived as alien to leave these fortifications and their southern land in peace. The coastal and island military bases, however, were another matter. With access to the sea, many were ordered to stay their ground, buy stores from the locals, and, if necessary, await reprovisioning by sea. If, however, the security of their position was deemed untenable, the base commanders were allowed to relocate to available nearby island installations. As a result, the North and South continued to stare each other down, each hoping the other's cooler head would see reason.

For the first few months, the climate indeed seemed cordial between the two parties, but before long, Confederate patience wore thin. Governor Pickens of South Carolina, for example, communicated to the Confederate government that the Federal forces inside an old Charleston Harbor American Revolutionary fortification, Fort Moultrie, were a threat to his state's security. Thinking an overt threat of force might shake the North's confidence, the Confederacy took a more aggressive posture. First, they authorized Pickens to move his southern forces to secure the harbor. Next, they rapidly dispatched a military strategist and Mexican War army engineer, Confederate

Brigadier General P.G.T. Beauregard, to oversee the crisis, applying a level of officialdom to the pressure applied to the fortification.

Major Robert Anderson, watching the numbers of southern militia grow larger than his men could handle, was forced to transfer his command from Fort Moultrie to a tiny island outpost near the mouth of the harbor—Fort Sumter.

The southern forces, watching the retreat, rejoiced.

For the first time, an overt threat of force had given the Confederacy a tactical success, but the limited military achievement also led to a series of even greater mistakes. With their immediate goals now achieved, the Confederate leaders thought their regional managers would sit in peace as negotiations continued. They were mistaken. The regional players thought a little more might shake the divided North from their precarious perch. They were wrong again. They also thought military force would send the Lincoln administration running like the yellow-bellied bullies many in the South were now imagining them to be. They were wrong about that, too. Besides, if it came to open war, the Union, they thought, would grow tired within a few weeks and leave the South alone. Oh boy, were they ever wrong about that one!

In light of these new developments, the Confederacy gave Beauregard theater discretion "to act as if he were in the presence of a hostile force with whom at any moment he might be in conflict." Instead of crafting a state of defensive preparedness, Beauregard and his men methodically forged a crucible. There would be only one acceptable conclusion: the Confederate occupation of Fort Sumter. Mail to the fort was stopped and any attempt to safely resupply the fort by land or sea was neutralized. As a result, Beauregard, South Carolina, and the Confederacy assured a Confederate tactical victory within a matter of days and certain long-term doom for their cause.

By using force unnecessarily, the South subverted its reasoned arguments on state sovereignty with renewed unilateral demands and aggressive action. Few northerners were willing to go to war over slavery. Similarly, a state's legal rights were a concern with which most states could sympathize. Yet acts of aggression, threats, and violence perpetrated against Union soldiers crossed a line. In light of Fort Sumter, the southern actions were viewed by Republicans as desperate acts of imbalanced and evil people that needed to be forcibly put down. Moreover, instead of compassion, the now coalescing North was gaining a taste for blood. If the Rebels allowed the Union to keep the island, they would be perceived as impotent, the southern populace would likely fragment, and the philosophical issues behind the current crisis might forever remain unresolved. As a result, whether impotent or arrogant, the Confederacy would now look like fools.

On April 10, 1861, the Confederates authorized the South Carolina commander to remove the Union from Fort Sumter. In response, Beauregard both ordered his men to gather additional supplies of gunpowder and sent a delegation to ask Anderson to surrender.

Anderson refused.

On the following night, Beauregard sent one last ultimatum to Anderson.

Anderson refused an unconditional surrender, but conceded he would surrender on certain terms. Instead of accepting the terms, this time Beauregard's adjutants boldly refused to compromise, rebuked the surrender, and rowed away.

At 4:30 A.M. on April 12, Edmund Ruffin, a Virginia farmer, agrarian expert, publisher, and ardent secessionist, fired the first shot in the bombardment of Fort Sumter. For the next thirty-four hours, Confederate fire rained down on the tiny island from three sides.

When the Union fort surrendered on April 14, the South had achieved its victory. Beauregard promptly took control of South Carolina's long-sought prize, but in seizing the island, he had lost the Confederacy. Diplomacy was now irrelevant. Gone were the possibilities of a peaceful settlement, a separate peace, and/or a reunification with the North. Moreover, where the North had boundless war-making capabilities in both men and supplies, Confederate leaders, hampered by the region's lack of industrial capabilities, now no longer had the luxury of time to stockpile goods and prepare for war. Finally, in taking an offensive posture over a largely insignificant fortification, Beauregard's act in Charleston Harbor had now injected a sense of bloody entitlement into a high-minded debate which flew in the face of the distracted North.

As the South should have anticipated, the battle for Fort Sumter rapidly replaced the secessionist crisis in northern minds. The unprovoked attack on the Federal installation, indeed, brought clarity to the Union. First, the debate within Lincoln's cabinet was replaced by war planning. Second, the once disparate factions of the Republican Party rallied behind the president's standard as fellow protectors of the Union and prosecutors of the war against the Rebels. Third, those living in the North who sympathized with the South became less open in their opinions for fear of being labeled unpatriotic or, worse, charged as a traitor. Finally, although Lincoln's move to call for troops would previously have been considered political suicide, the president's rally cry for action in the wake of Fort Sumter was met with a swarm of eager political supporters and a stream of volunteers with which he could defend the capital.

Prior to April 12, 1861, few would have challenged the prediction that the South might win their way through the crisis, but by losing their patience and acting the bully in their aggression against the Federals at Charleston Harbor, the secessionists had actually given Abraham Lincoln Christmas in April.

Grant's Rough River Road to the South

April 6–7, 1862: The Battle of Shiloh

—

Doug Niles

As the Civil War commenced, Ulysses S. Grant had to be rated as very unlikely to become the most famous and successful commanding general of Lincoln's armies. Born in Ohio in 1822, he had been a mediocre student with no fondness for working in his father's tannery. He managed to earn an appointment to West Point, though the application process somehow converted his given name of Hiram Ulysses Grant into the cognomen he would make famous as a soldier, a commanding general, and eventually a two-term United States president.

None of this future greatness was heralded by his term at the military academy, where he finished ranked twenty-first out of a class of thirty-nine. About the only area where he displayed mastery at West Point was horsemanship. He served as a young officer during the Mexican War, and while he didn't cover himself with glory, neither did he make any significant mistakes as he participated in nearly every major engagement of that conflict. He finished the war as a captain, winning several citations for bravery under fire. (Whatever faults, and there were many, that would be charged to Grant during the rest of his life, cowardice was never one of them.)

Following the war, he spent most of a decade in mundane army garrison duties on the west coast. Separated by distance from his beloved wife, Julia, he displayed a serious weakness for alcohol. He was mediocre in performance of his duties on the coast, and his decision to resign from the army in 1854 was at least in part motivated by a desire to avoid the prospect of impending court-martial for drunkenness.

He spent the rest of the 1850s in Missouri, where he failed as a farmer and bill collector, and in Galena, Illinois, where his father finally hired him to help in a family-owned leather and harness shop. He was barely scraping by when the secessionists of South Carolina bombarded Fort Sumter in April 1861. Like many of his countrymen, he accepted the challenge of President Lincoln's call to arms. For several months he served as a clerk in Illinois's military mustering process, organizing recruits into training units. After serving as commandant of the militia's camp of instruction, he was eventually promoted to colonel in command of an Illinois militia regiment, the 21st Illinois Volunteers.

The impression he made upon his new men was, to say the least, rather underwhelming—which was to be the common first impression of Grant pretty much everywhere he went, even as he gained in experience and reputation. He was slightly shorter than average, and tended to dress in plain clothes, either civilian or military. He was not loquacious, merely smiling tightly when he was pleased, or frowning when his mood was the opposite. Still, there was something in his manner that commanded attention, and within a few days the men of his regiment—who had earned a reputation as vandals and carousers under their previous commander—were shaping up and behaving like soldiers.

At that time, more and more western regiments were gathering at the southern Illinois town of Cairo. Because it was located at the confluence of the Ohio and Mississippi Rivers, and both were important avenues for military maneuver, during 1861 this city was the most strategically important Union position in the western theater of war. Promoted to brigadier general during the summer, Grant quickly earned command of the more than 10,000 recruits from Illinois, Iowa, Wisconsin, and other (at that time) western states. When the Rebels violated Kentucky's neutrality by taking the Mississippi River city of Columbus, Kentucky, Grant on his own initiative sent a force across the Ohio River to occupy and hold Paducah, Kentucky, in early August. This protected the Union position at Cairo and denied that key river town to his Confederate opposite, Major General Leonidas Polk.

In November, Grant took command of an understrength division (two brigades) and struck a Rebel encampment across the Mississippi River at Belmont, Missouri (just opposite Columbus). Utilizing navy gunboats in support, Grant's force took the enemy by surprise and inflicted damage before withdrawing in some confusion and disorder. The general's personal courage under fire went a long way to rallying his men in the battle, and the fact that he proudly proclaimed the battle a victory (it was really more of a draw) did wonders to the morale of his now-not-so-raw recruits. In addition, this early example of the smooth coordination between the army and river-based navy units would become a staple of Grant's operations in the western theater.

Ceding control of the important river junction to the Union, Polk determined to follow a defensive strategy designed to block the northern forces from using Kentucky as an avenue to invade the Confederacy. Columbus was a natural strong point on the Mississippi, with a bluff some 150 feet high. A series of earthen forts crowned the bluff, and rings of artillery formed positions lower down, including a rank of batteries right at river level. Manned by some 17,000 Rebels, the position was called the "Gibraltar of the Mississippi" and was in fact strong enough to deny river passage to any hostile ship trying to navigate on the Father of Waters. Crowning the defenses was a 128-pound rifled cannon, known to the Rebels as "Lady Polk."

Two more deep, navigable rivers offered routes through western Kentucky into Tennessee, however: the Cumberland and the Tennessee. Two well-garrisoned fortified positions, Fort Henry on the Tennessee and Fort Donelson on the Cumberland, commanded these rivers. Each fort was located just south of the Tennessee–Kentucky border, and as the year 1861 came to an end, those forts and the position at Columbus effectively blocked any Union attempt to use the waterways as paths of invasion to the South.

Northern operations against Kentucky and Tennessee were divided between Grant's immediate superior, General Henry Halleck, and General Don Carlos Buell, who was in charge of areas east of the Cumberland River. Halleck, disapproving of Grant's widely reputed drunkenness, was suspicious of his subordinate—and also concerned that Grant's accomplishments and reputation might somehow eclipse Halleck's own. Nonetheless, he gave the junior general authority to commence operations.

Now Grant's most significant military attribute came to the fore: if there was an enemy position within reach, he would figure out some way to attack it. Ably supported by United States Navy Flag Officer Andrew Foote, who commanded a fleet of riverines and gunboats affectionately known as the "brown water navy," Grant moved against Fort Henry in early February 1862. His infantry, transported by river, were landed some distance away from the enemy position and began to close in over difficult terrain.

In the meantime, the brown water navy went to work, bombarding Fort Henry from armor- and timber-clad gunboats on the Tennessee River. The fort proved to be poorly placed, lying so low that the barrage of Foote's gunboats was able to overwhelm the defending batteries and essentially flood the fort. After little more than an hour of this shelling, the Rebels abandoned the fort and fled eastward over the neck of the land between the Tennessee and Cumberland Rivers. Grant's men were not yet in position, so nearly all the enemy troops reached Fort Donelson. Still, the result was a signal victory for the Union.

Grant followed up immediately, moving his men overland and surrounding Fort Donelson while Foote's gunboats steamed down the Tennessee, a short distance up the Ohio, and then up the Cumberland, until they were in position to strike at Fort Donelson. The Confederate garrison was under the overall command of Major General John Floyd, assisted by fellow Major Generals Gideon Pillow and Simon Bolivar Buckner. Pillow led an expeditionary force that struck Grant's troops in a desperate and nearly successful attempt to break out of the trap. The failure to anticipate any Rebel thrust was a lapse that almost resulted in disaster.

The lack of preparation was compounded by a vacuum in command. At the time of the attack (February 14), Grant was absent from his headquarters, consulting with Foote on his own intended offensive, and he had neglected to delegate any of his subordinate officers to command in his place. Furthermore, he had ignored warnings about the lightly held right flank of his position, and it was here that Pillow's attack fell. After some savage fighting, the Rebels had achieved their breakthrough. Still, in confused fighting in the tangled, gullied forests, several Union formations—most notably the division commanded by General Lew Wallace—managed to stem the tide until Grant arrived on the scene.

Realizing that the enemy was attempting a breakout, Grant refused to characterize the Rebel attack as a success—rather, he portrayed it as an act of desperation by men who knew their position was hopeless. Also, he surmised that Floyd must have weakened his own right flank to make such a strong attack with his left. Bolstered by his calm self-assurance, the Union troops charged forward against the enemy's right flank and soon found themselves advancing into the ramparts of Fort Donelson. On the other flank, the counterattack sealed the breach, though not before the Rebel cavalry under Nathan Bedford Forrest made its escape—as did Generals Floyd and Pillow. But the rest of the garrison, and the fort itself, had fallen into Union hands.

When General Buckner asked for terms of surrender, Grant issued his famous reply, stating that "no terms except an unconditional and immediate surrender can be accepted." Buckner, an old friend and army comrade of Grant's, had no choice but capitulation. With Fort Donelson, Grant took some 16,500 prisoners and captured large quantities of supplies as well as fourteen siege guns and forty-three pieces of field artillery. It was, by a large measure, the most astonishing Union victory of the war to date, and it propelled Ulysses S. Grant to immediate national prominence. Many pundits suggested that his initials stood for "Unconditional Surrender."

With the Cumberland River open to allow for naval support, the brown water navy moved on Nashville. General Buell marched southward from central Kentucky and quickly occupied the Tennessee capital with troops. The next step was clear to Grant: he should move down the Tennessee River to divide the western part of that state from the remainder and stab a wedge into the heart of the Confederacy.

For a short time, however, politics intervened to put a hold on this advance. Envious of his subordinate's success, General Halleck used imaginary accusations of disloyalty and unfounded rumors of drunkenness to remove Grant from command. However, President Lincoln was not about to shelf the only general in his army who displayed a willingness to vigorously prosecute an offensive, and after less than two weeks Grant was restored to command of the force that was now named the Army of West Tennessee. He immediately traveled down the river to join his forces at Savannah, Tennessee.

In fact Grant, while undoubtedly an alcoholic, seems to have spent the entire war—with the possible exception of one rumored incident, well away from the front—stone-cold sober. In this he was supported by a loyal aide, a former lawyer named John Rawlins who served with Grant throughout the war. Though he performed valuable service as an aide-de-camp, his most significant contribution to the war seems to have been a sincere, and successful, attempt to make sure that his commanding general never had the chance to succumb to the temptations of alcohol.

Still driven by his offensive mind-set, Grant moved his army another nine or ten miles down the river, putting the men ashore at a place called Pittsburg Landing, just a short distance north of where the Tennessee River flowed from the state of Mississippi. He was ready to march into Mississippi, where the Rebels were reported to be gathering at Corinth, but Halleck ordered Grant to wait until Buell could join him from Nashville.

At Pittsburg Landing, Grant's army numbered nearly 50,000 men, organized into six infantry divisions. Lew Wallace's division was some six miles north of the rest of the army, posted there to ensure that the Rebels didn't post a battery that could command the waterway. The rest of the army, including the divisions of Sherman, Prentiss, Hurlbut, McClernand, and W.H.L. Wallace, was encamped in the area of a small church named Shiloh.

Displaying again the trait that had almost led to disaster at Fort Donelson, Grant seemed to give no thought to what his enemy might be up to. Instead of positioning his troops for defense, he placed them in a sprawling camp where they had room to drill and practice while they waited for Buell's 18,000 men to arrive. Grant himself supervised these drills until a riding accident, in which his horse fell on top of him, temporarily disabled him. After the fall, he took up quarters on a gunboat based up the river at Savannah.

Indeed, the Confederates had a plan of their own. Commanded by General Albert Sidney Johnston, seconded by General P.G.T. Beauregard, the Rebels who gathered at Corinth took the field with some 47,000 men as the Army of Mississippi. They marched on April 3, with Johnston hoping to move the twenty miles to Pittsburg Landing in time to attack Grant on the 4th. In the event, the movement did not go as smoothly as planned, and it was late on the night of the 5th that the Confederates moved into position. Still, they were barely two miles from the Union positions, and the Yankees had absolutely no expectation of an immediate attack. Nor had they yet made any attempt to prepare defenses, or even to scout and picket the approaches to the large camp.

Johnston's plan was to strike hard at the Union left, separating the troops from their base and line of retreat at Pittsburg Landing. The plan was audacious, but sound—had it succeeded completely, Grant's army could have been shattered, the remnants forced to retreat through a tangled region of swamps and creeks and dense underbrush. But Beauregard, who commanded the forces following the initial attack, lacked a clear understanding of his superior's intentions. Furthermore, the subordinate general was not enthused about the attack to begin with, preferring to wait for Grant to make an offensive move.

In the early morning of April 6, the Rebels attacked with almost complete surprise, emerging from the forested terrain to the south and southwest of the Union position in full battle order. With the exception of the warning provided by a small scouting detachment from General Prentiss's division, every Yankee formation was taken by complete surprise. General William T. Sherman's division, on the far right of the Union position, was driven hard, as were, subsequently, the divisions of Generals McClernand, Prentiss, and Hurlbut.

However, the tactical finesse of Johnston's plan became lost in the confusion of the desperate fighting. Instead of a solid punch with the Confederate right, the attack evolved into a straight linear attack along a front almost three miles long. The Rebels had the distinct advantage of surprise, and many Federal troops were killed or captured in the first minutes of fighting. The rest of the northerners were pushed back, though their fighting mettle began to show as the morning progressed.

Sherman was the initial commander on the scene, as Grant, still recuperating from the fall, remained about ten miles north of Shiloh. Though he couldn't move without crutches, the commanding general heard the sounds of the guns and quickly ordered the gunboat that served as his quarters to steam southward. He arrived at Pittsburg Landing before 9 A.M.

By that time, Prentiss's men, supported by some of W.H.L. Wallace's division, had taken up a position along a (barely) sunken road, where they resisted sternly. Instead of bypassing the site that would become remembered as the "Hornets' Nest," the Confederates pressed a series of frontal attacks with increasing desperation and ferocity. The stubborn Yankees held out for many hot hours, despite the loss of General Wallace and many hundreds of men. It wasn't until midafternoon, when the Rebels massed some forty cannons to smash the Hornets' Nest, that the position was finally taken. By then the staunch defenders had given Grant enough time to form a final redoubt right along the river at Pittsburg Landing.

At about the same time, the Confederates suffered a grievous loss when General Johnston was shot in the leg. Disdaining medical attention, and unaware that an artery had been severed, the Rebel commanding general quickly lost consciousness and died from loss of blood. Beauregard took command from the rear, but by then the weight of the attack had begun to dissipate.

Furthermore, instead of driving the Yankees away from their base, the encircling pressure of the Confederate attack had served to push the Union divisions into a strong defensive position on the bluff above Pittsburg Landing. Here Grant had mustered some fifty guns, ably supported by two gunboats on the river itself. Late in the day Lew Wallace arrived with his division (after a meandering march that caused his reputation to fall several notches in Grant's estimation) and the first of Buell's troops were ferried across the river to bolster the Union line. By 6 P.M., with darkness arriving within the hour, Beauregard called off the attack.

The Rebels were in possession of almost all of the Union camps, and had taken many prisoners. Beauregard cabled President Jefferson Davis to announce a "complete victory" and proceeded to make plans to reduce the small Yankee bridgehead the following day. He did not take into account the fact that his men were desperately tired, low on ammunition, and disorganized, and had suffered more than 8,000 losses, many of them in the brutal and unsubtle attempts to reduce the Hornets' Nest. He further discounted a report from Forrest's cavalry that Buell's men were reinforcing Grant.

In fact, the Army of the Cumberland was across the river and solidly melded into the Union position several hours before dawn. Nathan Forrest's cavalry scouts spotted and reported this movement, but the news either did not reach the Rebel commander or was discounted as inaccurate. In the event, Beauregard and his men were in the midst of planning a deliberate resumption of the offensive when they were surprised themselves as the Yankees attacked at first light.

Once again battle raged across the fields and woods around Shiloh Church. On the second day of the battle, it was the Rebels who stubbornly gave ground, the Union that grimly attacked. Both Grant's and Buell's men pressed the offensive relentlessly, and though the Confederates mustered some counterattacks and established a line of batteries near Shiloh Church, Beauregard could not stem the Yankee advance.

By the end of the second day, the northern men had regained control of the ground they had held before the battle, but were too exhausted to pursue the withdrawing Rebs. Grant, as senior officer in command, and Buell, who was determined to retain control of his own army, argued about how to follow up the battle. Meantime, Beauregard's men fell back to Corinth. And in truth, it seems likely that neither army possessed the morale or energy to immediately resume combat.

In fact, the Battle of Shiloh was the bloodiest battle to date in the American Civil War. Union losses were more than 13,000 men, including 1,700 killed; the butcher bill for the Rebs was some 10,700, also with 1,700 dead. These casualties, added together, exceed the battlefield losses of all previous American wars, combined! The numbers were shocking to the nation as a whole, and resulted in a lot of people in the North calling for Grant's removal from command. Lurid tales of Yankee boys bayoneted in their tents—exaggerated in the press, but based on kernels of truth—led to a crescendo of blame directed at the army commander.

While in fact Grant's army had been taken by surprise, and was poorly positioned to receive an attack, it was the general's steadiness and determination that had proven invaluable in salvaging victory from potential disaster. As he would many times in the future, he would simply shake off the memory of the losses, reward those subordinates who had performed well (notably William T. Sherman, in this case), and move forward to the next campaign.

Abraham Lincoln himself put to rest all the recrimination, the criticism, the cries for Grant's head. In one of his characteristically blunt and very well-remembered statements, the president merely said:

"I can't spare this man. He fights."

Lee Looks Smart Beating a Stupid General

August 28, 1862: Second Battle of Bull Run

William Terdoslavich

Big battles often start with small skirmishes.

And so it was on the evening of August 28, 1862. The division of Brigadier General Rufus King was marching from Gainesville, Virginia, east along the Warrenton Turnpike when its brigades skirmished with Confederates posted on a wooded hill on his left called Stony Ridge. King was ill and could not make the brigades under his command fight as a single division. Two brigades exchanged volleys with elements of Major General Thomas "Stonewall" Jackson's corps, then broke contact.

King's division fell away as evening twilight darkened into night; they retraced their steps to Gainesville, then marched four more miles southeast to New Market. This was to be the first of many errors that would punctuate the Second Battle of Bull Run. Too bloody to be a comedy, too flawed to be a tragedy, this battle was one the Union did not have to fight, but one that the Confederacy *had* to win.

Pope's Infallibility

The Union's Army of Virginia was a bastard child fathered by incompetence and born of defeat.

Its three independent corps, now bundled into an army, were commanded respectively by Major Generals John Frémont, Nathaniel Banks, and Irwin McDowell. Stonewall Jackson had whipped all three of them in a brilliant campaign of battle and movement in the Shenandoah Valley earlier that spring. The more senior Frémont refused to serve under the army's new commander, Major General John Pope, and was quickly replaced by Major General Franz Sigel.

Pope, previously a corps commander in the Union's Army of the Mississippi, was brought east following his victories at Island No. 10 and the siege of Corinth. Despite his reputation, Pope got off on the wrong foot that July when he issued an address to his troops: "I have come to you from the West, where we have always seen the backs of our enemies." Pope never wanted to hear phrases like "taking strong positions and holding them," or "lines of retreat" or "bases of supply." Study the enemy's line of retreat, he exhorted, and "leave ours to take care of themselves." The only position the Army of Virginia shall have is the one that allows it to advance against the enemy, he thundered.

This sounded great if Pope was leading a brigade, where he only had to worry about fighting the enemy in front of him. But generals who command armies had to worry about "bases of supply" (logistics), "taking up strong positions and holding them" (defense), and "lines of retreat" (maneuver). Pope did not understand that there was more to army command than just ordering attacks.

Pope's army was supposed to occupy central Virginia while Major

General George McClellan's Army of the Potomac was pulled off "the Peninsula" southeast of Richmond. The assorted corps either went to Washington or the landing at Aquia Creek, just east of Pope's army. The goal was to unite Pope and McClellan's forces. *No battle needed to be fought to do this.*

General Robert E. Lee could not afford to let that happen, as the far larger combination would easily crush his army. In late August, using the corps of Major General James Longstreet as his "shield," Lee marched his troops along the Rappahannock River, occupying Pope's attention. Lee then used Stonewall Jackson as his sword, ordering his corps to march northwest, then east along a slightly roundabout route. Jackson covered more than fifty miles in thirty-six hours to reach Manassas Junction, well in Pope's rear, and threaten Washington, D.C. Lee was breaking the rules by dividing his army in front of a larger force. But he had no choice, for playing the game by the rules risked defeat.

All Pope had to do was avoid battle so that the two Union armies could combine. But there was no gain or glory in that. That left Pope with two choices: He could attack and destroy Longstreet's smaller force, leaving Jackson's corps to the tender mercies of the Army of the Potomac, now strengthening in Washington. Or he could march back with the Army of Virginia and destroy Jackson. He chose to focus on Jackson and ignore all else.

Meanwhile, Lee marched north with Longstreet's corps, hoping to reunite with Jackson and destroy the Army of Virginia before Pope's headstrong retreat produced results. He had earlier maneuvered Pope out of central Virginia.

Hide and Seek

Pope had two of his corps from the Army of Virginia to work with, supported by three more corps from the Army of the Potomac. (Banks would sit out the battle with his command at Bristoe Station, to the south of the Manassas battlefield. Holding Bristoe Station was supposed to cover the Union left with Major General Fitz-John Porter's corps.) As the sun rose over Virginia on August 29, Pope hoped to crush Jackson in a three-pronged attack, but he did not know that only one prong was handy.

King's division of McDowell's corps was supposed to be facing Jackson's corps at Stony Ridge, but was in the wrong place, at New Market. McDowell's other division, under Brigadier General James Ricketts, was supposed to block Thoroughfare Gap, about seven miles west of Gainesville. But Longstreet outnumbered Ricketts by at least four to one and had no trouble outflanking the lone division, forcing it back east toward Pope's army.

Pope's orders showed little situational awareness, nor did he know where his units were or what they could do. McDowell was supposed to bring the remainder of his forces to attack Jackson from the west *and* cover Thoroughfare Gap to stop Longstreet. It was beyond McDowell's means to do both.

McDowell at least posted two cavalry brigades to cover Longstreet's corps and report back. At 9 A.M., the move paid off. "Seventeen regiments, one battery five hundred cavalry passed through Gainesville three-quarters of an hour ago, on the Centreville Road," reported Colonel John Buford. Did McDowell pass on the message to Pope? Nope. He just put it in his pocket.

Sigel's corps began its attack in the morning. Had King's division held its ground the night before, Sigel would have had better information to plan with. But he had to find out Jackson's dispositions the hard way, launching a broad attack with five brigades to probe the enemy line.

The base of Stony Ridge was fringed with a railroad cut that acted like a well-placed trench, strengthening Jackson's position. Sigel's bri-

gades were blindly "probing" into a strong position and getting shredded, with regiments bleeding half or two-thirds their strength. Sigel's
and Jackson's brigades attacked and counterattacked over the same
ground, but by late morning, Jackson was still king of his hill. He had
brushed back the "probe" on his left, while his center held.

Meanwhile . . .

McDowell was marching north toward the battle with Porter's corps.
Pope's order to McDowell showed some vague awareness that Longstreet's corps was coming, and also gave McDowell the discretion,
but not the command, to attack this force. With dust clouds to the
west and gunfire to the north, McDowell had to make a decision.
McDowell ordered Porter west to mask Longstreet's approach while
he galloped north to the sound of the guns.

Porter's corps was well positioned to confuse Longstreet. It just
dangled off to the southeast, ready to knife into Longstreet's right
flank should he advance his troops to relieve pressure on Jackson's position. Longstreet could not make a move until Porter did. And Porter
did nothing. (The average Union corps commander in 1862 was good
at that.)

By early afternoon, Pope brought the corps of Major Generals
Samuel Heintzelman and Jesse Reno to bear on Jackson from the east,
supporting Sigel. Badly pressed on his left, Jackson carefully shuffled
brigades and reinforced threatened sectors, and actually came close
to losing several times. But Pope didn't know how to press the blade
home. His corps commanders continued making stupid, straight-
ahead attacks with single brigades up and down Jackson's line. These
attacks were annoying finger pokes, not corps-sized fists smashing
into Jackson's positions.

By day's end, Pope had still gotten nowhere. He tried once more to bring Porter's corps into play, ordering it to attack Longstreet *and* march north to attack Jackson's right flank. Porter got a second order from Pope ordering his corps north immediately. Porter would later face a court-martial for "disobeying" these contradictory orders. In 1862, Union generals rarely exceeded orders on their own initiative, no matter how screwed up. Porter would eventually move his corps north to join Pope's line—*after* Longstreet's move.

That night, Pope held a meeting with his commanders. He finally got the morning message from McDowell about those all those Confederate regiments Buford sighted. Pope assumed Longstreet would line up on Jackson's right and extend the line westward. Instead, Longstreet joined Jackson's line at a forty-five-degree angle, facing Pope's flank. Pope never saw it.

Any ground gained against Jackson convinced Pope that the Confederates were retreating. On that basis, Pope stayed to renew battle the next morning, issuing orders to pursue "the broken Confederates."

Overnight, Longstreet's corps received reinforcements: the division of Richard H. Anderson and S. D. Lee's artillery battalion. Lee and Longstreet contemplated a corps-sized attack driving east into Pope's left flank. With the inactive Porter no threat to Longstreet's flank, this move was possible.

Denial Before Truth

As the sun rose on the second day of battle, Lee and Pope prepared to make the right move. One of them had to be wrong.

With Porter's corps in hand, Pope launched an attack on Jackson's right while Heintzelman's corps attacked Jackson's left. Already bled white from the previous day's fighting, Jackson's line was buckling under the large Union attacks. Jackson urgently asked Lee for a division to reinforce his hard-pressed line. But Lee and Longstreet judged that it would take too long to get there. The crisis was happening now. And it was at times like this that the cautious Longstreet was most dangerous. Whenever an opportunity beckoned to mess up the enemy, he pounced.

Noticing how his line flanked Porter's attacking waves, Longstreet posted S. D. Lee's artillery battalion on high ground with a good view. It took S. D. Lee's eighteen guns less than eighteen minutes to destroy Porter's attack. The corps broke and retreated in disorder. Now McDowell screwed up by ordering the division of John Reynolds, which faced west toward Longstreet, to pull out of line and fill the gap left by Porter's retreat. Only two brigades were left on Chinn Ridge to cover Pope's left flank.

General Robert E. Lee gave Longstreet the green light. Five divisions sprang forward, looking to overrun Chinn Ridge and seize Henry House Hill just a half mile beyond. Taking that hill would bring the entire Union Army under Confederate artillery fire. But Longstreet had to work fast. It was 4 P.M. Only three hours of daylight remained.

The two Union brigades on Chinn Ridge were little better than speed bumps quickly flattened by Longstreet's massive attack. McDowell saw his mistake immediately, pulled the nearest brigade out of reserve, and sent it to hold Chinn Ridge. The brigade under Colonel Nathaniel McLean should slow Longstreet's assault long enough for other units to rush to the scene.

The Texas brigade that spearheaded Longstreet's attack had already blown through the two Union brigades in just forty-five minutes. But losses from the attack had already weakened the brigade as it was climbing the last stretch of high ground to face McLean's brigade. Union artillery fire from the north was raking the flanks of the Confederate follow-on brigade to the rear of the Texans, robbing the assault of some punch.

The two southern brigades attacked in quick succession, but McLean held. Those were even-money fights. But the division of Brigadier General James Kemper followed, and its lead brigade climbed Chinn Ridge to the south of McLean's position and wheeled left, facing McLean's flank. One Union regiment turned to meet the threat, outnumbered. The two lines exchanged volleys at close range. Men dropped by the dozens. The Confederate brigade simply outnumbered the enemy, its extra regiments outflanking both sides of the thin blue line. The Yankees broke. More than 400 Union dead were left behind, but they had purchased thirty precious minutes with their lives.

Jackson's corps was fought out and did not attack, so now idle Union units could be rushed to backstop McLean's position. Two brigades from Ricketts's division would have to do. Brigades from Sigel's corps soon followed.

The Union reinforcements were beaten back by Longstreet's men, who eventually captured Chinn Ridge in ninety minutes of hard fighting. It was 6 P.M. An hour of daylight remained. Henry House Hill was only a half mile away. Lee tried to take the hill by sending one of Longstreet's divisions around the Union's line, but the attack proved tired and halfhearted while the Union's left held fast.

Pope's sense of denial ended at sunset. Knowing his left flank was smashed, he pulled in his line to front Henry House Hill and began an orderly retreat across Bull Run. Jackson's worn corps did nothing. Pope pulled back east to Centreville.

Fixing Problems? Fixing Blame?

In the days following the Second Battle of Bull Run, Pope oscillated between depression and optimism before he settled down to blame his defeat on the poor performance of corps commanders from McClellan's army, principally Porter. Pope's forces fought one more battle at Chantilly, checking Jackson, before Union General-in-Chief Henry Halleck ordered Pope to fall back on Washington. Pope was then relieved of his command.

The Army of Virginia was turned back into a bunch of corps for McClellan to reorganize within the Army of the Potomac. Within a week, it would be ready to move—a stunning example of McClellan's organizational talent.

The blood price for Second Bull Run was still steep, even by Civil War standards. Lee lost 9,500 men out of 55,000 compared to the 14,500 lost by Pope out of a force of 62,000.

With Pope out of the way and McClellan in Washington reorganizing his troops, Robert E. Lee was now free to invade Maryland. Little did he know that he was soon going to face McClellan again near an obscure town named Sharpsburg, which lay beside Antietam Creek.

When Not Losing Is Victory

September 13, 1862: Battle of Antietam

—

William Terdoslavich

It was dumb luck at first touch.

The 27th Indiana Regiment was going into camp near Frederick, Maryland, on September 13, 1862, when Corporal Barton Mitchell discovered a bundled paper in a field. Surprise! It was wrapped around three cigars. Surely this was his lucky day.

Then he looked at the "wrapper"—dated September 9, 1862, Special Order 191, detailing the dispositions of the Army of Northern Virginia as it invaded Maryland. Quickly, the captured order went up the chain of command to Major General George McClellan, the reinstated commander of the Union's Army of the Potomac.

McClellan had spent the previous days advancing slowly out of Washington, again fearing that Confederate General Robert E. Lee was lurking somewhere out there with 120,000 men, ready to pounce. But McClellan's fears vanished once he had Lee's order in hand. Now he knew exactly where each of Lee's detachments was located, and in what strength—a major advantage at a time when generals never had complete information of enemy whereabouts.

This spurred McClellan to get his forces moving—sixteen hours after he received "the Lost Order." Word also got back to Lee via southern sympathizers about what McClellan knew. The dream of shifting the cost of war onto northern soil turned into a nightmare. Lee had already split his Army of Northern Virginia into five parts, all in different places, each vulnerable to defeat by any portion of McClellan's larger army. Lee had broken the rules of war before and won. Now the calculated risk was turning into a rash gamble.

Those Who Dare Can Win

Knowing that defense alone never wins a war, Lee looked for ways to take the offensive. Invading Maryland might seem far-fetched, but Lee had a line of reasoning that took him there. Staying in Virginia would only continue the hardship of local farmers, already tapped out from supplying Lee's hungry forces. In Maryland, Lee's army could live off the bountiful land tilled by many southern sympathizers. Burning the bridge at Harrisburg, Pennsylvania, would slash the only direct rail route linking the eastern United States with the Midwest. Lee would then be free to turn on Philadelphia, Baltimore, or even Washington, D.C.

Okay, some of these goals were the stuff of daydreams, but a Confederate win on Union turf might—just might—influence Great Britain to recognize the Confederacy and mediate an end to the war. Also mindful of the war's political dimension, U.S. President Abraham Lincoln was keeping a secret scrap of paper in his desk, waiting for a Union victory before making it public.

The Army of Northern Virginia was on a winning streak when Lee took it north of the Potomac on September 4. Lee knew from previous experience that McClellan was not a quick or decisive commander in the field, more likely than not to take counsel of his fears. Banking on that, Lee assigned two-thirds of his forces to Major General Thomas "Stonewall" Jackson, which would assault the Federal arsenal at Harpers Ferry from three directions. This move stopped the garrison of 11,500 Union troops from reinforcing McClellan. Harpers Ferry was also a major supply base, whose capture would be a huge prize for Lee's poorly supplied force.

A fourth division would be posted around South Mountain to bag any retreating Union troops fleeing east. Major General James Longstreet would take his command north to Hagerstown, Pennsylvania, hopefully to block any mustering Pennsylvania militia. "The hallucination that McClellan was not capable of serious work seemed to pervade our army, even to this moment of dreadful threatening," Longstreet would later recall.

Approaching Folly

As of September 13, McClellan knew where all the pieces were on the chessboard, but Lee did not. But McClellan still had to move his forces through two passes at South Mountain to get at Lee's army. The division of Major General Lafayette McLaws covered Crampton's Gap, which led to Pleasant Valley, then on to Harpers Ferry. Farther north, Major General D. H. Hill blocked the way through Turner's Gap and nearby Fox's Gap.

McClellan assigned one corps to barge through Crampton's Gap on September 14 to relieve Harpers Ferry. McLaws gave ground grudgingly before the overcautious Major General William B. Franklin's force. The Federal garrison at Harpers Ferry fell to the three surrounding Confederate divisions in the nick of time early on the 15th, making moot Franklin's relief effort.

Meanwhile, the grossly outnumbered D. H. Hill held Turner's Gap for much of September 14 against the two corps of Major Generals Joseph Hooker and Jesse Reno, both under the overall command of Major General Ambrose Burnside. By sunset, Hill's position was outflanked on both sides, so his battered division retreated. No matter, Hill and McLaws bought time for Lee to send southward the mountain of supplies captured at Harpers Ferry and pick a defensive position for the impending battle.

Lee's choice of ground was reckless. The Army of Northern Virginia was making its stand just east of Sharpsburg, Maryland. Looking east from the town, there was a mix of farms, fields, and woods, bracketed by Antietam Creek in the east and the Potomac River to the west. The only crossing over the Potomac was Boteler's Ford, two miles south of Sharpsburg. There would be no way Lee could funnel his entire army through that single ford in a hurry if he had to retreat. If pressed, his army could be pinned against the Potomac and destroyed. Worse, Lee's army of around 40,000 was not "all there." Longstreet's corps was fully deployed, but not all of Jackson's divisions had arrived as of the evening of September 16, just as McClellan's Army appeared three or four miles away.

Did Lee really think he could break every rule in the book, just because he was facing the once-beaten McClellan? Was Lee being smart—or arrogant?

Cockiness Turns to Desperation

The Battle of Antietam began on McClellan's right, at the northern third of the battle line. At dawn on September 17, Hooker's corps crossed Antietam Creek and approached Jackson's corps, just on the other side of a cornfield, its line running through two stands of woods. Within ninety minutes, attack and counterattack pretty much wrecked both corps. A third of Jackson's old division was dead, dying, or wounded. The division of Major General John Hood suffered 60 percent losses driving back Hooker's corps, which also lost one-third of its number. Bodies clad in blue and gray carpeted the blood-christened ground. To veterans and historians, this became "the Cornfield," set apart from the mundane by such fearful bloodshed.

The corps of Major General Joseph Mansfield marched to reinforce Hooker. Mansfield insisted on leading his corps from the front—and was gunned down when his lead brigade made contact with what was left of Hood's division. Command devolved upon Brigadier General Alpheus Williams, Mansfield's senior division commander. The two divisions of Williams's command pushed through the woods east of the Cornfield, getting to within two hundred yards of the Dunker Church to the west, in the next stand of trees. Jackson was desperately reorganizing his line, dragooning anybody who could work a cannon or shoulder a musket to hold the line. Hooker was rallying his broken units to renew his attack when he took a bullet to the foot and had to leave the field. That attack stalled with the loss of its leader.

It was 9 A.M. Williams held his ground and requested reinforcements, his signalman rendering the message into semaphore. Two miles away, another signalman peering through a telescope relayed the message to McClellan, who always led from the rear. He now sent in Major General Edwin Sumner's corps to restart the assault.

Sumner's tactical ability was limited to attacking straight ahead, provided he had orders and a clear picture of the situation. He was typical of many Union commanders in the war's earlier years—too reluctant to exercise initiative, too reliant on written orders, which were never exceeded. Sumner arrived with his corps to find no one with a clear view of the entire situation, as both corps commanders were stricken and Williams only had partial knowledge of what was happening around the Cornfield. As Sumner tried to figure out what to do, his two divisions under Major Generals John Sedgwick and William French marched off in separate directions toward the enemy, thus ensuring that Sumner would not be fighting his corps as a single force.

With few reserves handy, Lee committed McLaws's division to reinforce Jackson and counterattack Sedgwick's division, causing it to break and retreat. French's division hit the sector controlled by D. H. Hill, whose regiments were strengthened by their placement in a sunken road that acted like a natural trench. Hard fighting would also rename this ground as "the Sunken Road," also known as "Bloody Lane." (By battle's end, Bloody Lane would be paved with Confederate dead.)

The division of Israel Richardson from Sumner's corps arrived to reinforce French's attack. The Confederate batteries posted on the rise behind D. H. Hill's line were losing the artillery duel to the Union guns. A Confederate brigadier tried to swap out a used regiment with fresh men at the right end of the Sunken Road, only to have his entire brigade break and run in front of Richardson's division. This unwound Lee's center. Two divisions fell back in disorder. Richardson pushed his division farther, taking the high ground behind the Sunken Road and trashing Lee's center. But the attack lost steam when Richardson was mortally wounded by artillery fire.

It was now early afternoon. Another corps under Franklin was close by, just behind the forces of Sumner and Williams. But Sumner thought it folly to press the attack with Franklin's fresh troops. McClellan concurred via signal flags, proving once again that misfortune favored the knave. (Lee's luck depended on fools such as these.)

McClellan was expecting Lee to attack his center, and so he kept Fitz-John Porter's corps and the cavalry of Alfred Pleasanton handy to repel it. The Army of Northern Virginia was fighting for its life, unlikely to attack. But the repulse of Sedgwick's division made McClellan fearful that Lee might pull another trick out of his hat that could win the battle.

A Bridge Too Near

This battle, like a play, would have three acts. With the first two acts having passed through Lee's left and center, act three would take place on Lee's right flank, starring the inept Ambrose Burnside. His overall command consisted of the corps commanded by General Jacob Cox, filling in for Reno, who died in battle at Turner's Gap.

Cox's corps was facing the Rohrbach Bridge, which spanned a deeper stretch of Antietam Creek, where crossings were few and far between. The bridge acted like a bottleneck, preventing Burnside from bringing many men to bear against the defenders on the other side. Wooded high ground overlooked both banks of the creek, giving advantage to the Confederates, who could concentrate their fire on the bridge.

Around 9 A.M., as all hell was breaking loose for Hooker, Mansfield, and Jackson, McClellan ordered Burnside to take the bridge and pin Lee's forces from the south. Burnside spent the next three hours trying to rush the span with a few regiments making piecemeal attacks. Lee thought so little of this threat that he actually peeled off a division and a brigade from this sector to reinforce his left.

Burnside tried to turn the enemy position by marching a division south to find a ford across Antietam Creek, then march back north to outflank the 3,000 men holding Lee's right. Poor reconnaissance turned that march into a fool's errand until a good crossing could be located. The division eventually arrived too late to make a difference.

Finally, a two-regiment task force charged across the Rohrbach Bridge around noon, just as Confederate fire slackened for lack of ammunition. Like all bloody landmarks at Antietam, the Rohrbach

Bridge became Burnside's Bridge. It took 500 Union and 120 Confederate dead to rename it. Now Burnside's exhausted lead brigades were nearly out of ammo. More time was wasted as he ordered a fresh division over the bridge. It would be 2 P.M. before it arrived—roughly two hours after taking the bridge.

Lee was also playing a game of patience. He did not shift any troops from his left to meet the growing threat to his right. He had one last card up his sleeve: A. P. Hill's Light Division of Jackson's corps. Starting the day at Harpers Ferry, A. P. Hill's division received orders at 9 A.M. to hurry to Sharpsburg, some seventeen miles away. He marched the five brigades of his division there in less than eight hours, with his lead brigade arriving around 3 P.M. And it was in the nick of time.

Burnside had ordered Cox to lead a two-division assault toward Sharpsburg, hoping to cut the road south to Boteler's Ford—the lifeline of Lee's army. But the thrust was blunted as the Light Division's brigades ran into Cox's lead units. Cox cautiously pulled his forces back to cover the approaches to the Rohrbach Bridge.

At the north end of the battlefield, Lee tried one more time to outflank McClellan's right, but it came to naught quickly when the attack met fire from a thirty-four-gun line placed on high ground by acting corps commander George Meade, filling in for the wounded Hooker. Daylight was fading, and Lee was out of options. It was 7 P.M. when the roar of battle faded into a spattering of potshots.

Sundown, Cease-fire, Spin

It took just twelve hours to make the Battle of Antietam the worst single day of combat in the Civil War. McClellan lost 12,350 men out of 70,000 and failed to bring roughly one-third of his force into battle. Even badly handled, the Union's greater numbers could have destroyed Lee's army by attrition alone. Lee's losses were far more severe—13,700 out of 39,000 troops.

Lee held the field for one more day, then pulled his troops back across the Potomac. McClellan did not pursue. By possessing the battlefield after the last shot was fired, McClellan "won." That was good enough for Lincoln to pull out the scrap of paper he had been hiding in his desk, better known as the Emancipation Proclamation, freeing the slaves in the Confederacy as of January 1, 1863. Lincoln had just moved the Union's war goal from reunification to revolution. Once word of the battle and the subsequent emancipation made it to Europe, the window of opportunity for British intervention was firmly nailed shut. Great Britain, which had freed its own slaves decades before, could not side with the Confederacy without the government of Prime Minister Palmerston risking electoral defeat.

Lincoln then nagged McClellan to cut Lee off from further retreat and destroy his army. The Army of the Potomac didn't start moving until October 21, long after Lee's forces made their getaway. It became apparent to Lincoln that McClellan had no strategy of what to do next. On November 7, after the midterm elections, McClellan was fired. Command was now turned over to Burnside—not a great improvement.

Lee would repeat his pattern of brilliant generalship, racking up two more decisive victories at Fredericksburg and Chancellorsville. Then he would again succumb to overconfidence and arrogance, fighting over some little-known Pennsylvania town called Gettysburg.

The Campaign for the Big Muddy

1862–1863: Western Theater

—

John Helfers

When the Civil War began, General-in-Chief Winfield Scott proposed a two-part plan to crush the new Confederacy, primarily by water. The first part consisted of a blockade of the southern ports on the Atlantic Ocean and the Gulf of Mexico, where the enemy shipped and received needed goods to. fund and equip its army. The second part consisted of sending a force down the Ohio to seize the Mississippi River, effectively cutting the South in half and encircling the main part of the Rebels. Pressure from the northern army on top, on the left from the captured Mississippi, on the south from the Gulf of Mexico, and on the right from the Atlantic would ensure the enemy's surrender.

Critics derided the plan's feasibility and goals, particularly since the Union didn't have the necessary ships to carry out a river campaign at the start of the war. They compared it to an anaconda crushing its prey in its coils, and the name stuck. However, Scott would be proven right in one aspect of his plan—the campaign to take the Mississippi River would prove to be every bit as important as the famous land battles to the east.

Caught with a lack of men, equipment, and boats, the South would respond poorly at best, suffering from communication and command issues, as well as a lack of an overall plan to defend the river. They ended up leaving the individual cities and outposts to block the Union advance, and, not realizing their jeopardy until it was too late, let them all fall like dominoes, and with them the river, into Union control.

The western portion of Scott's plan began in early January 1862, when Flag Officer David G. Farragut received orders to take his fleet of four steam sloops, twelve gunboats, and twenty-one mortar boats and capture New Orleans. Farragut assigned the floating artillery to shell the enemy force while the rest of his ships bypassed them and captured the city on April 25. Two weeks later, he seized the navy yard at Pensacola, Florida, depriving the South of another source of vessels. Emboldened by his successes, Farragut sailed upriver, taking Baton Rouge, then Natchez, Mississippi. However, in July he met his match in the heavily fortified city of Vicksburg, then the shipping crossroads of the Confederacy. Although Farragut's attempt to conquer the city lasted throughout the month, he was forced to admit defeat, leaving the toughest nut on the river to be cracked by someone else.

That someone was Brigadier General Ulysses S. Grant, who had already established himself with his campaign to capture Forts Henry and Donelson, taking the Tennessee and the Cumberland Rivers from the Confederacy. He'd also gained his nickname of "Unconditional Surrender" by demanding exactly that from the enemy at Fort Donelson. Grant knew Vicksburg was the key to seizing the entire Mississippi River, but capturing it would require a major campaign.

First, he had to get there. Heading south on the river, the next target on Grant's list was Island No. 10, another strongly defended outpost north of Memphis. With continual bombardment provided by Captain Andrew Hull Foote, General John Pope led his men across the river and captured Tiptonville, cutting off the garrison, which surrendered soon afterward.

Only one obstacle remained before Memphis—Fort Pillow. Foote had been injured in the Island No. 10 battle and was replaced by Captain Charles Davis. Although the Union ships suffered a surprise attack by fast, lightly armed Confederate gunboats that damaged two vessels, it was little more than a desperate feint. The Federal navy held fast, and the Rebels were forced to retreat, leaving the way to Memphis wide open.

The Confederate force defending Memphis, however, was determined to hold the city. To combat the fast southern gunboats, Davis turned to an invention that had been around for thousands of years: the ram. Colonel Charles Ellet brought six ram boats downriver to help take the city, and in a pitched battle they destroyed seven of the eight Confederate ships. They also didn't lose any men during the battle, although Ellis himself was wounded in the fight and later died from his injuries.

The way to Vicksburg was now open, but conquering it would be difficult indeed. Called "the Gibraltar of the Mississippi," its defenses were mounted on cliffs high above the river, making any approach or dash past on the river subject to heavy cannon fire. Although the rest of the river was now under Union control, the stretch between Vicksburg and Port Hudson, Louisiana, was a vital shipping artery for the increasingly commerce-strangled South—it had to be closed, and the sooner the better.

At first, Grant's attempts to get close enough to the city to capture it resembled the relatively ineffective efforts of the South to defend the Mississippi—unorganized and ineffectual. Unwilling to retreat all the way back to Memphis to bring his army down, he was determined to reach his objective by using either the Yazoo River or the Mississippi and tried several plans on both. During the winter months of 1862, construction was begun on two canals, one below Vicksburg, the other from Duckport, Louisiana, into bayou country, both of which met with failure. He also tried opening another waterway from the Arkansas–Louisiana border to Lake Providence and from there into bayou country to the Red River, and back to the Mississippi, which also failed due to the spring floods. A fourth option, digging to join Moon Lake to the Yazoo Pass to the Coldwater River, which flowed into the Tallahatchie, and from there into the Yazoo River, was stymied by a powerful Confederate battery on the Coldwater that couldn't be approached. A fifth route, passing through a bewildering series of various rivers and creeks, failed when Confederate soldiers drove off the Union force in a narrow waterway.

With all other options exhausted, Grant persuaded Admiral David Dixon Porter to chance a run past the Vicksburg batteries on the night of April 16. Although his twelve ships were all hit several times by the shore guns, only one failed to make it downriver. A week later, six barges towing twelve transports tried the same maneuver, with less luck; only half survived the trip. But the damage had been done—Grant could now begin maneuvering his army into position.

On April 30, the first Union forces landed on the Vicksburg side of the river. They pushed the Rebels out of Port Gibson and Grand Gulf, then marched north. Against them was a force of about 50,000 men, led by Lieutenant General John C. Pemberton. Although urged by his superiors to defeat Grant's army at all costs, Pemberton considered defending the city his highest priority, and felt that sallying out to meet Grant on the field would leave the city vulnerable to other Union forces, so he dug in and waited.

Aware that Confederate reinforcements were being mobilized at Jackson, Mississippi, forty-five miles away, Grant decided to take the potentially risky route of moving between Vicksburg and its relief force, and taking on first one army, then the other. Grant moved aggressively against the forces at Jackson, forcing General Joseph E. Johnston to try to hold the city long enough to evacuate cannon and supplies to the north, where he might meet up with Pemberton. Although Johnston had sent an order for Pemberton to attack Grant from the rear if he could, Pemberton refused to risk the city and stayed where he was. Grant intercepted the message, and if an attack had come, he would have been ready for it. By the time Pemberton marched his own men out, his and Johnston's forces were headed in opposite directions. Before the mistake could be rectified, Pemberton's force was defeated at the Battle of Champion Hill, then at the Black River.

Pemberton retreated to a ring of forts around Vicksburg to await Grant's army, despite Johnston's telegraph message urging him to abandon the city and save his troops. Grant attacked on May 19 and 22, but both assaults were unsuccessful, despite a small breach in Pemberton's line. Realizing he couldn't take the city by force, Grant hunkered down for a siege, acquiring enough men to increase his army to 71,000, and enabling him to turn some of them eastward to hold off Johnston, who was still gathering reinforcements with dimming hopes of breaking the Union forces and saving Vicksburg.

It was not to be. Throughout June, Grant set up 220 guns to pound the city day and night. Hearing more news of Johnston's growing army, Grant was planning another assault on July 6, but on July 3, Pemberton met with the Union general to discuss surrender terms. The next day, the garrison at Vicksburg marched out to give up their arms.

The last remaining bastion of Confederate power on the Mississippi was at Port Hudson, whose defenders had valiantly held off three Union attacks. But upon hearing the news that Vicksburg had fallen, the 5,500-man garrison surrendered on July 8. The Mississippi was once again in Union hands, allowing President Lincoln to remark, "The Father of Waters again goes unvexed to the sea."

In the battle for the Mississippi, the Confederate forces were outmatched at every level. From Grant's superb mastery of maneuver warfare during the campaign to the Union Navy's performance on the river itself to the final blow at Vicksburg, Joe Johnston and John Pemberton were always at least one step behind the canny northern general. But the failure reached beyond these two men. General Albert Sidney Johnston vacillated between a passive defense—letting most of the Tennessee River fall into enemy hands after barely contesting it— and attacking haphazardly, reducing the available Confederate forces without blunting the advance of the Union Army, until he was killed in 1862. The South also never allocated enough men or supplies to the western theater, partly due to Jefferson Davis never giving it the attention it deserved until it was too late. But by that time, the coils of the Union anaconda had completed its western encirclement, trapping the Mississippi River in its coils and cutting the Confederacy in two.

We Don't Need No Stinkin' Habeas Corpus!

1861–1865: The Union States

—

Paul A. Thomsen

hroughout the war, Abraham Lincoln struggled daily to both hold the North together and compel the surrender of the South. Although the South had coalesced into a Confederate force his military could fight, the Union was a bitterly factionalized populace. His policies were questioned by his own party and ignored by many of his generals. Governmental actions were daily criticized by a growing dissident movement of northern Confederate sympathizers known as Copperheads. None were more contentious than Lincoln's subversion of the Constitution to selectively militarily detain, try, and sometimes execute civilians deemed an imminent danger to a country at war. In fact, the efforts would have been unconscionable in peacetime. Still, in his wildest imagination Lincoln never considered that one of his own generals, Ambrose Burnside, would plunge the president into one of the biggest domestic policy blunders of the Civil

War by imprisoning the North's leading Peace Democrat, Clement Vallandigham.

Although the North had an industrial capacity far in excess of the South, the Union consistently suffered from a deficit of capable and willing field commanders. Winfield Scott, pushing seventy-five at the start of the war, was well past his prime to lead men into battle. At the Battle of First Bull Run, Irvin McDowell proved his gross inexperience in being routed by an inferior number of enemy troops. Similarly, George B. McClellan, an able Union trainer, also later proved to be a poor strategist and a fear-driven battle commander. At one point, the president suggested he could outperform his generals with an army in the field under his own command. Try as he might, Lincoln, however, could not find a general worthy of the rank.

With the Confederate forces making daily advances with far less men and supplies, Lincoln was forced to contend with what he had on hand and hope for the best. In November 1862, Abraham Lincoln replaced McClellan with a man he hoped could fight, Ambrose Burnside. Burnside, however, was by no means a strategic thinker or a consummate warrior. In fact, he wasn't even much of a financial manager. Upon graduating from West Point in 1847, Burnside left the army and promptly fell on hard times. By the onset of the Civil War, Burnside had narrowly managed to dig himself out of financial ruin by working long hours for the Illinois Central Railroad. Sadly, his battlefield career was, likewise, unremarkable. In 1861, for example, Burnside had been one of the routed brigade commanders at Bull Run. Worse, at Antietam in 1862, Burnside also dubiously chose to funnel his men across a stone bridge into withering enemy fire rather than ford the shallow nearby creek little guarded by the enemy. Worse still, his ordered attack repeatedly delayed the Federal advance, gave the Confederates room to escape, and caused the loss of approximately 500 Union soldiers in the single engagement.

Although the president hoped Burnside would at least be more willing to fight than McClellan, Lincoln's hopes in his new commander of the Army of the Potomac rapidly disintegrated. In December, Burnside executed an ill-conceived uphill, winter battle against entrenched Confederate positions at Fredericksburg, Virginia. According to the United States Army Center of Military History, in just this one engagement, Burnside lost 1,284 dead, 9,600 wounded, and 1,769 missing men. Lincoln was apoplectic. While McClellan had been slow to attack, Burnside's continued poor battle planning would soon drain the Union Army dry. With little choice, in January 1863 Lincoln was forced to relieve Ambrose Burnside of command and send him to the rear of the army, where, Lincoln believed, the failed commander would stay out of trouble.

Oh boy, was the president ever mistaken. . .

Instead of being neutralized by the transfer off the front lines, General Burnside's new command created an even greater problem for the president. In March 1863, Burnside was assigned command of the Department of the Ohio and tasked with rebuilding the army's regional presence. He was supposed to quietly reorganize the army's reserve elements. He also should have defended the region from enemy privation, waited for more competent commanders to break the enemy, and wired Washington for instructions should something unforeseen arrive. Instead, when Peace Democrat Clement Vallandigham, a former congressman and southern sympathizer, made appearances at rallies in Ohio against the war, Ambrose Burnside decided to settle the matter himself.

Over the course of the war, Abraham Lincoln had shown certain deftness in handling matters of civil liberties, but Burnside was not a subtle man. First, the general revised Lincoln's early war habeas corpus and military trials policies, including the charge that treason could be considered "expressed or implied" in his Ohio military command. Next, he ordered the creation of a military tribunal panel to enforce the previous order. Finally, when Vallandigham next spoke out against the war in Ohio, on May 5, 1863, Burnside's men swept in, arrested the man on charges of treason, and sent him before a five-man military tribunal. Given Burnside's new orders and the purview of field commanders during the war, the jury speedily convicted Vallandigham and he was sentenced to imprisonment for the duration of the war.

When the president learned of the incident, he was apoplectic. Not only had Burnside exceeded his authority and made a martyr of a minor political nuisance, but in prosecuting Vallandigham, the Ohio commander also threatened to upend a delicate legal matter vital to national security. Over the past several years, the president and his staff had taken great pains to negotiate a precarious balance between the issue of freedom of speech in wartime and military necessity. Although Lincoln had suspended the writ of habeas corpus (required by arrestees when someone is charged with a crime) and had installed military courts, the president had intended the measures to remain limited and administration control to protect domestic security interests. For example, in April 1861, the army moved troops from the North to defend Washington City against a potential Confederate invasion. The transfer, however, had been hampered by violence in Maryland, through which the rail lines ran. Some transiting troops were pelted with bricks and threatened by mobs. In another instance, eyewitnesses reported that Maryland militiaman John Merriman and a contingent of armed men forced a group of Union soldiers back across a Baltimore bridge at gunpoint and then set fire to the structure. The subject threatened not only to plunge the state into chaos, but also to drive Washington's northern neighbor into the waiting arms of the Confederacy.

With the security of Washington at stake, the Lincoln administration had been forced to take desperate measures. On the night of April 27, 1861, Federal soldiers kicked in the doors of several Maryland homes and dragged John Merriman and others out of their beds. They were then identified as national security threats and hauled off to military bases, where they were to be imprisoned indefinitely.

"If at any point or in the vicinity of the military line," wrote Lincoln on April 27, 1861, to commanding General of the Army Winfield Scott, " . . . you find resistance which renders it necessary to suspend the writ of Habeas Corpus for the public safety, you . . . are authorized to suspend that writ."

Yet Burnside's arrest of Clement Vallandigham was not of military necessity, had no such national security stricture, and, worse, severely undermined the Lincoln administration's public standing. During the trial, Vallandigham had refused to enter a plea, claiming his imprisonment was unlawful and the trial a mockery of justice. The trial itself also generated considerable negative press for the Lincoln administration in Ohio and across the nation. Furthermore, upon conviction, Vallandigham petitioned the Supreme Court to intercede on his behalf, generating still more bad press for Lincoln. Worse still, when the petition was denied, the court invoked District Judge Humphrey H. Leavitt's ruling, saying "the court cannot shut its eyes to the grave fact that war exists. . . . Self-preservation is a paramount law." Finally, and most unfortunately for Lincoln, the Supreme Court's refusal left the president as the only man capable of ending the farce and indirectly nullified the validity of his past national security measures.

The incident could not have come at a worse time. Due to the trial, Union public support for the war was once again waning. The economy likewise was faltering. The body count for each engagement continued to climb steadily higher. Consequently, more northerners were flocking to pro-southern organizations. Some scholars, such as David

Stephen Heidler, Jeanne T. Heidler, and David J. Coles in the *Encyclopedia of the American Civil War*, even estimate that pro-southern elements in the North grew from approximately 200,000 members to as many as 300,000 members during this period. Furthermore, Lincoln had recently been forced to replace Burnside's Potomac Army replacement, Joe Hooker, with another officer, Gordon Meade, for failing to perform adequately. As a result, one could have misconstrued that Burnside was really fighting for the other side.

Rather than let the problem grow as Vallandigham played the role of martyr for the southern cause, Lincoln rapidly moved to correct Burnside's mistakes. In a short time, the president quietly commuted Vallandigham's sentence to banishment from the Union to the Confederacy, and ordered the man escorted to the limits of Union territory and released into the Confederacy. There the Peace Democrat's pleas were rendered moot. With the double threat of Vallandigham now effectively neutralized, the president finally turned to the architect of the Union's great public relations mistake. Through the War Department, Lincoln directed Burnside to limit his remaining time in Ohio to attacking raiders and supporting Union operations in Tennessee. Now much chagrined, Burnside did what he should have done months before: he followed the orders of his superiors, kept his mouth shut, and contributed to the fall of the Confederacy in the West.

For a man whose major claim to fame remains popularizing sideburns, Ambrose Burnside's prosecution of Vallandigham did some serious damage to the credibility of the North. Coupled with Robert E. Lee's menacing thrust into Pennsylvania, Vallandigham's headlining presence won a sea of supporters for the Confederacy. It also emphasized the heavy-handedness of Federal governance and stoked the spiritual fires of dissent against Lincoln, which ignited in the anti-conscription riots of the summer of 1863. Burnside's vendetta against Clement Vallandigham also had an enduring negative impact on Lincoln's own reputation. Whereas other Civil War civil liberties cases involving military arrests of civilians (most notably, *Ex Parte Merriman* and *Ex Parte Milligan*) have painted the nineteenth-century president of the United States as a savvy lawyer who knew the limits of his abilities, the poorly handled Vallandigham case paints Lincoln as both a dupe for allowing Burnside to act as well as a hypocrite for pardoning a man his own system validated as dangerous. Above all, the case also serves as a palpable reminder of the boundlessness of alleged wartime necessity and national security.

Against a Rock and a Hard Place

December 13, 1862: The Battle of Fredericksburg

—

Doug Niles

By mid-autumn of 1862, Abraham Lincoln had had enough of General George B. McClellan. Although "Little Mac" (aka "the Young Napoleon") had finally won a victory, of sorts, at Antietam, McClellan—true to form—had never gotten his entire army involved in the battle, and had allowed Robert E. Lee and the Army of Northern Virginia to retire unmolested across the Potomac River. McClellan was a genius at organizing, training, and preparing an army, but he seemed almost pathologically unwilling to bring about a decisive battle, a clash that—while risky—stood at least a chance of destroying the Army of Northern Virginia and bringing about a speedy end to the war.

After the bloody but indecisive fight at Antietam, Mac resisted all of the president's entreaties to pursue the retreating Rebels, arguing—again, as usual—that he lacked supplies, that he was outnumbered, that his troops needed more preparation before they could be employed in combat operations. In effect, he refused to obey the direct orders of his commander in chief, except in the most reluctant, glacially deliberate fashion.

When McClellan replied to yet another of the president's prodding suggestions with several telegrams declaring that, now, his horses were too weakened and broken down to move the army's heavy equipment properly, Lincoln became positively waspish. "Will you pardon me for asking what your horses have done since the Battle of Antietam that fatigues anything?" he demanded.

Finally, on November 7, 1862, President Lincoln removed George McClellan from command of the Army of the Potomac. In his place he appointed Major General Ambrose Burnside, a general who had earlier won some small successes along the coast of North Carolina. Lately Burnside had been one of the army's corps commanders, where he had displayed stolid determination but little imagination. His corps had been badly bloodied at Antietam with little to show for its efforts, save that one stone bridge across the eponymous creek, forever after known as "Burnside's Bridge." He didn't ask for the army command—and he privately admitted that he was not certain he was capable of handling a force that numbered more than 100,000 men.

But he was a soldier—indeed, a West Point graduate, ranked eighteenth in a class of thirty-eight—and he would obey orders. When he took command, Robert E. Lee and the Army of Northern Virginia had retreated south to the Rappahannock River, where they were resting and refitting following the withdrawal from Maryland. Lincoln wanted a general offensive against Lee, so an offensive he would get.

Burnside's initial plan was not a bad one: instead of relying on the single rail line through Manassas as his supply corridor, ever vulnerable to Rebel cavalry raids, he proposed to move the army nearer to the coast and rely on the navy to keep him supplied as he began a drive on Richmond. He wasted little time in moving the Army of the

Potomac to the small town of Falmouth, Virginia, on the northern bank of the Rappahannock River across from the city of Fredericksburg.

So swift was the movement that Burnside had two corps in Falmouth, with the rest of his now 110,000 men closely following, before Lee had time to react. But here the first example of Burnside's great shortcomings popped up to delay further Union operations: the commanding general needed to have his engineering units and their pontoon bridges in place before he could advance across the river. Yet Burnside had an uncanny knack for failing to communicate his wishes to his subordinates. In this instance, in early December 1862, the result was that it took more than a week for the bridging companies to join the army.

By this time Lee had his entire army, some 75,000 men divided between Longstreet's and Jackson's corps, entrenched around and behind Fredericksburg. The city itself had been evacuated of most of its civilian population, and the Army of Northern Virginia occupied a very strong position indeed. Since here the Rappahannock flowed around a bend so that it passed the town from the north to the south, the Yankees were to the east and the Rebels to the west of the deep waterway.

Longstreet's corps, on the Confederate left, dug itself in on a series of hills that, while not very high, commanded the entire city. The most formidable of these was called Marye's Heights and was distinguished by a fine antebellum mansion with a classic columned portico that provided a splendid view of the city and river valley below. Longstreet's left was protected by the river itself, which curved westward just north of the city, while his right extended along the hills for another two miles south of Fredericksburg.

There Jackson's position took over, extending two miles more to the south until the hills gradually petered out. Jackson's right was posted at a small crossroads and rail junction known as Hamilton's Crossing. Beyond that crossing, J.E.B. "Jeb" Stuart's cavalry had charge of the far right of the Confederate line.

On the whole it was a very strong position, and it was an obviously tough objective to the Union soldiers looking at it from across the river. While secure against a frontal attack, it could conceivably have been flanked either upstream or down, but now that Burnside had his objective in his sights he wasn't about to waver in his focused and determined concentration. He realized that Lee might anticipate a sudden move to the left or right flank, so Burnside resolved to surprise his opposing commander by attacking right here!

Lee was surprised, all right—surprised that any army commander could be so foolhardy as to attack his obviously strong position. But for Burnside, the bridging companies were up, and it was high time to move.

The commanding general planned to make his attack with two of what he styled as grand divisions. Each of these consisted of two corps, while a fifth corps would remain on the east side of the river, ready to exploit any success that might be gained by the initial attack. Major General Sumner was in charge of the right grand division, the one charged with taking Fredericksburg itself, while Major General Franklin commanded the left, which would cross the river south of the city and try to turn Lee's flank.

A total of six bridges would be thrown across the river, three to support each side of the attack. Beginning in the chilly predawn hours of December 11, the engineers started to place their spans. To the south, the bridges would cross from the Union shore anchor to an exposed field along the riverbank, and—since there was no place for Rebel soldiers to conceal themselves in opposing the crossing—these were established with little resistance. Under the protection of a steady artillery bombardment, the engineers did their job handily, and by midday on the 11th all three bridges in front of Franklin's position were installed and ready to handle traffic.

Things were not so sanguine on the Fredericksburg waterfront, however. Though darkness and, for a few hours after dawn, a thick fog concealed the labors of the engineers from Rebel observers, there was no doubt that the enemy knew what was happening. Despite their most diligent efforts at silence, the men building the pontoon bridges could not help making audible clues as to their activities. As the fog began to lift around midmorning, Confederate sharpshooters—most notably a brigade of Mississippians concealed in the houses and other buildings of Fredericksburg—started to find targets.

Constructing a military pontoon bridge in the Civil War era was a fairly straightforward enterprise. The "pontoons" themselves were flat-bottomed, open-topped boats anchored with their hulls oriented up- and downstream. As these pontoons were placed side by side, gradually extending out from the near shore, stringer beams would be placed across them to stabilize the bridge—think of the boats as railroad ties, the stringers as railroad tracks. These stringers would then be covered by planking, so that the bridge surface would be solid enough for marching men, horses, and wheeled conveyances. Most significantly, each boat anchored, each stringer and section of planking, had to be placed by men who stood fully exposed at the end of the completed section of bridge. The farther the bridge extended, the closer these men were to the rifleman on the far side of the river.

As soon as the fog cleared enough for them to see their targets, the Mississippians opened up, killing and wounding many of the engineers while the rest raced for the security of the friendly bank. At first the northerners replied with volleys of musketry, hundreds of infantrymen lining up to plaster the city with their slugs. The sharpshooters, unscathed, would duck down and wait for the engineers to venture forth again, and then the whole process would resume. The cycle was repeated several times with nothing to show for it except more dead engineers.

Clearly some heavier persuasion would be required, and to this end Burnside turned to his artillery commander, Brigadier General Henry Hunt. Hunt had some 140 guns—the heaviest and longest-range pieces in the Yankee arsenal—in commanding positions on the high ground on his side of the river, and he turned the full force of these batteries against the city of Fredericksburg. Each crew was ordered to expend fifty rounds, taking deliberate aim with each shot.

For nearly two hours the thunderous barrage wracked the brick and timber buildings of the city. Witnesses on the Union side reported it to be the largest barrage of the war to date, and they watched uneasily at the wholesale destruction unleashed upon an essentially civilian target. (The entrenched Rebel army mainly occupied the heights beyond the town.) Beams and bricks flew through the air, walls tumbled, and fires erupted, all concealed within a churning murk of smoke and dust. Finally the bombardment ended and the engineers sallied forth again—only to discover that, while the explosive shells could knock down buildings, they could not kill all, or even most of, the men taking shelter therein. The Mississippians had taken some losses, to be sure, but they still numbered enough to make the exposed bridges deadly zones for any Yankees who dared to venture there.

Finally, Burnside and Sumner sent across several regiments in boats. These men, too, took losses in the crossing, but they fought their way ashore and, after being reinforced, were able to drive the Rebels from the town by nightfall so that the spans could be completed. For the next twenty-four hours, Sumner moved nearly all of his men across the bridges. They took up positions in the city, many of them embarking on an orgy of looting and pillaging among the battered buildings of Fredericksburg. Many eyewitness accounts report garish scenes, with men capering about in women's dresses and undergarments, and pianos and other musical instruments hauled onto the streets to be kicked into splinters amid the chaos. Any stocks of unbroken liquor bottles were quickly confiscated to further the war effort. Meanwhile, to the south, Franklin moved the men of his grand division across the river, after which they took up assault positions on the plain in front of Jackson's position.

As December 13, the day of battle, dawned, Burnside had already made enough mistakes to doom his offensive. He intended for Franklin to make a strong effort to break into Jackson's position and then turn the Rebel army by driving in the right flank. Yet his written orders to his grand division commander suggested to Franklin only that he advance part of his force to determine where in his front the enemy had strong positions. The commanding general never directed Franklin to prosecute a vigorous attack! There was no chance of him executing Burnside's plan, since he had no clear understanding of what the plan was.

Nevertheless, as the fog lifted in the midmorning, some of Franklin's men moved forward. A division of Pennsylvanians under the command of General George Meade encountered success when it forced its way into a ravine that split Stonewall Jackson's defenses. That erstwhile Rebel general had failed to appreciate the lone weakness of his position, and for an hour or more Meade's men met with considerable success, driving a deep, sharp wedge between the two halves of Jackson's line.

Yet Franklin (who was thinking "reconnaissance in force") failed to send any more men to support the Pennsylvanians' potential breakthrough, while Jackson and Lee wasted no time in countering the Federal thrust. Several Rebel divisions advanced against Meade, hitting the spearhead in front and from both sides, driving him back from the breakthrough and closing the breach in the Confederate line. Before long they pushed the Pennsylvanian division right out of the woods and into the open, where, finally, Union artillery posted across the river broke up the counterattack. But the damage had already been done, as the only Yankee thrust with any potential for success on this grim day was soundly bloodied and rebuffed.

On the plain between Fredericksburg and Marye's Heights, the day's drama was just getting started. The fog's dissipation raised the curtain on one of the most futile and bloody acts in a long and bloody war. Here, too, Burnside's communication failures manifested themselves in thousands of Union dead and wounded. It was his wish that Sumner's men attract the attention of the Rebel defenders, fixing them in place until Franklin's attack to the south should develop into a solid blow against the enemy's flank.

Sumner intended to attack Longstreet's corps with a broad front of blue waves, many brigades organized into a powerful blow, but the terrain just outside the city proved sufficient to block his intentions. The ground over which these brigades were to attack was discovered to be scored by ravines and a muddy drainage ditch, and was bracketed by sections of impassable marshy ground.

Instead of cautiously holding his foe's attention, Sumner, who also seems to have been hazy on Burnside's actual plan, dispatched his men in a series of attacks—fourteen of them—that all yielded the same result. Because of the constricting terrain, only one brigade could form up and attack at a time. This they did, heroically, each brigade marching forward under a hail of shot and shell from the Rebel cannons emplaced all across the steep slopes of Marye's Heights.

At the bottom of that hill, placed almost diabolically so as to block the Union advance, was a sunken roadway protected by a solid stone wall more than half a mile in length. Rebel soldiers could stand behind this wall, almost fully protected from enemy fire, and blast away at the fully exposed Yankees with so much musketry that the effect of the volleys resembled the lethal blasts of the machine guns that would come to characterize later wars.

The Federal brigades each followed the same pattern, marching stolidly, enduring the deadly storm, until they reached a very low, almost unnoticeable rise the ground, some hundred yards short of the Sunken Road. Here the Yankees would fire, almost impotently, against their sheltered tormentors, and die in great numbers. First was Nathan Kimball's brigade, and then the other two brigades of French's division, II Corps. Hancock's division of the same corps was next: one, two, three more brigades advancing in order to provide fodder for the Rebel guns. The proud Irish Brigade of New Yorkers went into the attack with 1,400 men; that night, 250 made it back to the regimental camps. And for the whole of the afternoon this butchery was repeated like some factory assembly line in hell, with divisions from the III and V corps joining the carnage, and always one brigade at a time. They kept coming through the afternoon and into the evening, apparently because Burnside was determined to attack and couldn't think of any other way to go about it.

After those fourteen brigades had been shattered against this impregnable position, with countless officers and men sacrificed in one of the most useless attacks of the war, darkness finally called a halt to the madness. One northern reporter recorded his reaction: "It can hardly be in human nature for men to show more valor, or generals to manifest less judgment," than he had witnessed on that bloody day.

Burnside, distraught by the disaster, wanted to personally lead a charge against the position the next day with his old VI Corps, but his subordinate commanders talked him out of it. Finally, on December 15, the Army of the Potomac withdrew to the north bank of the Rappahannock, and the Battle of Fredericksburg was over.

It was one of the most horrifyingly costly, one-sided, and futile battles of the war. Union losses numbered more than 12,500 men, while the Rebels lost a little more than 5,000. Absolutely nothing had been gained. Following a few weeks of muddy maneuvers at the end of the year, Burnside was relieved of his army command (January 26). Yet another general commanding the Army of the Potomac had been bested by Robert E. Lee and his Army of Northern Virginia.

And the war marched into its third year.

When Second-Best Generals Fight

December 31, 1862–January 2, 1863:
The Battle of Stones River

William Terdoslavich

"Can you hold your present position for three hours?"

Major General William Rosecrans put that question to his right wing commander, Major General Alexander McCook, the day before battle.

McCook casually answered, "Yes, I think I can." They knew they were facing a Confederate army nearby. McCook ordered his right-most units to build campfires that night, extending far to the right of his actual line, hoping to fool Confederate Lieutenant General Braxton Bragg into thinking he was facing greater numbers.

The Battle of Stones River was a bloody struggle over an ill-chosen battlefield. Bragg could have picked higher ground behind the Duck River, farther south. That would have made a Union attack more difficult. But no, Bragg concentrated his army around Murfreesboro, Tennessee, with the bulk of two corps west of Stones River. The hills that dominated the landscape went overlooked. Instead the fight would be scattered around a mix of cedar woods, occasional hills, and a few farms.

"In few other battles were the characters of the commanding generals so completely eccentric," wrote historian Peter Cozzens. He had a point. Neither Bragg nor Rosecrans could be called the sharpest knife in the drawer.

Robert E. Lee easily eclipsed Bragg, his winning streak standing in stark contrast with Bragg's inability to win a battle. Lee had already notched several victories around Richmond and the decisive wins at Second Manassas and Fredericksburg. Bragg only had his loss at Perryville, Kentucky, made worse by his talent for snatching defeat from the jaws of victory. Worse, Bragg was a strict disciplinarian, remembered by his contemporaries as too quick to find fault with his subordinates, who were not shy in finding fault with Bragg behind his back.

Ulysses S. Grant also overshadowed Rosecrans. Grant had wins scored at forts Henry and Donelson as well as at Shiloh. Rosecrans served under Grant after Shiloh and proved a slow and diffident subordinate. At Iuka, Mississippi, Rosecrans failed to do his part to trap a larger Confederate force in a pincer movement with a second Union force under Grant's remote command. Thus Rosecrans failed to earn Grant's confidence.

Subordinates and contemporaries recall Rosecrans as being harsh on some officers under his command, but that never got to the men in the line. Whether it was in battle or in camp, the troops always saw Rosecrans, and he made damn sure they had everything they needed. He would drive the War Department crazy, firing off fifteen or twenty telegrams a day, demanding more men, supplies, and horses. In reply, the War Department always demanded that Rosecrans take action. He was even threatened with relief if he persisted in waiting for "the right moment." By late December, he heeded the call of his superiors and advanced his army of 47,000 south from Nashville to face Bragg with 38,000 men at Murfreesboro.

Bragg and Rosecrans both planned to launch major attacks on their left against their enemy's right. So it was with some urgency that Rosecrans asked McCook: can you hold? Rosecrans sought a breakthrough on the left to take Murfreesboro. He needed his right to hold steady.

McCook said yes and went back to doing nothing. He never did ride the length of his line to make sure all the units of his command were properly posted, all brigades in line, ready to defend. One brigadier was so sloppy that he had only two of his five regiments actually facing the enemy.

As two of McCook's division commanders snoozed that night, a third perked up. Brigadier General Philip Sheridan took to heart the worries of one of his brigade commanders that "something might happen," given Confederate activity beyond his front. Sheridan reinforced that troubled brigadier's position with two regiments and roused his division to readiness before sunup.

Off to Sheridan's right, the groggy Federals got a rude awakening at 6:30 A.M. on December 31, 1862. A gray mass of Confederate infantry poured out of the tree line several hundred yards away. Formed up in ranks, the division of Major General John P. McCown came crashing into the disorganized division of Brigadier Richard Johnson's division, holding the extreme right of McCook's line.

Johnson's division slowly disintegrated. As men fell in greater numbers, each brigade would falter and fall back to the rear. This would unpeel the line, exposing the flank of the next brigade, which would also fall back to avoid being attacked from its vulnerable side. Eventually, Johnson's division retreated in disorder.

The right flank of Brigadier General Jefferson Davis's division became uncovered. The same sequence repeated itself, as units seeing their right flank exposed fell back to re-form their lines, only to fail rallying. Retreat turned into a rout as regiments, then brigades, sought the safety of the rear.

By 8 A.M., Rosecrans's right flank was collapsing. Then Sheridan's division became the thin blue line that must hold back the gray wave, lest it sweep away an entire army. Rosecrans's plan to launch a major attack with his left wing became moot.

The battle was going all wrong.

Sheridan Stands Firm

McCown's division belonged to Lieutenant General William Hardee's corps, whose morning attack kicked the divisions of Johnson and Davis like battered tin cans. The division of Major General B. F. Cheatham, belonging to Lieutenant General Leonidas Polk's corps, formed up to support that attack by taking a whack at Sheridan's line, which threaded its way through a scruffy stand of cedars. Cheatham sent three brigades piecemeal at 8 A.M., each hitting different sections of Sheridan's position. A pair of Union artillery batteries caught the Confederates in a crossfire, ripping bloody holes in their advancing ranks.

Cheatham sent in his fourth—and last—fresh brigade to breach Sheridan's line, to no effect. By failing to attack with all four brigades at the same time, Cheatham allowed Sheridan to shuffle his regiments and batteries to meet each crisis separately. Sheridan gave ground in good order and again reordered his line, but he looked with worry at his right. Union units still streamed back, uncovering his flank. No one was rallying the broken brigades. It was only 9 A.M.

Sheridan made sure he was seen by his men, and in turn controlled his battle. McCook, the corps commander, was nowhere to be seen. He'd be spotted, now and then, among the fleeing mob of blue. His order was inspiring: fall back.

Rosecrans knew none of this. He was at his headquarters, far away from seeing failure. He received one generic message from McCook seeking reinforcements, to which Rosecrans replied with a generic "hold your ground." But a staff officer delivered the second report, telling Rosecrans his right flank was collapsing. That was when Rosecrans sprang into action like an unguided missile.

Rosecrans was excitable in a crisis, often issuing a stream of orders, many of which were contradictory. But he made a couple of good decisions early, despite being in a jabbering near-panic. He committed Major General Lovell Rousseau's reserve division and the army's Pioneer Brigade to form a line behind Sheridan's right, giving the position some strength and depth. Next, Rosecrans abandoned his planned attack on his left with the wing commanded by Major General Thomas Crittenden. The movement across Stones River was halted, while Rosecrans pulled two brigades from this force to become the new army reserve.

By 10 A.M., Sheridan's line looked like a V, his right flank pulled back as far as it would go. McCook showed up and ordered a brigade to the rear, uncovering a section of line. That stupid move allowed Polk's corps to overrun a Union artillery battery that had helped hold the line all morning. By 11 A.M., Sherman reluctantly pulled his division out and fell back. But Rousseau's division was in line, ready to block the next attack. Hardee was not going to score his outflank easily. He pushed McCown's division to attack, looking to get around Rousseau's right, but Rosecrans checked the move by slotting in his last two reserve brigades to extend Rousseau's line. Sheridan lined up his division on Rousseau's left, while Major General James Negley's division fell in by Sheridan's left.

Bragg's Punch Loses Force

Now Bragg had to reinforce Hardee's slackening attack. Posted across Stones River on his right was the division of Major General John Breckenridge, just south of a series of hills that Bragg and Rosecrans overlooked. (Too bad: they offered commanding views of the battle-field.) Bragg ordered Breckenridge to release two of his four brigades and march them over to Hardee as reinforcements. But Breckenridge feared a suspected Union attack on the Lebanon Pike off on his right. He kept the two brigades.

By noon, Major General George Thomas, commanding the Union center, got word from Sheridan that his division was running low on ammo and needed to pull out of line to replenish. That withdrawal created another gap. Hardee tried to push his corps between Rousseau's and Negley's divisions. Always calm in a crisis, Thomas pulled back these two divisions to higher ground and made a stand. One brigade under Colonel William Hazen held fast near the Round Forest, blunting further attacks. It was the only unit of the day not to give ground.

Rosecrans's line was holding. It was sloppy, running at a right angle to the line originally held in the morning, with both flanks resting on Stones River. Johnson's and Davis's divisions were rallied on the right. Sheridan now had a new position behind them. Confederate cavalry was picking off Union supply trains. But the northern men were holding.

By 4 P.M., Breckenridge figured out that no Union troops were heading toward him. He sent the two brigades to Polk for an attack against the Union line. But Polk rushed them piecemeal into the fray. Like Cheatham's attacks earlier in the day, the unsupported brigades got cut down to no purpose.

The sun set on a messed-up battle that neither Bragg or Rosecrans fully controlled. Neither could deliver the killing blow.

Happy New Year

As midnight approached, Rosecrans rang in the New Year with a council of war with his generals. Accounts vary about the meeting.

"There is no better place to die," Thomas reportedly said as he favored holding. In the end Rosecrans decided to stay and fight rather than quit and run. Both armies spent New Year's Day doing nothing, hungover from the previous day's battle. Only Polk launched one attack, trying to push through Thomas's section of line, but to no effect.

Come January 2, Bragg decided to renew the battle on his right. Breckenridge's division was the freshest unit left, despite Polk's mishandling of its two brigades earlier in the battle. Bragg ordered the division to assault north into the chain of hills now held by a Union division. Breckenridge obeyed with gritted teeth, knowing his command would be mauled, but he would do his best. The attack drove the Union back, almost succeeding. But on the west bank of Stones River, upon a hill with a good view, the Union posted a gun line fortyfive pieces strong. The artillery let go, shredding Breckenridge's left flank. The division fell back.

That night, it was Bragg who took counsel of his fears. Believing that Rosecrans was about to be reinforced, he ordered his army to withdraw southward to Tullahoma. One brigadier protested, noting that all of the Union's troops in Tennessee were there at Murfreesboro. Rosecrans had nothing left to draw on. But Bragg clung stubbornly to his illusion. The Confederates withdrew, thus giving up the last meaningful remainder of Tennessee to the North.

Each side suffered about 12,000 casualties. But the Union could make good its losses. The South could not. Credited with a meanly won victory, Rosecrans provided some needed political boost to the Lincoln administration, which was eager to prove that the victory at Antietam was no fluke and that emancipation was no empty promise.

Rosecrans did not pursue Bragg, but instead kept his army at rest, building up another horde of replacements, horses, and supplies to fuel his next advance, months away.

Bragg, meanwhile, wallowed in recriminations. He had lost the confidence of his officers before Stones River, and so the call to replace him was taken up again. Subordinates spoke out of turn, communicating through back channels to the Confederate press or to President Jefferson Davis himself about how an army of lions was being led by a chicken. But Bragg had the one vote that mattered, and that was Davis's. Bragg would stay in command, and the dysfunctional agony of his army would continue. Victory muted the same internal discord inside the Army of the Cumberland . . . for now.

Fighting Joe Hooker Does Everything Except, um, Fight

May 1–6, 1863: The Battle of Chancellorsville

—

Doug Niles

After the Fredericksburg debacle, President Lincoln wasted little time in removing the clearly overmatched Burnside from command of the Army of the Potomac. On January 26, 1863, that exalted position was awarded to another of the army's veteran corps commanders, General Joseph "Fighting Joe" Hooker. Unlike his predecessor, however, Hooker had actively campaigned for the job, scheming with other corps commanders to undermine first McClellan's, and then Burnside's, performance.

This subterfuge had reached the point, by mid-January, that Burnside traveled to Washington and demanded that Lincoln remove corps commanders Hooker and Franklin, and a host of other ranking leaders from the army, or else replace Burnside himself. The president opted for the latter choice, and it is doubtful that Burnside was very disappointed—and it is certain that Hooker embraced the promotion with all the delight of a very ambitious and confident commander of men.

In some respects, the promotion was surprising. Hooker had a somewhat unsavory reputation, with one observer referring to his headquarters as "a combination of barroom and brothel." Still, the seasoned veterans of the army, bitterly resenting the lives wasted at Fredericksburg, reacted to Hooker's appointment with a modicum of hope. The Army of the Potomac was proving to be a very resilient army indeed, filled with soldiers who seemed determined to prevail in battle not so much because of their leaders as in spite of them. In Hooker, with his bellicose reputation and proven aggressiveness, they felt at least a common desire for success.

The new army commander took immediate steps to improve the lot of his soldiers, and these steps did much to further improve morale. He aggressively cracked down on corrupt quartermasters, men who had been growing rich by skimming profits off supplies that were intended for the army. He saw that rations for the common soldier were improved, opening up warehouses stocked with fresh vegetables and other delicacies that had been essentially lost in the ranks of the vast army bureaucracy. For the first time in months, the troops had fresh, soft bread instead of tough, dried hardtack.

Hooker granted furloughs, offered amnesty to AWOL soldiers— many of whom returned to the ranks—and had distinctive badges designed for each corps. These insignia, apparently trifling though they might be, went a long way toward improving unit cohesion and instilling soldiers' pride in formations that went beyond their immediate regiment, brigade, or home state. Finally, he reorganized the Union cavalry arm, melding the many small formations attached to the various Yankee corps into an independent force. There were enough troopers to form an entire corps of cavalry, and Hooker, based on the Confederate model, determined to use his riders as a single, powerful entity. This latter step went a long way toward propelling the Union horsemen into an arm of service that would soon match, and eventually surpass, the southern foe.

By contrast, Robert E. Lee's men were in bad shape as the winter of 1863 warmed into spring. General Longstreet, with two of his veteran divisions, was detached southward to support Rebel positions along the coast of Virginia and North Carolina. It was hoped that he could also garner some fresh provisions from those prosperous regions that had yet to feel the scourge of war. The troops remaining along the Rappahannock numbered only about 60,000 men, or about half the size of Hooker's army. With supplies running out throughout the region, troops ate wild onions and sassafras buds to avoid scurvy. Many horses starved because of a lack of forage.

But like their opponents across the river, the soldiers of the Army of Northern Virginia retained a very high morale, with an almost spiritual belief in the infallibility of their legendary army commander and his chief lieutenant, Major General Stonewall Jackson. From his position in unspoiled territory, Longstreet was soon able to send grain and hogs to replenish the army's commissary, strengthening the men and further improving morale. Still anchored around Fredericksburg, the army occupied a strongly fortified position that now reached some twenty-five miles in length. When Hooker's army began to stir, Lee was ready to watch, wait, and eventually to counter his opponent's activities.

Hooker possessed a confidence that was so sublime as to worry President Lincoln, who warned that his army commander was just a trifle too cocky. When Hooker boasted that the question was not "if" he would take Richmond, but "when," Lincoln pointedly remarked: "the hen is the wisest of all the animal creation, because she never cackles until the egg is laid." Still, Hooker's enthusiasm was unabated. As he began to put a plan of campaign together he was heard to say, "May God have mercy on General Lee, for I will have none."

As the plan took shape, Hooker continued to prove himself a master of military events. He had a clear objective: he wanted to maneuver Lee out of his entrenchments and force him to accept battle in the field, where the Union superiority in numbers should prevail. To this end, he divided his army into three large detachments. Some 40,000 men under Major General John Sedgwick would remain in the Union positions opposite Fredericksburg, there to demonstrate against the entrenched Rebels, hopefully to hold them in place.

Hooker also dispatched 10,000 Union cavalry, the largest such force yet to take the field, under the command of Major General George Stoneman. Their assignment was to raid far to the south in an effort to break Lee's lines of supply and communications with Richmond. While sound in concept, this task proved a little too audacious for the recently expanded cavalry. In the event, this proved to be an early mistake by the commanding general—though he had created a strong and concentrated cavalry arm, in its first action he sent it so far away from the main engagement that Stoneman's riders were unable to provide the traditional screening and scouting roles performed by the horsemen. Lee, on the other hand, refused to let Jeb Stuart's cavalry be drawn away by the distraction, and thus he gained much better intelligence about his enemy's movements. At the same time, the Rebel horsemen were able to screen Confederate operations very effectively and provide accurate intelligence about Federal deployments during the imminent action.

Finally, Hooker himself took command of the bulk of his army, some 70,000 men—a force that, on its own, outnumbered Lee's entire army. He intended to march them upstream, well beyond the left flank of the Rebel lines, and then cross first the Rappahannock and then the Rapidan River, placing his large force squarely on Lee's flank, where the southerner's entrenchments would be useless. He expected that the Army of Northern Virginia, thus outwitted, would pull out of its prepared positions and begin a southward march—whereupon the Army of the Potomac would advance, face its foe in a mobile fight on an open battlefield, and attain the battle of annihilation that had thus far eluded both sides.

This was a complicated plan, but the Army of the Potomac executed the movement with precision and speed. Though Lee's scouts informed him that much of Hooker's army was on the move, Hooker moved well beyond Lee's left flank and was able to cross first the Rappahannock and then the Rapidan before the Rebels could react. He moved into a region known locally as the Wilderness, a relatively tangled forest of new-growth trees, dense underbrush, and frequent swamps. Only two known roads traversed the Wilderness, and Hooker planned to use both of them to converge his forces at a remote crossroads known as the Chancellor Plantation.

By the end of April, Hooker's plan was very near to a dramatic payoff. The four corps under his direct command were advancing through the Wilderness toward Chancellorsville, though passage through the dense woods was a little more difficult than anyone on the Union side had expected. Still, all units were able to move into their assigned positions, and in his wing alone Hooker possessed more men than in the entire army arrayed against him.

Back at Fredericksburg, Lee and Jackson kept a wary eye on Sedgwick's 40,000 men, who sidled downriver on their bank, and made as if to cross and attack the Confederate right. However, neither of these veteran Rebel leaders was fooled, and together they concluded that they were watching a feint. Stuart's cavalry, meanwhile, had brought them news of the Federal presence in the Wilderness. Lee, ever the gambler, decided to violate one of the basic tenets of warfare by dividing his force in the face of a larger enemy army. It was a gamble that would pay off, in spades.

He left Major General Jubal Early with 10,000 men at Fredericksburg, well entrenched on Marye's Heights, with orders to keep an eye on Sedgwick. With the rest of his men, some 43,000, he marched swiftly westward, reaching the edge of the Wilderness on April 30. The Rebels plunged into the woods and, on May 1, met the advance elements of Hooker's force, General George Sykes's division of Meade's corps.

The resulting clash became a sharp little firefight, with Union General Darius Couch bringing up reinforcements at Hooker's command. The Rebels on the front seemed to be growing in strength, but so were the Yankees. It seemed to Couch, Meade, and most of the rest of Hooker's command group that things were developing according to plan. After all, if each side kept pouring men into the fight, lengthening the front, the simple law of arithmetic meant that the Federals would soon outstretch their foe and the victory would be won.

But they had not taken into consideration the army commander. Now, as the battle was beginning, Fighting Joe Hooker seemed to be getting very cold feet indeed. After another hour or so of the growing skirmish, he abruptly ordered Couch and the rest of his advance units to fall back to Chancellorsville, ceding the bit of contested high ground to the Rebels. Couch and Meade both protested vigorously, but Hooker's mind was made up—the men were to retreat, now!

"If he thinks he can't hold the top of the hill, how does he expect to hold the bottom of it?" Couch grumbled as he glumly obeyed orders, bringing his men as a rear guard back to Chancellorsville. That night Hooker tried to reassure his subordinate, boasting that he had Lee right where he wanted him. The reassurance didn't work, and later Couch would say, "I retired from [Hooker's] presence with the belief that my commanding general was a whipped man."

For their part, Lee and Jackson let the Yankees retreat unmolested, and paused to consider a plan of action. Thanks to a topographical engineer and some help from locals, Jackson learned of some narrow back roads that theoretically would allow him to move a force across the face of Hooker's army and come upon the Yankees from the west—that is, from the rear of Hooker's eastward-facing army. Lee approved the plan, and Jackson put it into motion as quickly as possible on May 2. This meant that, once again, the Army of Northern Virginia would divide itself in the face of a stronger foe, as Lee retained about 16,000 men to face Hooker while Jackson took some 25,000 for the flanking maneuver.

But, as usual, Robert E. Lee had taken accurate measure of his foe. Even as his corps commanders chafed at the inaction, Hooker seemed like a changed man, now determined to simply wait and see what developed. When III Corps commander Daniel Sickles located a relatively open bit of high ground in his front, Hooker allowed him to advance to the place, called Hazel Grove, with some of his corps. But for the rest, the army would stay in place.

On the right (westernmost) flank of Hooker's force was posted General Oliver Howard's XI Corps, composed mostly of German immigrants—commonly called Dutchmen in the vernacular of the time. These men had received little respect and affection from the rest of the army, and perhaps this prejudice was reflected in their being posted at what was assumed to be the far rear. Howard had recently replaced the previous commander, Franz Sigel, a fellow Dutchman. Howard had little affection for his men, and they reciprocated.

On May 2, Sickles reported large columns of Rebels moving past his position. He and Hooker assumed that this indicated that Lee was retreating, though Hooker did send one message to Howard warning him to watch his flank. There is no record that Howard passed this warning on to his men. Indeed, as more and more signs of activity began to stir in the woods to the west of XI Corps, many junior officers went to Howard's headquarters to warn of enemy activity. Howard and his non-German staff officers dismissed these men as worrywarts, even implying cowardice in some cases. The general would not authorize a change in his corps' facing, or anything more than a couple of lonely artillery pieces swiveled to face west.

By 5:30 in the afternoon, Jackson had his men in position, and they came swarming out of the woods like a hurricane. Though some individual units fought gallantly, Howard's corps was soon shattered, survivors streaming back to the Chancellorsville plantation in confusion and dismay. It was only the late hour that saved Hooker's force from complete disaster, as darkness finally broke the impetus of the attack and gave the weary Yankees a chance to catch their breath and reorient their lines.

Disaster did come in the darkness, but in a capricious act of cruel fate it struck the Rebels very sharply indeed. Stonewall Jackson, determined to keep the offensive moving, rode forward in the twilight to try to spur his men on to greater efforts. As he was returning with his staff to the Confederate lines, a group of pickets mistook his mounted party for Yankee cavalry and unleashed a volley of musketry. Stonewall was badly wounded by several shots that shattered his arm. He fell from the saddle and was carried to the rear, wrapped in blankets. The arm was amputated later that night. Though Jackson would show signs of recovery in the immediate aftermath of the battle, the wounded general would fall victim to pneumonia and die on May 10.

On May 3, Jeb Stuart took command of Jackson's corps and resumed the attack. By then Hooker's men had established a fairly strong defensive perimeter and, in fact, still possessed superiority in numbers that would have allowed the Federals to assume the attack in any direction that they chose. But Fighting Joe seemed to be all fought out. Much to Sickles's disgust, Hooker ordered him to fall back from his "exposed" position at Hazel Grove. The Rebels immediately claimed the spot, which was about the only good artillery ground in all the Wilderness, and used it to relentlessly hammer the Yankees for the rest of the battle. One of those cannonballs struck a pillar of the Chancellor mansion while Hooker was leaning against it, the resulting concussion knocking him out for several minutes. Fortunately for the Rebels, he recovered soon enough to prevent any of his subordinates from taking decisive action.

In the meantime, Sedgwick was moving aggressively at Fredericksburg, and this time the Yankees drove the Rebels from their trenches on Marye's Heights. Early, outnumbered by four to one, was pushed westward, and once more the Army of the Potomac had a chance to close on a portion of the enemy force. But again Lee acted quickly, virtually abandoning his position before the immobile Hooker and sending reinforcements eastward. On May 4 they clashed with Sedgwick's corps at Salem Church, sending the Yankees reeling backward.

Over the next two days, the Army of the Potomac withdrew carefully back across the Rappahannock until, by the end of May 6, that deep river once again divided the two armies. "Fighting Joe" Hooker's ambitious plan had come to naught, not for lack of a good plan but for a simple lack of fight.

Take Nothing for Granted

May 1863: Vicksburg Campaign

—

William Terdoslavich

War is fought by rules that all generals can understand. To defend, fortify. To advance, build up supplies, then march. If the enemy gets between you and your supplies, fall back. Then try again.

Major General Ulysses S. Grant played by those rules at Vicksburg and for a while gained nothing. His opponent, Lieutenant General John C. Pemberton, did the same and successfully defended his fortress on the Mississippi. Holding Vicksburg maintained the last link to Arkansas and Texas, vital sources for beef and supplies for the Confederacy. At the same time, the fortress cut the Mississippi in two, denying full use of the river to the Union from end to end.

Grant's capture of Vicksburg was more than just a siege. It marked a very serious change in Grant's thinking, the point where he discarded the rulebook and produced the turning point of the war.

So how did Grant pull it off? And how did Pemberton fail?

The Textbook Approach

Terrain did much to strengthen Vicksburg, long before any Confederate fortifications appeared. Its bluffs overlooking the east bank of the Mississippi marked the highest ground between Memphis and Baton Rouge. The town had few roads leading to it, usually perched on high ridges overlooking waterlogged lowlands that made it difficult for troops to march cross-country.

The orthodox approach to taking Vicksburg was an overland advance from a supply base. That is what Grant did in December 1862, moving his army south from Memphis, then building a supply base at Holly Springs, Mississippi, to support the next push. But that plan went up in smoke when General Earl Van Dorn led a cavalry raid against the base, burning the supplies. It was one of the few instances in the Civil War when a cavalry raid worked. Grant pulled his forces back to Memphis, scrounging supplies from surrounding towns and farms. (He admitted in his memoirs that this technique would be useful later, but at present it was only a means to an end.)

Concurrently, Major General William T. Sherman led a corps-sized attack against the bluffs north of Vicksburg, hoping to take the heights by frontal assault. It was a very conventional attack that failed. Grant was forced by circumstances in January 1863 to take the situation in hand when a political appointee, Major General John McClernand, took command of Sherman's corps and combined it with his own.

As a department commander, Grant outranked McClernand, so he took command of the latter's combined force and shipped this army to the west bank of the Mississippi, opposite Vicksburg. He now depended on the navy to deliver supplies, making his logistics impervious to Confederate cavalry raids. But Grant still had to find a way to take Vicksburg after failing twice.

Further downriver, a smaller force under Nathaniel Banks was maneuvering its way north from New Orleans to take the smaller fortress at Port Hudson, Louisiana. Banks made constant demands for more troops, which Grant always found a way *not* to provide because the army was "too busy."

Grant wasn't kidding. If he could not go to Vicksburg, he would try going around it. Army-navy cooperation was excellent, so Grant asked Admiral David Dixon Porter to use his flotilla of ironclads to probe the waterways north of Vicksburg, looking for an opportunity to outflank it. Porter tried more than once, but the efforts proved fruitless. Digging a canal through a peninsula across the river from Vicksburg failed. One scheme called for excavating shorter canals to link a myriad of lakes and bayous that peppered the Mississippi's west bank, hoping that such an improvised route would bypass Vicksburg. But in the end that plan was abandoned due to low water, numerous complications, and insufficient time.

Now it was April. Grant pursued every logical approach, by the book. Nothing worked. A lesser mind would have written off Vicksburg as impossible to take. Blessed with a lesser mind, Pemberton was banking on that conclusion to be his solution.

The answer was to break the rules. Grant now planned to march his army down the west bank of the Mississippi to a point south of Vicksburg. Admiral Porter would run his flotilla of ironclads and steamboats past the Confederate guns, ready to ferry Grant's men across. For Porter, there would be no return upriver. The Mississippi's six-knot current would slow down the ironclads, making them lingering targets for Confederate artillerists. Once on the east bank, Grant's army would be free to maneuver against Pemberton and Vicksburg.

Where Is Grant Going?

Pemberton's command in Mississippi was caught between two stools. He reported directly to President Jefferson Davis, who told Pemberton never to give up Vicksburg. The Confederacy was depending on

Texas and Arkansas for a significant portion of its beef, grain, and manpower to fight the war. Vicksburg was the vital link.

But Pemberton had to obey orders from the theater commander, General Joseph Johnston, whose responsibility ran from the Appalachian Mountains to the Mississippi River. Johnston was more than willing to give up Vicksburg if he could combine Pemberton's army with other forces to defeat Grant in open battle, provided it was in the right place and at the right time. (Johnston usually could never find the right place at the right time to fight anyone.)

At first, Pemberton handled his problems successfully, by the book. Sending Van Dorn forth to raid Holly Springs forced Grant back. Defending the bluffs north of Vicksburg checked Sherman. Vicksburg itself was well fortified, so attacking it from any point of the compass would not be easy for the Union.

But what was Grant up to? The naval probes into the Yazoo River and Steele's Bayou were checked by a few brigades and some well-placed artillery holding a few patches of dry ground. As for all that digging on the west bank, what was all that about? Pemberton hunkered down, ready to defend against the next conventional attack. Only conventional attacks were possible, so Pemberton thought.

Then the Union Navy ran past the guns at Vicksburg on the night of April 29. Sure, the guns scored hits, but only one steamer was destroyed. The rest of the flotilla got through. Grant had marched his army down the west bank to Hard Times, Louisiana, ready to cross over to the east bank.

While Grant was making his big move, he befuddled his opponent with two smaller actions. First was massing Sherman's corps against the bluffs north of Vicksburg, again. Pemberton kept his forces ready to repel the attack that never came. (It was this or let Sherman walk in.)

Then came the Union cavalry raid, led by Colonel Benjamin Grierson. Starting in mid-April, Grierson's brigade spent the next two weeks knifing its way from Tennessee south through Mississippi into Louisiana. Pemberton had no cavalry handy to stop it. Grierson's raid didn't wreck anything irreplaceable. But it distracted Pemberton, who dispatched a few infantry brigades hither and yon to protect a few rail junctions, hoping Grierson would cross paths with one of these "mobile garrisons." Grierson never did.

Crossing the River

Grant wanted to cross his army from Hard Times to Grand Gulf, but the Confederates were too strong there. Pemberton figured out this was the objective and dispatched 5,000 men to reinforce Brigadier General John Bowen, who commanded another 4,000 men in that area. After getting information from a local escaped slave about a steamboat landing farther south at Bruinsburg, Mississippi, Grant made that his crossing point. That put his army forty miles south of Vicksburg. After landing, McClernand's corps marched to Port Gibson, some ten miles inland, to face down Bowen's force, which covered the back way to Grand Gulf.

Pemberton could not move his entire army to Port Gibson to stop Grant. The forty-mile road back to Vicksburg could supply no more than one division. Bowen did his best to hold off McClernand's corps, but the battle on May 1 only delayed the inevitable. Bowen retreated once he saw the blue hordes outflanking his thin gray line. Grant pushed his troops, but could not trap Bowen, who evacuated the garrison from Grand Gulf.

Pemberton began calling in his scattered forces from all over Mississippi. Grant paused, preparing to detach McClernand's corps to work with Banks to take Port Hudson. But Banks was away, undertaking a fruitless foray up the Red River into Arkansas. Grant could not afford to wait for Banks to return. Action was needed now. So Grant broke another rule: get rid of his supply line and have his army live off the land, free to move anywhere except back the way he came.

Grant resumed his campaign. By May 7, Sherman's corps had marched down the west bank of the Mississippi and crossed over to Grand Gulf. The two corps belonging to McClernand and James B. McPherson were operating twelve to eighteen miles to the northeast.

Pemberton figured Grant would now turn northwest, cross the Big Black River, and strike Vicksburg from the south. He dispatched the divisions of William Loring and Carter Stevenson to block such a move. Pemberton wanted to advance his army southeast from Vicksburg to cut Grant's supply line. (He's supposed to have one, right?) None existed, but Pemberton didn't know that. Pemberton was playing the game by the rules. Grant wasn't.

Pemberton, with 32,000 men under his command, also expected Johnston to show up with 6,000 additional troops at Jackson, the capital of Mississippi. The opportunity existed for the two generals to combine their forces against Grant's 44,000—not quite even odds, but good enough.

Grant had to keep the linkup from happening. So he did what Pemberton did not expect—he marched northeast to Jackson. McPherson's corps got there on May 13. Discretion being the better part of valor, Johnston withdrew in the face of a larger force. With Jackson in pocket, Grant pushed McClernand's corps west toward Vicksburg while using his other two corps to trash the rail line from Jackson westward. This cut any hope of resupplying or reinforcing Pemberton, who now shifted his army to the east to block Grant.

What to Do?

Pemberton was ordered by Jefferson Davis to defend Vicksburg.

Johnston issued orders to Pemberton on May 14 to abandon Vicksburg and join forces.

Pemberton had to make a decision.

In a "council of war," many of Pemberton's generals wanted to link up with Johnston, but a few wanted to fight Grant and hang on to Vicksburg. Pemberton took the advice of the few. He advanced eastward down the Vicksburg–Jackson rail line, blundering into Grant's picket line at Champion Hill on May 15.

The battle pitted three Confederate divisions against six divisions under Grant, with Pemberton enjoying the advantage of high ground. Stevenson's division held Champion Hill while Loring's and Stevenson's divisions were posted on a ridge running south.

McClernand's corps attacked, with one division taking part of Stevenson's line and the other two mounting halfhearted pinning attacks against Pemberton's two divisions. McClernand sent a messenger back to Grant, asking for instructions. The reply was simple: attack. Grant rushed McPherson's corps to reinforce.

But McClernand was not a fighter. Noting the diffident pinning attacks, Pemberton yanked out his two divisions and sent them to his left to reinforce Stevenson. Grant made a mistake, pulling a division from his far right to hold the line against Pemberton's reinforced attack. This threw away any chance of cutting Pemberton off from his line of retreat. By 4 P.M., Pemberton saw he could not win the fight against increasing Yankee forces, so he withdrew his force, leaving a single division as a rear guard. Pemberton lost close to 4,000 men out of his force of 21,000. Grant suffered the loss of almost 2,500 out of 29,000.

Retreating to the Big Black River, Pemberton posted 5,000 men to guard the crossing while the rest of his force retreated to Vicksburg. But the defensive position was turned when a Union brigade attacked on its own initiative. This forced out the Confederate rear guard, but also spoiled a chance for Sherman's corps to cross the river farther north and score another outflank.

Pemberton finally got his force back to Vicksburg. Grant reached the town on May 18, getting word back to Washington of recent developments and calling for reinforcements. Trying to capture the town on the cheap the next day, Grant tried to rush the defenses. McClernand claimed to have taken a stretch of the Confederate line, and Grant maintained his attacks to pin Pemberton's forces elsewhere so McClernand could exploit the foothold. But McClernand's report proved false, so men died for nothing. Grant built his siege lines, truly cutting off Vicksburg. He deployed incoming reinforcements to screen all avenues of approach to the north and east, thus keeping Johnston away. (McClernand was eventually relieved by Grant for speaking out of turn to the press, claiming credit for more than he actually did.)

By July 4, southern troops and townspeople were starving. No relief could be expected for Vicksburg. Pemberton acceded to Grant's demand for an unconditional surrender.

The Score

Grant read the situation shrewdly, paroling the defeated Confederates, knowing they would "quit the war" and go home. Banks returned from his idiot errand to Arkansas and took the surrender of Port Hudson later in July.

The blood price was cheap. From May 1 to July 4, Grant lost about 9,300 men. Pemberton surrendered with 29,500—a total loss for the Confederacy. The Union now had undisputed control of the Mississippi. Grain from the inland states could flow again to New Orleans for export. The South lost all supplies coming from its western states. Grant's victory also coincided with Meade's win at Gettysburg. That battle was certainly the dramatic climax of the war, but the true strategic turning point was Vicksburg.

Grant came out of the campaign a changed general. Conventional thinking was a straitjacket he discarded in favor of fierce, ruthless common sense. As he later wrote: "I don't underrate the value of military knowledge, but if men make war in slavish obedience to the rules, they will fail. No rules can apply to conditions of war as different as those which exist in Europe and America. Consequently, while our generals were working out problems in an ideal character . . . practical facts were neglected."

Five Generals in Two Years

1861–1865: The Union Army's Command-Level Failures

John Helfers

One of the most striking differences between the North and the South during the Civil War was in the choice of commanders for the two armies. Like everything else in the Civil War, the Union and the Confederacy had very different ways of organizing and leading their armies—but the Union had particular difficulty in finding aggressive leaders for its new army.

The Confederate president, West Point graduate Jefferson Davis, had served in the field as colonel during the Mexican War, and was committed to installing trained and experienced officers to lead his army. Almost immediately, the South made Robert E. Lee, one of the finest tactical and military minds of his generation, one of the first five generals in charge of the Confederate Army. Lee would lead the Army of Virginia against the northern forces in most of the major battles in the east. The others, skilled officers Thomas J. "Stonewall" Jackson, James Ewell Brown "Jeb" Stuart, Jubal A. Early, and Joseph

E. Johnston, would make their own valiant contributions to the southern war effort.

On the other hand, the North suffered the resignation of hundreds of military officers across all branches of service at the start of the war—many to join the Confederate cause. The Union Army also did not have a fixed command in place when the war began, and had to slowly create one while also trying to fight. The lack of firm, aggressive leadership would hinder the Federal army, particularly the Army of the Potomac, especially in the early years of the war, when a skilled, confident commander might have been able to bring the conflict to a swift conclusion. Although each potential general selected was an experienced military officer, their skills were often not the ones needed by a general-in-chief. (For those wondering why this essay, which details a problem the *winning* side had, is included, please remember that while the Union ultimately triumphed, if the North's upper-echelon commanders had kept failing to defeat the Confederacy, history might have turned out very differently.)

The first commanding officer for the Union Army was General-in-Chief George Brinton McClellan. (When the war began, General Winfield Scott was serving in the position, despite being too old and unfit to go into battle.) McClellan had gained acclaim for his swift carving of northwestern Virginia from the rest of the state (even though he left most of the fighting during the campaign to his subordinates). He took command of the Army of Northeastern Virginia from General Irvin McDowell after the disastrous action at Bull Run on July 21, 1862, where, after a day of back-and-forth fighting, two forward Union batteries were overrun, leading to the army's defeat.

Aware that this would not be a swift war, McClellan took the rest of the summer to train the new recruits swelling the Union Army. He didn't order any major troop movements, despite the presence of Confederates near Washington, D.C., including at an outpost ten miles away that allowed them an unobstructed view of the main road south of the capital as well as the army's advance camps. The unit withdrew in September, and when the site was investigated, their covering artillery was found to be "Quaker guns"—logs painted black, which made McClellan the butt of jokes in the northern press.

Still, Lincoln kept his faith in McClellan, making him the general-in-chief of all Union forces in November after Scott's resignation due to age and ill health (a third reason may have been his acrimonious relationship with McClellan). McClellan's first action upon receiving this promotion was to prepare . . . and prepare . . . and prepare his troops some more. The only action during this time was an ill-handled reconnaissance at Ball's Bluff, where Union regiments were routed and their commanding officer, Colonel Edward D. Baker, killed in action.

And still McClellan delayed, arousing the ire of hawkish Republican leaders in Washington, including Edwin M. Stanton, the secretary of war. They all felt McClellan lacked the will to fight, with some even accusing him of being a Confederate sympathizer, since he refused to ally with the hard-core abolitionists, feeling that slavery was protected under the Constitution. Whatever the reason, McClellan dragged his heels so long that in March 1862 he was demoted back to the commander of the Army of the Potomac. Lincoln had to directly order him to go after Richmond, figuring to capture the enemy's capital and cut off the head of the Confederacy in one stroke.

But even when McClellan entered the field, he was unable to do so effectively. He'd planned to take a massive army down to Fort Monroe, then back up the Virginia peninsula toward Richmond. He was hoping a war of maneuver would allow the Union Army to defeat the southern nation while avoiding a head-on collision between the two armies, and allow a swift, bloodless reunification of the two sides.

Lincoln and Stanton, however, demanded that enough men be

left behind so that Washington, D.C., would be adequately protected in the event of a Rebel attack on the city. McClellan promised to do so, but didn't follow through, forcing the president to separate an entire army corps from his command and place it between Washington and Fredericksburg. Now McClellan only had 100,000 men at his disposal (which still should have been plenty). He also relied too heavily on his head of military intelligence, Allan Pinkerton, who constantly overestimated the Confederate force's strength, an error that slowed McClellan's advance to a crawl.

By this time, McClellan's psyche was weakening, both from his demotion as well as the suspicion that the politicians in Washington were plotting against him (which was most likely correct in some cases). When Lee and his troops struck during the series of battles and skirmishes that would later be known as the Seven Days' Battles, McClellan provided hardly any leadership, apparently overcome by the idea of actually sending tens of thousands of men to their deaths. He led from well behind Union lines, including from a ship, the *Galena*, in one instance, and even leaving the field of battle twice. The series of clashes at places like Mechanicsville, Gaines' Mill, Savage's Station, Frayser's Farm, and Malvern Hill halted the Union advance, with the Confederates taking more losses than they could afford—3,286 dead and 15,909 wounded to the Union's 1,734 dead and 8,066 wounded. Still, a victory was a victory for the South, and it also hammered a big nail in the coffin of McClellan's military career.

Back in Washington, the cabinet cast about for another general-in-chief, and found what they thought was an ideal candidate in Henry "Old Brains" Halleck, who had been fighting on the western front as part of the Union's Department of the Mississippi. Halleck's first action was to assess the state of the Army of the Potomac. McClellan was requesting reinforcements to continue his advance, despite believing he faced an army of 200,000 Rebels. Instead Halleck ordered the withdrawal of the army to northern Virginia. McClellan took most of August to plod his army out of harm's way.

Reassigned to bolster the defenses of Washington, D.C. (Lincoln justified his order by saying, "If he can't fight himself, he excels in making others ready to fight"), McClellan received word of Lee's advance into Maryland in early September, and slowly sallied forth at the head of 84,000 men to carefully pursue the Rebel army. Although McClellan had the infamous "three cigars" orders found by a Union soldier, informing him of Lee's plan to divide his army, he was still the same cautious, stolid leader, and advanced at a snail's pace.

A brief series of battles was fought for three passes at South Mountain on September 14, but when night fell, the Confederates still held two of them. This allowed Lee to assemble his main force at Sharpsburg and prepare for the Union Army to come to him, which it did at Antietam Creek on September 17. When the smoke cleared after the bloodiest day of fighting in U.S. military history, more than 3,500 men had been killed and a staggering 22,719 were wounded on both sides. Although outnumbered almost two to one, Lee had fought McClellan to a draw, able to shift his men to meet each of the three Union Army's attacks in turn.

Although in hindsight the battle was a win for the Union, since it both stopped the Rebel advance and allowed Lincoln to announce the Emancipation Proclamation, it was also the end of McClellan's military career. When he refused to pursue the tattered Confederate Army for more than a month, Lincoln removed him from command on November 7, 1862.

His replacement, Henry Halleck, had made his reputation leading first the Department of the Missouri, then the Department of the Mississippi in the west (again, there is controversy as to whether Halleck or his subordinates, which included Ulysses S. Grant and John Pope, were responsible for the Union successes). After securing the upper half of the Mississippi River, Halleck was called to Washington, where Lincoln hoped he could prod the Union generals to action. Alas, if McClellan was a better administrator than commander, Halleck was McClellan multiplied by five. An aloof, abrasive man, he did not inspire confidence in his subordinates or Lincoln's cabinet. Even the president himself assessed Halleck as "little more than a first-rate clerk." Under his jurisdiction, the Union Army was well equipped and trained, but Halleck did not direct its movement in the field, leaving that up to Lincoln and Secretary of War Stanton, both of whom, it should be noted, micromanaged the war effort.

But no matter who was issuing the orders, the Union was rocked by a series of mismanaged battles due in part to the installation of two more generals to lead the Army of the Potomac who would be defeated by Lee.

Major General Ambrose Burnside had fought under McClellan in the Peninsula Campaign and at Antietam. He managed to orchestrate a crushing defeat for the Army of the Potomac at Fredericksburg on December 11 to 15, 1862. His army's quick advance to the field of battle stopped upon crossing the Rappahannock River, allowing Lee to set up his troops on Marye's Heights. Instead of finding another attack route, Burnside ordered wave after wave of futile charges that cost them 1,284 dead and 9,600 wounded, compared to the 608 killed and 4,116 wounded Confederates. Burnside tried to strike at Lee once more in January, but his plan was ruined by rainy weather (today it is referred to as the "Mud March") and Lincoln replaced him with Major General Joseph "Fighting Joe" Hooker.

Hooker had chafed under the ineffective leadership of both McClellan and Burnside since the war began, and he welcomed the chance to lead. After reinvigorating the Army of the Potomac's morale by improving the care of the men under his command, his elegant plan seemed very feasible. First, his cavalry would swing behind Lee's army to disrupt his supply lines, then Hooker's army would outflank Lee, then attack and defeat him. Unfortunately, the reality was less glorious. The cavalry didn't accomplish its goals, and Hooker was defeated at the Battle of Chancellorsville, fought on April 30 to May 6, 1863. The typically aggressive Lee divided his force of 60,892 men and struck hard at elements of Hooker's massive 133,868-man army, beating them soundly and forcing Hooker to leave the field. Almost incapacitated by a near miss from a cannonball that hit a wooden pillar he'd been leaning on, Hooker was timid and unaggressive in command, unable to muster his large army in a concerted effort. He would resign his command three days before one of the most critical battles of the war—Gettysburg.

His replacement, Major General George Gordon Meade, would serve as the commander of the Army of the Potomac until the end of the war. With only three days to assume command before the start of the fighting at Gettysburg, Meade finally stopped the tide of Union losses. Outside a small Pennsylvania town, he and his subordinate officers held off Rebel assaults in heavy fighting from July 1 to 3, 1863, halting Lee's second invasion of the North. The casualties were heavy on both sides (Union: 3,155 killed, 14,531 wounded; Confederates: 4,708 killed, 12,693 wounded), but the decisive victory was exactly what the Union needed. Unfortunately, Meade did not follow up on his opportunity to pursue and defeat Lee's army once and for all, despite the Confederates being trapped on the rain-swollen Potomac for a few days. Just as Pickett's Charge was a high-water mark for the South, Gettysburg was the high-water mark for Meade, who would go on to undistinguished service for the rest of the war.

By March 1864, Ulysses S. Grant would replace Halleck as general-in-chief of the Union Army, and under his leadership, the final blows would be struck to bring the Confederacy down once and for all. But why weren't the other generals able to defeat Lee's seemingly (at least until Gettysburg) unstoppable army?

In the case of McClellan and Halleck, the answer is obvious—

both men could handle localized military actions where the goal was clearly identified, but the pressure of creating a strategy with the entire Union riding on it was more than they could handle. Add to this a hostile press ready to lampoon them for the slightest mistake, as well as a cabinet that could turn on them for that same mistake, and they found themselves in a thankless, grueling job where success demanded more of the same, only better, and a single failure marked them as targets. If some theories are correct, and McClellan and Halleck rode to their success on the coattails of others, then it would be only logical that, when faced with the true challenge of coordinating all of the Union Army across the huge front, they would simply not be up to the task.

As for Burnside and Hooker, not only did they allow themselves to be beaten by smaller Confederate forces that used terrain more effectively, but they were also up against a foe almost impossible to defeat—the already burnished legend of Robert E. Lee. Both generals became timid and unaggressive when facing the leader of the Army of Virginia (although for Hooker, one could say the near miss by the cannonball played a part as well). It is not to say that Lee's reputation alone defeated either Burnside or Hooker—how he deployed his officers and men took care of that. However, when all is said and done, the simple fact is that both generals, each a capable officer in his own right, were outmaneuvered and outfought by the brilliant southern general.

And in the end, it was a hard-drinking, plain-speaking general, Ulysses S. Grant, who understood that the only way to win the war was to grind down the South's military and economy until it could not fight anymore. That would lead the Union Army to victory.

Lee Gambles at the Right Time, in the Wrong Place

June 3–July 14, 1863: The Gettysburg Campaign

—

Douglas Niles

From the outset of the American Civil War, the strategic imperatives of the Union and the Confederacy had been diametrically opposed. Since the southern states had already seceded, and they began the war in control of their own territory, they simply needed to maintain the status quo in order to conclude the conflict victoriously. There was no manifest need for the Rebel armies to conquer, or even attack, the Union.

President Lincoln's goal, of course, was to restore the United States to its original boundaries, which required him to gain control of the rebellious states by force or other means, and compel them to rejoin the Union. This could only be done by carrying the war into the southern states. In one form or another, all of the Union-initiated campaigns were designed to bring the country closer to this goal.

This strategy was articulated right from the start by the hero of the Mexican War and U.S. Army Chief of Staff Winfield Scott. When he suggested that a long and complicated series of campaigns of relentless pressure would be necessary to win, however, his idea was widely derided as the "Anaconda Strategy." It was nowhere near lively or imaginative enough to appeal to a population that expected the war to be over in a matter of months. In fact, Lincoln's first call for volunteers created regiments that were only planned to last for ninety days! As the months turned into years, however, it became increasingly obvious that the Anaconda Strategy was the only way for the Union to prevail.

Sometimes the method employed was direct and physical, as in the campaigns in the western theater where Grant, Buell, and others moved into the Confederacy in a more or less straightforward attempt at conquest. The same was true in the east, at least in concept, as McClellan launched his ill-fated Peninsula Campaign in his own timid way as an attempt to move against the Rebel capital of Richmond.

Other methods were more indirect, most notably in the Union Navy acting to blockade ever-greater stretches of the southern coast in an effort to deny supplies and commerce to the Rebels. Such, too, was the aim of the diplomatic offensive engaged by American statesmen in Europe who strove to keep England and France from coming to the aid of the South. Even the president's Emancipation Proclamation, announced after the Pyrrhic victory at Antietam, served this purpose: by publicly striking at the institution of slavery, it clearly staked a claim to the moral high ground, making any European sympathy for the South a very distasteful proposition.

All these offensives, direct and indirect, chipped away at the borders, the resolve, and the resources of the Confederacy, though by the spring of 1863 none had come close to striking a lethal blow. Still, it was becoming clear to some Rebel leaders, Robert E. Lee prominent among them, that a slow war of attrition in the face of implacable Union pressure could have only one outcome—an outcome that would be very bad for the independence of the Confederate States of America.

In the most important theater of the war, the fertile and populated lands around the respective capitals of Richmond, Virginia, and Washington, D.C., the Rebels had accomplished some startling successes with their very capable and well-led armies. While some of these battles had been defensive on the part of the South—Fredericksburg being perhaps the most vivid example—some of Lee's most dramatic successes had involved taking his army on the attack. The stunning setback of Second Manassas had shattered a Union army and opened the road into Maryland for a large-scale raid. That campaign had ended at Antietam, where, even though Lee had been forced to fall back from the field, a strong Confederate defensive position coupled with McClellan's well-known penchant for hesitation had allowed Lee to escape while inflicting terrible damage on his enemy.

The Battle of Chancellorsville, in May 1863, was perhaps the most perfect example of Lee's idea of a defense-by-offense. Following its brutal and (at least temporarily) demoralizing defeat, the Army of the Potomac, still under the command of Joe Hooker, was pushed back north of the Rappahannock River, there to lick its wounds and contemplate how in the world it had been savaged by a Rebel army only half its size. It seems clear that neither the troops, nor Hooker himself, knew the answer.

Meanwhile, just south of that same river, Bobby Lee was already plotting his next move. Buoyed by the dramatic, if incomplete, success at Chancellorsville, and realizing that the southern supply and reinforcement reserves were down to the bottom of the barrel, General Robert E. Lee knew that it was time for the Army of Northern Virginia to do something very dramatic.

By this time in the war, Lee and the Army of Northern Virginia had a certain sense of destiny and infallibility about them. Lee had proven time and again to be a master strategist and tactician, and his subordinate generals and hardy, veteran soldiers had yet to let him down. The fullness of this success, however, had gone a long way toward masking some key weaknesses in General Lee himself, while the strength of his military reputation had made him virtually untouchable by even the highest authorities in all the Confederacy. After Chancellorsville, it seemed clear that what Robert E. Lee wanted from his government, Robert E. Lee would get (if it was available).

And what Lee wanted, now, was to go on the attack.

There were, in fact, many sound reasons for this idea. Prominent among them was forage and supply. Both armies had been encamped and operating in Virginia since Antietam, the previous September. The lands around Fredericksburg, and for a great distance in every direction, had pretty much been ravaged and scoured by the presence of nearly 200,000 hungry soldiers, not to mention their tens of thousands of mounts and livestock. As the summer growing season was commencing in 1863, Lee argued persuasively that a movement of his army northward into Maryland and Pennsylvania would put the burden of supporting those troops onto the northern states that had, as yet, barely felt the harsh scythe of military operations. Beyond just the army's subsistence, a raid into Pennsylvania would provide opportunities for the capture of livestock and horseflesh that could be returned to Virginia to further replenish the sadly depleted local herds.

Furthermore, Lee argued that, after Chancellorsville, the Army of the Potomac would be badly demoralized. He believed he had the measure of Hooker as an army commander and was eager to have another crack at a decisive battle. In the former assumption, Lee was mistaken, for the Army of the Potomac proved once again to have an almost surreal ability to survive a terrible defeat and emerge with troops not only confident and courageous, but eager for an opportunity to redeem their previous failure. These hardy veterans fought with pride and resolve that came from within themselves, and seemingly made them immune to even the most glaring ineptitudes of their commanders.

And as for Hooker, his glaring weakness in combat management at Chancellorsville had concealed some genuine skill in leadership and maneuver. As it happened, these attributes would be essential to the upcoming campaign. When it finally came to battle, the Rebels would not in fact find Fighting Joe Hooker in command of the Union Army—though in May 1863 that was a development unknown to both sides that lay several weeks in the future.

Lee took his arguments, persuasively, to Jefferson Davis himself. The Confederate president was facing pressure from many directions, for his beleaguered nation was proving to be a dike with more holes than he had fingers. Most significant, General Grant's Army of the Tennessee had been besieging Vicksburg, Mississippi, for months. That city was the last southern link across the great river, and if (when?) it fell, the Confederacy would be effectively sliced in two. While most of the southern armies were committed to ongoing and critical campaigns, General George Pickett, at Richmond, was in command of a veteran division detached from Lee's army. The Confederate secretary of war wanted to send Pickett west to help defend Vicksburg.

But there was no saying no to Robert E. Lee. He argued that Pickett was needed in the Army of Northern Virginia, and that he wouldn't even reach Vicksburg in time to make a difference—a true enough conclusion, as Vicksburg fell the day after the Battle of Gettysburg concluded, and Pickett barely made it to Pennsylvania in time to participate there. By the time Lee departed Richmond to rejoin his army, he had secured the return of Pickett's division, and been granted official permission to initiate a new invasion of the North. His wish for an offensive campaign had been granted.

Even before the movement got under way, a trait of Lee's command style began to manifest itself as trouble for the upcoming campaign. General Lee had always led his armies with an avuncular style in which he made suggestions to his key subordinates (rather than issued outright orders) and counted upon those subordinates to execute the army commander's desire. For the most part, this had worked very well—but that was when the main offensive wing of the army had been commanded by the late Stonewall Jackson. The loss of this brilliant, ascetic general at Chancellorsville put one dire nail in the coffin of the invasion before it even began. James Longstreet, Lee's other corps commander, was a competent and veteran soldier to be sure, but he lacked Jackson's aggressiveness and capacity for almost incomprehensible speed of operations.

Up through May 1863, the Army of Northern Virginia had been centered around two powerful corps, each significantly larger than a corps of the Union Army. The Rebel corps were numbered I and II, but were most commonly known as "Longstreet's Corps" and "Jackson's Corps." As the war had increased in scope and complexity, and Lee confronted the idea of a sprawling, mobile operation with more than 75,000 troops, he decided that this structure was too unwieldy. As a result, he took a division away from Longstreet, added it to what had formerly been Jackson's Corps, and created two new formations—II Corps and III Corps. With Jackson's loss, however, Lee had no subordinate experienced in handling such large bodies of troops. In the event, he gave command of II Corps to Richard Ewell and III Corps to General A. P. Hill. Both of these men had proven their worth as division commanders but were untried at this new level of leadership.

Lee could always rely on James Longstreet, of course, but here, too, his aloof and nonspecific command style would create problems. Longstreet was a perceptive leader who had readily grasped an increasingly obvious truth of mid-nineteenth-century warfare: a tactical defensive battle was clearly better than a tactical offensive. Improvements in firepower, including the range of infantry weapons and the speed with which they could be employed, rendered previous ideas of courageous charges by brigades in line of battle tantamount to suicide. More use was being made of entrenchments, even on battlefields, and these hastily erected works were becoming increasingly elaborate and effective at shielding defending troops from attacking firepower. The I Corps commander was an early advocate of the idea of selecting a fortified position and forcing the enemy to attack it.

Longstreet was already reluctant about the whole idea of an invasion of the North. He expressed his thoughts in several long, earnest conversations with the army commander. Realizing that the operation was going to happen, he argued forcefully that, when the Army of Northern Virginia was in Pennsylvania, it should be positioned on good defensive terrain. The Union Army then would inevitably be compelled to attack the invaders, and it would destroy itself in the process. Lee listened carefully to Longstreet's entreaties, but the conversations ended with a serious misunderstanding: Longstreet believed that Lee had committed to the corps commander's grand tactical idea, whereas in fact Lee had made no such decision.

Yet another one of Robert E. Lee's subordinates would have a key role to play in the upcoming campaign, and once again Lee's vague guidance, as opposed to specific orders, would play havoc with the operation. General J.E.B. Stuart was widely acknowledged, in both the South and the North, as the supreme master of cavalry operations. Since the Peninsula Campaign, more than a year earlier, he had been the eyes, ears, sword, and shield of Lee's army—a role most dramatically illustrated in June 1862, when he took his cavalry division on a wild raid that completely encircled McClellan's army, destroying supplies, rail lines, and depots before Stuart returned to Lee with complete and accurate intelligence on the Yankees' strength and dispositions. Lee had come to depend on Stuart's instincts, and to trust him to provide the support Lee desired. This trust, in the summer of 1863, would prove to be sadly misplaced.

Nevertheless, it was a sublimely confident army that departed from its camps around Fredericksburg on June 3 and began the long, carefully coordinated march to the north. Lee would rely on Stuart's cavalry to screen the move from Hooker, and counted on getting many days of head start while the Union corps would remain fixed on the position along the Rappahannock. His direction of march would take the army, with Ewell's II Corps in the lead, up through the Shenandoah Valley to a crossing of the Potomac.

On June 9, Hooker got wind of the movement when his cavalry divisions, under Major General Alfred Pleasanton, crossed the Rappahannock and made a surprise attack on Stuart's camp at Brandy Station. At first, however, Hooker was not convinced that Lee was making an audacious move to the north. On June 13, however, Ewell's Corps smashed aside a Union force in the valley, confirming the drive on the Potomac. Finally the Union forces, some 115,000 strong, pulled out from the Rappahannock and started after Lee.

By the 15th of June, Ewell's leading elements had begun to cross the Potomac (at Williamsport) and wasted no time in driving toward, and through, Chambersburg, Pennsylvania. The Rebels eagerly collected horses, cattle, and wagonloads of grain, sending the prizes southward along their route of advance. They captured African Americans, too, by the dozens if not the hundreds. It didn't matter whether they were escaped slaves or legal freemen living in the North—a black person that fell into the hands of the Army of Northern Virginia was very likely to be chained and marched south to slavery.

By the 24th, all of Lee's 76,000 men were across the river, while Ewell had moved north of Chambersburg to approach the important city of York. A suggestion from Lee that he consider taking York if possible became, in Ewell's mind, an order to do the same, so his leading elements pressed forward toward the Susquehanna River, extending the army into a very long column.

In the meantime, Hooker moved deliberately after. The Army of the Potomac was not across its namesake river until nearly a week after Lee's men had completed the crossing. However, Lee had yet to be informed of the Yankee maneuver, and continued into Pennsylvania in blissful ignorance of the fact that the Union Army was on his tail, and not terribly far away.

Still, the Union Army chief of staff in Washington, D.C., General Henry Halleck, and President Lincoln himself pressed Hooker to take a more aggressive approach toward disrupting the Rebel offensive— even as, privately, they both doubted his ability to handle troops during a large battle. Frustrated by this "interference from above," Hooker, in a fit of pique, offered his resignation on June 27. Much to his surprise and chagrin, the resignation was accepted that very night. Almost on the eve of battle (June 28), Major General George Meade, a corps commander since Fredericksburg, was given command of the army, becoming its fifth commander in ten months.

That same day, Lee learned that the Union Army was on the move. (In Stuart's absence, the information came from a private spy hired by Longstreet.) Realizing that his army was so spread out that it would be vulnerable to defeat in detail, Lee immediately sent orders recalling Ewell from his advanced position, and urging A. P. Hill and Longstreet to bring their men up as quickly as possible.

All the pieces were in place for the climactic battle of the war— a battle that would indeed be the largest ever fought on either continent of the Americas in recorded history. Lee's men were confident and their leader himself sanguine about the prospects for success. But mistakes and misunderstandings had placed many hairline cracks in the foundations of this confidence, soon to be proven as misplaced. Lee and his men seriously underestimated their enemy and overestimated their own abilities. These errors, coupled with a tactical plan that failed to acknowledge the new realities of war and the lack of cavalry at the time it was most needed, had planted the seeds of disaster. And already that insidious crop was beginning to sprout.

The place selected by Lee to concentrate his army was a small village in Pennsylvania called Cashtown. The men of A. P. Hill's corps were the first to take station there. While he waited for the rest of the army to join him, Hill granted permission for one of his division commanders, Henry Heth, to conduct a reconnaissance down a well-paved road leading from Cashtown through a pass in the mountains called Cashtown Gap. Legend says they were looking to steal some shoes, though no one knows for sure if this is true. But Heth's destination is known, and it remains a name that resonates through American history:

Not too far beyond that gap lay a quaint but prosperous town of Pennsylvania Dutchmen, a place called Gettysburg.

Two Brigades Wasted

July 1, 1863: Harry Heth Blunders Toward Gettysburg

—

Mark Acres

After the Battle of Gettysburg, Confederate Major General Henry Heth, commonly called Harry, spent a lifetime admitting that he had blundered into a major engagement at Gettysburg, despite being ordered not to, and then explaining why it wasn't his fault. In the years after the war, "Why did we lose at Gettysburg?" became a great and contentious topic of debate among Confederate veterans and former generals. There was finger-pointing aplenty, much of it nasty and false. Heth no doubt felt vulnerable in this debate, and perhaps was dogged by a sense of personal guilt that he had brought it all on. The great irony is that Heth defended himself against the wrong mistake. Gettysburg was not his fault: it was ultimately Lee's. Heth's blunders that fateful morning of July 1 were tactical and operational, not strategic.

At 5 A.M. on July 1, 1863, Heth's division, just under 8,000 men, set out on the pike from Cashtown, Pennsylvania, marching east toward Gettysburg. The ground immediately west of Gettysburg consisted of rolling farmland and some woods, with three parallel and well-defined ridges running roughly north to south: Herr Ridge about a mile and a half from the town, McPherson's Ridge about eight tenths of a mile farther east, and Seminary Ridge just a few hundred yards east of McPherson's Ridge. The pike ran straight and true at a slight northwest to southeast slant from Herr Ridge to McPherson's and Seminary Ridges and then into the town.

BY 11 A.M., HETH'S DIVISION SAT ON HERR RIDGE WEST OF GETTYSBURG, licking its wounds. While two of his four brigades, including his largest and best, General James J. Pettigrew's, had remained unengaged, his remaining two brigades under Brigadier General James J. Archer and Brigadier General Joseph R. Davis, nephew of Jefferson Davis, had been brutally repulsed. Both were out of the battle for the day, serving as placeholders in the line as the first day at Gettysburg unfolded. Their fighting strength would be sorely wanted later that day.

The details of this engagement are well-known and have been covered in numerous histories. First, the dismounted cavalry of John Buford's Union cavalry division had delayed Heth's advance toward Herr Ridge, causing him to deploy a skirmish line to drive back the much less numerous cavalry pickets. When the Confederates approached Herr Ridge, Buford had a full regiment waiting in skirmish order. Heth halted and deployed. He put Archer's brigade in line of battle south of the pike, and Davis's brigade in line to the north. His remaining two brigades remained in reserve. With two brigades against their one regiment, the cavalry made a fighting withdrawal down the far side of Herr Ridge toward Willoughby Run, a shallow creek in the valley between Herr Ridge and McPherson's Ridge. The rest of Buford's division, in a long thin line along McPherson's Ridge, tensely awaited the Confederate onslaught.

General Archer didn't want to advance against the Union forces on McPherson's Ridge, despite Heth's urging, correctly observing that he had no idea what might lie in those woods to his front along that ridge. Heth listened, and an artillery duel began between Confederate and Union guns on their respective ridges. About a half hour passed. Then Heth again ordered Archer and Davis forward. Archer's brigade drove forward south of the pike as far as Willoughby Run and then stopped at the base of McPherson's Ridge, facing a steeply rising swell of ground partly covered by the Herbst Woods. Davis's brigade moved steadily toward the Union line to the north of the pike. Perhaps Davis's men did not immediately notice that Union infantry were relieving the cavalry to their front, and that their flanks were "in the air," as Archer's line did not extend far enough north to actually reach the pike.

Again Archer objected to continuing the advance but this time Heth would not relent. Reluctantly, Archer led his brigade forward. In a short while they found themselves in an intense firefight with the arriving elements of the Union's feared and elite Iron Brigade. In a short while Archer's brigade was flanked, then overwhelmed by the Union troops who had arrived just in time to save the hard-pressed cavalry. The brigade collapsed in a retreat that became a rout. At least 200 prisoners fell into Union hands, including General Archer himself, the first general of the Army of Northern Virginia to be captured in the war.

Davis's brigade fared little better. At first his three regiments did well, flanking and driving back the newly arrived Union infantry to their front. But more Union infantry had deployed in that gap between Davis's and Archer's brigades, forming a line parallel to the pike. The 6th Wisconsin Regiment from the Iron Brigade joined the other Union troops on this line and opened a galling fire on the Confederate flank. Davis's entire brigade turned to face this new threat, and soon his regiments were intermingled and taking cover in the now infamous unfinished railroad cut, a ditch that had been cut for the placement of railroad tracks. Rufus Dawes led the 6th Wisconsin and other Union troops in a now legendary charge against the railroad cut, and despite sustaining heavy losses, ended up capturing at least 200 and possibly many more prisoners in the cut, while the rest of Davis's brigade fled for their lives back to Herr Ridge.

By 11 a.m. the remnants of Davis's and Archer's brigades were back on Herr Ridge, where the remaining brigades of Generals Pettigrew and John Brockenbrough could offer protection. Heth halted his attack and reported to Lee. He did not resume operations until ordered to do so by Lee later that afternoon.

Heth had allowed himself to be surprised first by the strength of the resistance of the Union cavalry he encountered, and then by the surprise arrival of the cream of the Army of the Potomac. What's worse, this happened after General Pettigrew was sent to Gettysburg the previous day but had retired before entering the town, because he found a strong force of Federal cavalry there and suspected that infantry was nearby.

The question remains: why did Harry Heth blunder so badly?

It's no good asking Heth himself this question. Over the years he gave numerous and contradictory accounts of what he was thinking and what his orders were during this opening engagement of the Battle of Gettysburg.

In his official written report, the earliest written testimony we have from him, he acknowledged that Pettigrew found enemy cavalry at Gettysburg the day before, and states, "I was ignorant what force was at or near Gettysburg, and supposed it consisted of cavalry, most probably supported by a brigade or two of infantry." Was this accuracy of his "supposition" based on hindsight? Only much later, in 1877 after Lee, Hill, and Pettigrew were all dead, did he write his most often cited account, in which neither he nor Hill believed Pettigrew's report, and apparently concluded that any cavalry at Gettysburg was either militia or a detachment of observation—a very small force of perhaps a squadron or two. The "shoes" story—the tale that the Confederates came to Gettysburg to get badly needed shoes—takes its life from this 1877 account. Still later in life, Heth allegedly told a Union officer in an interview that General Lee himself had sent him a note that fateful morning, telling him to "get the shoes even if I had to fight for them." This whopper doesn't hold water, but it does show how desperately Heth did not want to be remembered as the man who started the battle that doomed the Confederacy.

Heth spent a lifetime trying to avoid blame for the wrong mistake. The truth is that even after Heth's force first delayed and then bloodily repulsed, it was Lee, not Heth, who decided to renew the battle that afternoon. Heth's real blunder was not in engaging; his real blunder was the sloppy way he engaged.

Harry Heth was a vibrant and lovable character with a well-known devil-may-care attitude. His genial, joking, outgoing nature made him one of the best liked of all the Confederate officers. Before and after the Civil War, fellow officers befriended him—Ambrose Burnside was his West Point roommate and lifelong friend; Winfield Scott Hancock loved Heth like a cousin if not a brother, and promised to "take care of" Heth if he won the presidential election of 1880; Robert E. Lee himself was under Heth's charming spell, and Heth was known to be the only officer Lee addressed by his first name. But Heth also had the impulsive and volatile nature shared by his first cousin George Pickett. (He also shared with Pickett the distinction of being last in his class at West Point.) This impulsive side of his character often served him poorly on the Civil War battlefield.

The trait showed in his first real Civil War engagement at Lewisburg, West Virginia, in May 1862. There, with a very slight superiority in numbers, Heth launched a force composed largely of raw conscripts in a straight-up frontal assault against much more experienced Union foes. The Union forces quickly recovered from any surprise Heth thought he had, and counterattacked the oncoming Confederates. Heth's force was routed.

Again, commanding a brigade at Chancellorsville in May 1863, he almost blundered into a fatal night assault against a superior Union force in strong defensive terrain. He was saved at the last minute by some alert scouts who got word to him in time to cancel the attack.

Oddly, Heth's career did not suffer from these seeming setbacks. In fact, he continued to be promoted—a strong affirmation that aggressiveness, even if overly impulsive, was rewarded in Lee's command. And at no time was this culture of the aggressive spirit more strong in the Army of Northern Virginia than in the summer of 1863 following Lee's incredible victory at Chancellorsville. There Lee had broken all the rules, twice dividing an inferior force in the presence of a superior enemy, and then driving that enemy to defeat and retreat. Indeed, Lee directed real anger after the battle at subordinates who he believed had failed to show a sufficiently aggressive spirit. Years later Heth wrote in his memoirs that Lee was the most aggressive general in the army.

At Gettysburg, Heth commanded a full division for the first time, and he almost certainly was not going to disappoint the mentor and guardian of his career by showing a lack of aggressive spirit. Furthermore, his orders from his immediate superior, III Corps commander General A. P. Hill, were to conduct a reconnaissance in force to see what Union force was in the vicinity of Gettysburg. A reconnaissance in force calls for aggressive action to provoke an enemy response. Given an impulsive general who has been rewarded for impulsive aggressive behavior, in an army with a cult of the aggressive spirit, and with order to recon in force, there is no question that Heth was going to attack anything he found.

TWO QUESTIONS REMAIN. WHY DID HETH SEND IN ONLY TWO brigades against a foe of undetermined strength, and why did he leave his two supporting brigades—Pettigrew's and Brockenbrough's—too far to the rear to support his lead brigades if they ran into trouble? Perhaps the answer lies in part with that nagging "other order" Heth had that morning—the order not to bring on a major engagement. A probe with a couple of brigades could still be called minor; throwing his whole command into the fray couldn't be seen as anything less than a major engagement.

Still, why did he allow himself to be surprised? At times Heth tried to blame the absence of J.E.B. Stuart's cavalry for the "surprise" at Gettysburg, and by implication for his own misfortunes on that first morning. In fact the unavailability of intelligence from Stuart is one of the most often cited reasons for the Confederate defeat at Gettysburg. This excuse won't hold for Heth that morning. Heth had been fore-warned by Pettigrew. Moreover, Buford's cavalry line was stretched thin; even a few officers sent on horseback to scout ahead could have ridden around the south end of Buford's line, and upon reaching the crest of Seminary Ridge they would have seen Union infantry hasten-ing toward the battlefield. In the end, it was his hasty impulsiveness that did in Heth that morning.

The morning defeat is often little noted, given the overall Confed-erate victory on that first day at Gettysburg. But a nagging question remains: what if A. P. Hill had had two fresh brigades available from Heth's division late in the afternoon when Lee wanted Cemetery Hill to be taken?

Confederate Command Failure

July 1, 1863: The First Evening at Gettysburg

—

Mark Acres

In the musical play *1776*, the John Adams character sings about the Continental Congress, "Piddle, twiddle, and resolve, not one damned thing do we solve." His words, an apt description of many congresses through the ages, also describe the activities of the Confederate high command in the late afternoon and evening of the first day of the Battle of Gettysburg.

After a series of initial reverses, the Confederate III Corps of Lieutenant General A. P. Hill, striking from the west, and the Confederate II Corps of Lieutenant General Richard S. Ewell, striking from the north, had driven the Union forces from the ridges and fields west and north Gettysburg. By 4 P.M. two Union Corps, the I and XI, were in full retreat toward Cemetery Hill just south of the town. A good portion of the XI Corps units panicked and routed when a blunder by Major General Francis Barlow exposed the right flank of his division (and the entire Union line) to a flanking attack by Jubal Early's Rebel division. A desperate battle against Major General Henry

Heth's and Major General William Dorsey Pender's divisions of Hill's corps on McPherson and Seminary Ridges, and against Major General Robert E. Rodes's division of Ewell's corps on Oak Hill, left the Union I Corps shredded, although it managed to retreat in good order. As the Union troops streamed in disarray, and some in panic, toward Cemetery Hill, Confederate General Robert E. Lee watched from Seminary Ridge. Lee immediately saw the necessity of occupying Cemetery Hill, and observed that it would be "only necessary to push those people" to drive them from the heights. Lee sent Colonel Walter Taylor to Ewell with word that he should go ahead and "take that hill, if practicable."

Lee's order started an ineffective discussion that began that afternoon, grew into a firestorm of controversy after the battle, and continues to this day. The sequence of events that ensued is a case study in the difficulty of communication and coordination on the battlefield in the Civil War. One of the Confederates' two best chances to claim victory at Gettysburg evaporated in the ensuing stream of piddle, twiddle, and hot air. While taking Cemetery Hill that afternoon or evening would probably have been difficult, perhaps impossible, the opportunity to seize Culp's Hill, the higher eminence just east of Cemetery Hill and the key to the Union right flank, was lost.

After the battle, many Confederates found it convenient to blame Ewell for the failure to drive straight on up Cemetery Hill immediately in the wake of the Union retreat. The question this criticism overlooks, but which Ewell could not overlook, is, drive up Cemetery Hill with what troops? Rodes's division had suffered heavily in the fighting on Oak Hill and was just closing the distance to link up with the right flank of Early's division as the Federals retreated. Early, meanwhile, had two brigades left relatively fresh. The rest of Early's command was in disarray as a result of chasing the Union troops through the narrow streets of Gettysburg. It would take an hour, probably two, to bring order out of the chaos engendered by the sudden Confederate occupation and wild chase through the town.

Ewell, with his great balding dome and his wooden leg, was new to corps command. Already he had formed a habit of consulting with his subordinates about important decisions or orders that confused him, as Lee's orders often did. Even before Lee's order to take Cemetery Hill reached him, Ewell turned to Jubal Early with his two fresh brigades, and General Rodes, who had slugged it out on Oak Hill. Ewell wanted to know if he should continue the attack—pursue the Federals onto Cemetery Hill. Early, normally an aggressive general, urged caution. Rodes agreed with Early. An attack could succeed, Early thought, but only with support from A. P. Hill's corps to the west, on Seminary Ridge.

Ewell sent word to Lee, asking if Hill's corps could coordinate in an attack on Cemetery Hill. (Tick-tock, tick-tock went the victory clock.) Ewell's message and Lee's order crossed each other in transit; Taylor arrived and got Lee's order to Ewell after Ewell had sent word to Lee asking if Hill's corps could help in an assault.

A. P. Hill, himself normally an aggressive commander ready for a hard march and a harder fight, failed to live up to his former reputation at Gettysburg. Like Ewell, he was new to corps command. It is also likely that Hill was ill the three days of the battle. Speculation has it that he was suffering from a bout of a "social disease" he had contracted during a visit to a house of ill repute in New York City during his West Point cadet days. In any event, Hill was hardly aggressive on July 1. Lee's arrival that morning in Cashtown on the way to Gettysburg had roused him from a late sleep, and he had exercised but scarce control over the fighting by his subordinates. Asked by Lee if he could assist Ewell in an assault on Cemetery Hill, the usually reliable General Hill decided his troops were too worn-out by the previous fighting for McPherson's and Seminary Ridges to participate in another attack. He did have one fresh division, Anderson's, just arriving on the field, but Lee himself wanted Anderson's division held as a reserve for the army. And so another rider galloped from Lee to Ewell: there would be no help from Hill's corps.

Meanwhile, a closer examination of the Federal defenses discouraged Ewell. It is easy to understand why. A ring of forty-two Union guns crowned Cemetery Hill. Clearly visible from the town below, their black tubes promised fiery death by ball and canister to any who dared the steep slope to assault the masses of men in blue who swarmed in confusion among them. Some order was already emerging from that swarm as Union lines began to form among the artillery batteries. (Unbeknownst to the Confederates, the Union's secret weapon—Major General Winfield Scott Hancock—had arrived about 4 P.M., taken command, and begun organizing the Union defenses.) Ewell would later write that he was also constrained by Lee's previous order not to bring on a general engagement until the full army was up. This shows the depth of Ewell's confusion; that earlier order was obviously no longer in effect since a general engagement had been under way since 1 P.M., with Ewell's own corps a major participant in it.

Then—Yankees on our flank and rear! Suddenly that desperate report arrived from William "Extra Billy" Smith's brigade of Early's division. The brigade, one of the two fresh formations available to Ewell, had been guarding the left rear of the Confederate line along the York Road. Now the brigade reported Union infantry, cavalry, and artillery advancing in force on Ewell's flank along that road. Smith sent a second rider, even asking for reinforcements. Early, with Ewell's consent, responded by sending his best brigade commander, Brigadier General John Brown Gordon, along with his reformed brigade, to take command of Smith's brigade, assess the situation, and bring Smith's brigade back onto Ewell's left flank. Smith's report proved false—there were no Yankees on the York Road. The result was to make both Smith's and Gordon's brigades unavailable for a later afternoon or evening attack.

As Ewell continued to ponder what to do—now with the worry of a possible Union force on his flank and rear—Lee rode in person to find Ewell. The two met, with Rodes and Early both present, sometime between 6 P.M. and 7 P.M. Lee was not in good spirits. Despite winning a significant victory, he had already heard sour notes of protest about continuing the battle here from his most trusted subordinate, Lieutenant General James Longstreet. Now Hill and Ewell were both balking at continuing the fight today. In their meeting, Lee told the officers of Ewell's corps that he wanted an immediate attack on Cemetery Hill. If they felt they could not attack, he wanted the entire corps moved from the north side of Gettysburg to the opposite flank of his army, south of Hill's corps along Seminary Ridge.

It is difficult to imagine Lee's consternation when Early and Rodes both objected strenuously to moving the corps as well as to launching an attack. Ewell, apparently diffident, did nothing to constrain the argumentativeness of his two division commanders. Lee did not insist; he left the meeting with nothing agreed upon and nothing accomplished.

Tick-tock, tick-tock went the victory clock.

Ewell no doubt sensed Lee's disappointment. He found a compromise idea: a new division of his corps, Johnson's division, was just arriving on the field. Perhaps he could use that division to attack the hill to the east of Cemetery Hill. Culp's Hill protected the Union's line of communications along the Baltimore Pike. It dominated Cemetery Hill. Taking Culp's Hill would unhinge the Union position. Ewell ordered a reconnaissance of Culp's Hill and learned it was unoccupied. (This intelligence was not entirely accurate, as remnants of the Iron Brigade were already deploying on the slope of the hill nearest to the Union lines.)

Back at his own headquarters, Lee could no longer contain his irritation nor brook inaction. A courier galloped off to find Ewell with a preemptive order: Ewell must either attack immediately or move his corps to the right of the army.

By the time Lee's new order arrived, Ewell had formulated his new idea based on the intelligence he had received about Culp's Hill. Johnson's troops had marched all day, but they had not engaged. Now they were taking position in front of Culp's Hill on Ewell's right. With Lee's permission, they could attack. Perhaps that would satisfy Lee's eagerness for an attack, keep Ewell's subordinates Rodes and especially Early happy, and avoid any movement of the corps that would involve leaving the town and the real estate they had already paid for that afternoon.

Rather than entrust this to a courier, Ewell himself rode over to General Lee's headquarters, and soon had a meeting with the commanding general. By now it must have been at least 8 p.m. and the last of daylight would be fading soon. Lee consented to Ewell's plan to attack Culp's Hill. No doubt Lee sought any plan that would bring about more decisive action.

Ewell rode back to his headquarters. (Tick-tock, tick-tock went the victory clock.) Orders were prepared for Johnson to attack. Johnson, appropriately, sent skirmishers forward toward the crest of the hill. By now the sun was gone and the attack would be a night attack. Johnson wanted to be sure what was in front of him.

What were in front of him were skirmishers from the 7th Indiana Regiment, the only fresh regiment from the Union's First Division. The Hoosier skirmishers opened fire in the dark as the Confederate skirmishers from Johnson's division approached the crest of the hill. After a brief firefight in the darkness and thick woods, the Rebel skirmishers withdrew. Johnson now knew that Federal troops were on the hill; it was not unoccupied as Ewell had thought. Johnson sent word to Ewell that the enemy possessed the crest and that it was now too late, darkness having fallen, to mount an attack on the unknown foe.

So it was that no further attack was made anywhere on the Federal line on the first day at Gettysburg. Responsibility for this failure to act rests with all the persons of the high command involved in the decision making: Lee, Ewell, Hill, and even Early. Brigadier Smith deserves some special distinction in the false alarm category. A determined attack, especially on Culp's Hill, that afternoon or evening would have been difficult for the Union to meet. While Henry Slocum's XII Corps was available, the command disarray on the Union side (despite Hancock's best efforts) might have made it difficult to bring that asset to bear in time. But tick-tock, tick-tock went the victory clock—and when it struck midnight, the Confederate chances disappeared. Culp's and Cemetery Hills would become the scenes of bitter fighting and bitter defeats for the Rebels over the next two days.

General Dan Sickles Proves to Be an Independent Thinker

July 2, 1863: The Second Day at Gettysburg

—

Doug Niles

The morning of July 2 dawned hot and sticky over southern Pennsylvania. The previous day's fighting had resulted in some real triumphs for the Confederacy, and two Union Army corps—the I and the XI—had suffered serious casualties. The I Corps had fought well before being forced to retreat, while the ill-starred XI Corps had been poorly placed by its commanders and had routed in panic and confusion under an attacking avalanche of Rebel divisions. Both corps had retreated to the high ground of Cemetery Ridge, where they joined some later arriving troops of the II and III Corps.

In the meantime, the rest of the Union Army had been marching to the sounds of the guns. General Meade arrived during the middle of the night after the first day of battle. Now Meade had almost all of his army on the battlefield, though Sedgwick's VI Corps was in the middle of a thirty-five mile forced march and would not arrive until midafternoon. Still, despite the first day's losses, the Yankee position was strong. The line was deployed on a shape vaguely resembling a fishhook, with the right anchored on the heavily fortified crest of Culp's Hill, situated against attack from the east and north. From Culp's Hill, the line traversed a short distance westward to the eminence of Cemetery Hill, overlooking the town of Gettysburg itself.

South of Cemetery Hill stretched Cemetery Ridge, the long shaft of the fishhook, and this is where the bulk of Meade's men had been ordered to make their stand. The line extended for nearly two miles, following the gradually descending crest of the ridge into a low swale. From there the land rose abruptly again, first to a steep, wooded hill named Little Round Top—with a top that included some clearings providing a good view of the field—and then to a loftier elevation known as Big Round Top. Though it was the highest hill in the area, Big Round Top was heavily forested and slightly removed from the rest of the front. For all intents and purposes, Little Round Top would be the solid left flank of the long, curving Union line.

Most of Meade's corps commanders were pleased with the position, recognizing that they possessed interior lines that would allow them to move reserves easily from one part of the front to another. Also, this time the Yankees had the high ground, with plenty of vantages for artillery positions and clear fields of view to the east, north, and west. The Confederates, conversely, were spread out beyond the Federal arc and had much more distance to traverse if they tried to redeploy troops from one sector of the line to another. More than one officer suggested that a Rebel attack against this line would give the army a chance to fight a "Fredericksburg in reverse."

The one dissenter to this point of view was the III Corps commander, Major General Daniel Sickles. Sickles was a unique character in many ways. He was the only non–West Pointer in all of the high command, and as an ambitious and suspicious fellow he suspected that the clique of military professionals did not show him the respect he deserved. He, in turn, viewed Meade, Hancock, Howard, and his fellow corps commanders as overly cautious and careful, more concerned with not making a mistake than in taking bold action to achieve decisive results.

And Dan Sickles was no stranger to bold action. The most notorious example of his character occurred in 1859. Having served as a local and state politician in New York, rising through the tangled byways of Tammany Hall, he had served as a diplomat on a mission to Europe under James Buchanan and had found a comfortable place in the United States House of Representatives. At thirty-three years of age he had married a pretty fifteen-year-old, Teresa Bagioli, though since then he had been known to be unfaithful to her on several instances during the 1850s. He was also a good friend of Philip Barton Key II, son of Francis Scott Key, who is best known for composing the national anthem.

When it came to his attention that Teresa and Francis Key were engaged in a very public adultery, Sickles acted. He encountered Key on the sidewalk at Lafayette Square, right across the street from the White House, and there he shot him dead. His trial was a media circus, perhaps most notable for the fact that he was the first defendant ever to plead innocent based on a period of "temporary insanity." His lawyer, Edwin Stanton (soon to become Lincoln's secretary of war), argued the case successfully to an understanding public and jury, and Sickles was acquitted and, in fact, welcomed back into the bosom of Washington high society. After all, it was reasoned, any self-respecting husband might be expected to do the same thing.

In the view of that society, however, a real outrage happened after the trial, when Sickles forgave his wife and welcomed her back into his home. While killing the man who cuckolded you was deemed acceptable behavior, reconciling with a known harlot was clearly not! For the next year and a half Sickles was ostracized throughout the city and even in the halls of Congress, until the Civil War gave the ambitious politician a chance to get his career moving again.

He wasted no time in organizing several companies of New York volunteers, eventually drawing so many that he was commissioned a brigadier general in charge of a full brigade. He took good care of his men, even paying for many of their expenses out of his own pocket as official commissary and payroll matters were resolved. (Reportedly he once rented an entire bathhouse and paid a dime apiece for each of his 1,400 men to get a shave, bath, and haircut.)

Despite the fact that he was clearly a political general, Sickles performed adequately in the field, and indeed had the presence of mind to seize the good position of Hazel Grove in the Battle of Chancellorsville, giving it up only reluctantly under direct orders from Hooker. After III Corps withdrew, of course, the Rebels made good use of the grove as an artillery park.

Now, at Gettysburg, Sickles feared that the same thing was going to happen all over again. His corps was assigned to anchor its right against Hancock's II Corps and follow the rapidly vanishing crest of the ridge to Little Round Top. From his line, however, Sickles could see a rise of higher ground about a mile in his front, with a peach orchard marking the apex of what looked like a natural position along the Emmitsburg Road. That road began in Gettysburg, very near to Cemetery Ridge, but as the ridge extended southward the road followed a southwesterly path, so that in front of Sickles's part of the line the road was more than a mile in front of where Meade had ordered III Corps to take up station.

During the morning of July 2, Sickles made several attempts to get Meade to come over and consult with him about the position, but the new army commander was (understandably) busy with a whole host of details and couldn't afford to take the time. After yet another personal visit from Sickles, Meade sent his artillery commander, General Henry Hunt, over to inspect the lay of the land for himself.

When the two men returned to the III Corps position, Sickles was further dismayed to discover that the Union cavalry of General Buford, which had been his flank support, had been sent away on some irrelevant mission by the overall cavalry commander, General Pleasanton. (Pleasanton's order was never satisfactorily explained, and had the result of removing one of the army's most effective and hard-fighting units from the rest of the battle.) Hunt suggested to the increasingly anxious Sickles that he might want to send a reconnaissance force out toward the Emmitsburg Road, and perhaps beyond, to see what the enemy was up to.

That was better than nothing, so Sickles dispatched three companies of sharpshooters, with an infantry regiment in support, to see what they could see. This small force moved up to and over the Emmitsburg Road without encountering any trouble, but when they advanced onto the southern part of Seminary Ridge they met a line of Rebel skirmishers. Scattering them, the patrol continued to advance but was soon met by massed volleys of musketry, discovering a whole formation of Rebel infantry marching to the south. After about twenty minutes of a firefight, the Yankees withdrew, their colonel reporting to Sickles that a large column of Johnny Rebs was trying to sneak around to the left.

Sickles had an idea of what had to be done, and he did it: he ordered his entire corps forward, marching them almost a mile to the position he coveted along the road. The center of his line was that peach orchard, and he posted infantry and guns throughout the widely spaced trees in a solid wedge. There was a wheat field nearby and he also garrisoned that with men and artillery. To his extreme left was a rocky nest of hillocks and gullies known to the locals as Devil's

Den, and he even managed to post a couple of cannons in this rough terrain at the far left of his line.

There were but two problems with this deployment, though those proved to be glaring problems indeed. First, Sickles didn't have enough men to cover the front of his position, which, because it bowed out into a considerable salient, was much longer than the front assigned to him by Meade. Thus Little Round Top was unoccupied by infantry or guns—it was only manned by a few men and officers of the signal corps, who had set up an observation post and flag station on top of the steep, dominating hill. Also, Sickles's advance broke contact entirely with Hancock's II Corps directly to his right, so that both of the III Corps flanks were essentially hanging in the air. (As one of Hancock's veteran division commanders, John Gibbon, watched Sickles move forward, he wondered if an order for a general advance had been issued and Gibbon had somehow not heard the news.)

The second problem with Sickles's deployment was that he didn't tell anybody from army headquarters that he was doing it. Right about the time his men were taking their new positions, General Meade decided to have a conference with his corps commanders. General Sedgwick and VI Corps had finally arrived, and the Army of the Potomac now had its full strength on the battlefield. Before the conference began, however, Meade got wind of Sickles's advance and rode over to III Corps to find out for himself what was going on.

The army commander, to put it mildly, was displeased with his subordinate. He rebuked him with some heat—in Bruce Catton's nicely worded description, when Meade "looked out at the new line he became wrathy." Perhaps slightly chagrined, Sickles asked if he should return his troops to their assigned position. Just as Meade was answering in the affirmative, a crash of guns roared across the battlefield, and plumes of smoke clearly indicated that III Corps was under attack. It was too late to do anything but stand and fight.

This opening salvo, coming in midafternoon, was the result of a long, reluctant march on the part of Longstreet's corps. That veteran general had spent much of the day trying to convince Lee not to attack here. When the Confederate commander insisted upon the offensive, Longstreet had grudgingly moved his men onto position to strike the Union left. Insisting upon a screened line of march, he had taken hours longer than Lee had expected, moving his two powerful divisions, Hood's and McLaws's, into position for a powerful attack from concealment. Now the full fury of the Rebel I Corps was about to explode against Sickles's dangerously exposed line.

But it turned out that Sickles's creative deployment was not just a surprise to his own commander. Perhaps because of his lack of enthusiasm for the attack, Longstreet had not conducted a thorough reconnaissance of his target. He trusted all of his battlefield intelligence to a cursory inspection conducted by one of Lee's staff officers much earlier in the day. Lee, for his part, maintained his hands-off approach to the operation: once he had ordered Longstreet to make the attack, he did nothing to influence the course of events.

As a result, Longstreet's advancing divisions were startled when they immediately encountered Yankee defenders—far forward of where they had expected them. In effect, Sickles would end up sacrificing his corps to form a trip line for the day's battle, and though the great strength of the offensive would do horrific damage to his exposed divisions, the battle would be fought in the Peach Orchard, the Wheatfield, and Devil's Den, instead of on the low eminence of Cemetery Ridge.

To his credit, Meade wasted no time in recriminations or regrets. He ordered Sickles to fight where he was, and told him he would send him as much support as he could. Galloping back to his headquarters, he immediately sent Sykes's V Corps, a unit he'd intended to hold in reserve, to bolster the far left of the line. Hancock, meanwhile, advanced one brigade after another to try to fill the gap between the two corps—even as another cannonade opened up against the Union right, signaling that Culp's Hill was also under attack.

Longstreet's attack didn't commence until late afternoon, but between then and the blessed relief of darkness occurred some of the most savage fighting of the whole war. The scenes of these clashes were soaked in blood and fire, and their names became the stuff of history and legend. For every fresh brigade marched into the carnage, another emerged, pathetically thinned, survivors shocked and bruised and bleeding. McLaws and Hood were bold, experienced commanders, and their men were some of the best the Confederacy had to offer. To meet them, Meade kept marching more and more of his brigades into the hellish inferno, stripping his right flank dangerously to try to cover the gaps on Sickles's flanks—and, before long, the gaping hole in the center as the bulk of III Corps was torn to pieces.

One of the most dramatic actions of the war occurred on Little Round Top, which was not even garrisoned with infantry at the start of the attack. Fortunately, it was occupied by Meade's chief engineering officer, Brigadier General Gouverneur Warren. Instantly perceiving the danger, he pulled Strong Vincent's brigade, of Sykes V Corps, out of the left wing and ordered it to deploy on the key hilltop. With its flank bolstered by the heroic stand of the 20th Maine Regiment on the left and Warren's perfectly timed reinforcement of the right, the brigade fought until half of its men had fallen and its ammunition was expended. When all else failed, the 20th Maine executed a bayonet charge with the men rushing downhill bearing their empty muskets, and Little Round Top—and quite possibly the Union itself—was saved.

The battle on July 2 was, in Wellington's words about Waterloo, "a very near-run thing." If Lee and Longstreet had planned, coordinated, and scouted more effectively . . . if Lee had taken a more direct role in command or been more flexible to Longstreet (and Hood's) ideas for a wider flanking move . . . or if Longstreet had followed his orders with more alacrity, the Rebels could very conceivably have broken through Sickles's malformed line, rolled up the Union line, and won the Battle of Gettysburg. But on this day, there were plenty of mistakes to go around, and many of them were made by commanders on each side.

At last, Hood's charge was broken. Nightfall brought an end to some of the most furious fighting that the world had ever seen. Sickles's military career was over, a cannonball having taken off his leg— though even then he didn't lose his sense of style, as he puffed a cigar and urged his men to valor while the stretcher-bearers carried him to the rear.

The second day of the Battle of Gettysburg, at last, was over.

The Amazing Mystery of Billy Mahone

July 2, 1863: Gettysburg

—

Mark Acres

Blunders, insubordination, miscommunications, and sand in the gears of command abound in the story of the Battle of Gettysburg. The bizarre behavior of Confederate Brigadier General William "Little Billy" Mahone on the second day of the battle ranks among the most amazing and mysterious of all the military mistakes that occurred over those dreadful three days. What did Billy Mahone do that remains one of the great unsolved mysteries of Gettysburg? Nothing—he did nothing at all.

The second day at Gettysburg began slowly for the Army of Northern Virginia. Commanding General Robert E. Lee met with his commanders that morning and gave orders for an attack that would drive up the Emmitsburg Road, strike Cemetery Ridge from the left flank, and roll up the Army of the Potomac all the way to Cemetery Hill. For whatever reason, it took Lieutenant General James Longstreet, commander of the Confederate I Corps, until almost 4 P.M. to position his troops for the assault. By then, events had outpaced Lee's plan. Union Major General Dan Sickles's III Corps occupied the ground directly in front of Longstreet.

A new Confederate plan rapidly evolved. The attack would be an echelon attack. An echelon attack begins at one point in the enemy line—usually a flank—with the object of drawing the enemy's reinforcements to that point. After a while, a second attacking force comes forward to attack the next point in the enemy line—hopefully drawing in more reinforcements. Then a third force advances, and so on, until the enemy has no reserves left and his line can be broken at what is now the weakest point. Echelon attacks can be quite effective, but require careful timing and coordination between all the participating units.

First, Longstreet would hurl the division of Major General John Hood against the Union left flank in the area of Devil's Den and the Round Tops. Then the division of Major General Lafayette McLaws would strike just north of Hood's division—moving through the Peach Orchard toward the low point in the Union line north of Little Round Top. Next up would be Major General Richard H. Anderson's division. Billy Mahone's brigade stood at the left, or north end, of Anderson's line.

After the battle, critics tore into Longstreet for taking so long to get his two divisions into position to lead the attack. It is no secret that Longstreet did not want to make this attack; he did not want Lee to attack at all. But when it comes to foot-dragging, recalcitrance, and doing nothing in a time of desperate need, Billy Mahone outshines Longstreet so brightly that the corps commander's mere dilatoriness disappears in the blinding light of Mahone's incompetent insubordination.

Longstreet's attacks finally went in. Hood's boys went first, and they, along with their Union foes, immortalized the names of Little Round Top, the Triangle Field, Houck's Ridge, Devil's Den, and a branch of Plum Run creek forever after known as the Slaughter Pen. McLaws's men followed Hood's, and their blood flowed freely in the Rose Woods, the Stony Hill, the Wheatfield, the Peach Orchard, and the Trostle Farm.

Union commander Lieutenant General George Meade, hampered by the actions of Dan Sickles, who led his III Corps forward contrary to orders, found himself forced to throw troops helter-skelter into the explosive mayhem that threatened to unhinge the left end of his line. He chose the ubiquitous Major General Winfield Scott Hancock to take command in the center. After nearly two hours of fighting, Hancock had thrown one of his entire divisions, most of the V Corps, and elements of the arriving VI Corps into the fight against Hood and McLaws, and still elements of the Rebel force were coming forward.

At about 6 P.M., it was time for Anderson's division to hit the Union line. Brigadier General Cadmus Wilcox led forward his brigade of Alabamians, accompanied by the tiniest brigade in Lee's army, one of three Florida regiments under the command of Colonel David Lang. Lang's men formed on the left or north side of Wilcox's brigade. Together, Wilcox and Lang crossed the ground between the Spangler Farm and the Emmitsburg Road, driving in the last remnants of Union Brigadier General Andrew Humphreys's Second Division of III Corps and elements of Brigadier General John Gibbon's Second Division, II Corps, sent to reinforce Humphreys. The charging Confederate line began to near Plum Run in the center of the battlefield and had an unobstructed path straight ahead toward Cemetery Ridge.

Desperately, Hancock searched the Union center for troops—any troops. He found the 1st Minnesota Regiment and ordered them forward in their famous charge that bought Hancock just enough time to draw even more troops up from the VI Corps and from his own II

Corps divisions farther north along the Union line.

Into this confused maelstrom Brigadier General Ambrose Wright brought forward the next Confederate brigade. His four regiments of Georgians, numbering just over 1,400 men, surged forward toward the Emmitsburg Road, the Codori Farm, and the Union-held ridge-line just beyond. Joining with Lang's brigade in driving back elements of Gibbon's Second Division, II Corps, Wright's Georgians advanced against terrible artillery fire, finally driving back a Federal battery and approaching the crest of Cemetery Ridge. According to many accounts, Wright's men actually reached the crest of that ridge, momentarily breeching the Union line. Whether they did punch a clean hole in that line or not—still a debated issue—here is the great secret about the fighting that day that many histories ignore or dispute: the echelon attack was working. Troops were being drawn from as far north as the area where the Union line turned, the Angle, to plug the growing gap in the Union center. Further, it was at about 6 P.M. that Meade ordered units of the XII Corps, stationed on his far right flank on Culp's Hill, to march to the assistance of the far left flank. This opened up Culp's Hill to attack.

If ever there was a moment to continue an echelon attack, this was that moment.

It didn't happen.

On Cemetery Ridge, Wright desperately sent word for support to come forward. His troops were now facing two Federal batteries firing from the crest of the ridge, a deadly fire from the 69th Pennsylvania at the famous stone wall in the Union center, and an advance of Vermont troops led by Union Brigadier General George Stannard. In fact, Wright's brigade was facing alone the very troops that on the next day would be instrumental in repelling "Pickett's Charge." Anderson, his division commander, sent word back that Confederate Brigadier General Carnot Posey's brigade would be coming quickly.

Anderson erred. He had ordered Posey forward to support Wright, but Posey no longer had control of his brigade. A minor skirmish at the Bliss Farm, a house and barn conveniently located in the no-man's-land between the two armies, sucked in one after another of Posey's regiments. When the time came to advance, at most one of Posey's regiments was available in any semblance of order—the rest were engaged in a hot skirmish and sniping from the Bliss property. In fact, Posey was so hotly engaged in this sideshow that he appealed for help to the brigadier commanding the brigade on his left—Brigadier General Billy Mahone.

At about the same time, a second plea for help from Wright reached Anderson. The division commander sent a courier to Billy Mahone with orders for him to advance his brigade at once to support Wright's.

Billy Mahone weighed about a hundred pounds when dripping wet. Standing five feet six inches high in his best boots, the wiry, hard-muscled man sported a huge beard down to his chest and favored a large cowboy-type hat. With his sharp, angular face and scrawny but tough limbs, he looked like nothing so much as a scrappy bantam rooster when fully decked out in uniform.

A Virginian by birth, educated at Virginia Military Institute, Mahone made his fortune in the railroad business prior to the war, and was active in Virginia politics, managing to win election to the Virginia legislature in 1863 while still on active duty with the army. By the time of Gettysburg, at the age of thirty-six, he was a veteran of the fighting in the Peninsula at Seven Pines and Malvern Hill, and had led troops at Second Bull Run, Fredericksburg, and Chancellorsville.

It was this veteran, scrappy little man who told Anderson's courier that his brigade would not move. Mahone claimed that General Anderson himself had told him to occupy his current position. The aide protested that he had just come from General Anderson with this urgent order. His pleas didn't move Mahone, and Mahone did not move. The courier returned to General Anderson in some consternation. Amazingly, Anderson took no further action!

After this strange incident, another courier arrived—this time from Posey—asking for help on his front. Mahone replied that he could not render aid to General Posey, as he had just been ordered to render aid to General Wright! And then Mahone continued to hold his ground. Not a soldier moved forward.

Wright's brigade, alone in the midst of a growing crowd of Union troops, retreated. All along the line to their south, the Union reinforcements drawn from the center, the Union right, and the newly arriving VI Corps advanced to throw back the Confederates. And north and east of Billy Mahone, the waiting brigades of Heth's, Pender's, and Rodes's divisions sat, never moving forward, since the key for their movement was the movement of the brigade to their right. Mahone broke the chain of the echelon attack at the very moment when it had the best chance of success.

There is more to the strange story of Billy Mahone. Not only did Anderson never take Mahone to task for his disobedience, he even defended Mahone in print. The only public criticism of Mahone appeared in a Virginia newspaper. When made aware of a public rebuke to Mahone, Anderson wrote to the newspaper defending Mahone, saying his subordinate had done nothing wrong, though Anderson didn't provide any details to back up his claim.

Mahone went on in his military career to become one of Lee's most respected generals. He performed with distinction in later fighting, and was the Confederate hero of the famous Battle of the Crater at the siege of Petersburg, Virginia, in 1864. After the war he was highly respected in both business and politics.

Why didn't Anderson take sterner measures to get Mahone moving? Where was corps commander A. P. Hill, and why wasn't he overseeing both Anderson and Mahone? Lastly, if the echelon attack plan was working—and it was working—why didn't Robert E. Lee himself step in to see why it was breaking down at the most crucial moment? These questions remain unanswered, as does the larger question: if Mahone had gone forward, followed by Pender's and then Heth's divisions, would the Union line have collapsed, turning Gettysburg into Robert E. Lee's greatest victory?

Where in the World
Is J.E.B. Stuart?

*June 26–July 2, 1863: The Rebel Cavalry
Takes the Scenic Route to Gettysburg*

—

Doug Niles

D id you ever take one of those road trips where nothing goes
right, where events and circumstances and geography itself
seem to act maliciously to delay and impede your progress?
Say you're off to join the whole clan for a big reunion. You know that
you can travel light, move faster than everyone else, so you decide to
take in some out-of-the-way sights along the route. But then you run
into one traffic jam after another, and are forced to detour far out of
your way.

Then, just when you finally start to make some time, you stumble
across a garish tourist trap filled with gaudy souvenirs, and your whole
traveling party wants to take a day off for shopping. And after they
burden themselves with piles of irresistible baubles, you're no longer
traveling light, or fast. So you prop some toothpicks in your eyes and

travel all night, trying to stay awake. You're almost to your destination, but you run into some local toughs who want to pick a fight—and of course, you can't just ignore a challenge like that! So in the end you arrive at the three-day party two days late. The clan patriarch isn't too happy with you, and all you get to do is help with the cleanup.

That narrative, in an admittedly whimsical sense, is an allegory of Confederate cavalry commander General J.E.B. Stuart's role in the Gettysburg campaign. In the real crucible of Civil War combat, the legendary cavalryman's loose interpretation of his orders and reckless disregard for the needs of his army commander directly contributed, in no small part, to the single greatest Rebel defeat of the war.

During the first two years of the Civil War, the performances of the cavalry arms of the two opposing forces were very mismatched indeed. The Confederate horse, under the command of dashing leaders such as Nathan Bedford Forrest and Jeb Stuart, consistently outperformed the Union riders. The Rebs regularly raided deep behind the Union front, tearing up rail and telegraph lines, capturing supplies and destroying depots, even menacing northern towns and cities. On two separate occasions, Stuart took his entire force for a fast-moving raid that completely circumnavigated the Union Army in the field. In each case, he returned to Robert E. Lee with valuable information about the enemy's strength and locations.

By 1863, however, the Yankees were starting to catch up. The more urbanized northerners didn't start with the tradition of lifelong horsemanship embedded in the southern plantation culture, nor did they cherish the romantic image of the cavalier that seemed to dwell so strongly in many a Rebel bosom. But these Yankees could learn, and learn they did. Beginning with Joe Hooker's reorganization of the Army of the Potomac's cavalry arm early that year, the Federal riders strived to meet the Rebs on a more equal footing. True, the first large cavalry operation by the Union, Stoneman's raid during the

Chancellorsville campaign, did little damage to the South and in fact removed a useful asset from Hooker's purview, but already the die was cast.

A month later, the Gettysburg campaign would provide the first example in the war of the Federal cavalry clearly and decisively outperforming the Confederates. The fault for the Rebel failure in these battles and maneuvers must be placed squarely on the shoulders of the legendary hero Jeb Stuart himself.

Stuart was an accomplished leader, brave in combat, skilled in tactics, bold in operational planning and execution. He gained more esteem, and commanded larger and larger numbers of troops, as the war progressed. He was also a proud, vain man who loved the pomp of uniforms and pageantry, cherished the attention of beautiful ladies, and warily guarded his reputation against any besmirchment. As Lee was getting his army moving north toward Pennsylvania in June 1863, any number of these traits combined in Jeb Stuart's heart, compelling him to order a grand review of his cavalry for the army commander's—and Stuart's own—edification.

At this time, the cavalry corps, five brigades strong, was camped around Brandy Station, a Virginia crossroads just south of the Rappahannock River, near the depot town of Culpeper and conveniently located on the route Lee's army would follow as it moved north. The date of the review was set for June 5, and the requirements were specific: each officer would acquire a new uniform, and all the horses must be splendid specimens, impeccably groomed. A great ball for the officers and as many of the ladies of Piedmont Virginia as could attend would be held the evening before, in nearby Culpeper.

The review, by all accounts, was a dazzling success. Stuart's troopers, some 9,500 of them, formed a line more than a mile and a half long. They entertained the watching galleries with a parade ground march, full-speed mock charges, and other displays of horsemanship.

Bugles sounded, sabers flashed, and the Rebel yell ululated across the field. The cannons of the horse artillery roared, belching smoke and fire (but no shot) for the entertainment of the gathered audience. The whole affair was followed by another ball, every bit as grand as the first, on the evening following the review.

The only problem was that the army commander was occupied by some important matters regarding the imminent campaign, and was unable to attend. But no matter to Jeb Stuart: he learned that Lee himself would be coming by in a few days, and that the commander wished to review the cavalry. So Stuart's riders would do it all over again on June 8—though without the galloping, the yelling, and the firing of blanks. (Lee suggested that the horses' strength, and the gunpowder, be conserved for use in the upcoming campaign.)

But the army commander was duly impressed with his mounted arm, and before Lee and General Longstreet moved toward the Shenandoah Valley for the northward march he praised his cavalry general highly, and left Stuart and his men full of pride and purpose, knowing their importance to the upcoming campaign. They were to screen the movement of the Army of Northern Virginia, gain intelligence on Federal marches and dispositions, and perhaps stir up a little trouble with some raids and fighting as the opportunity arose.

The Rebel riders retired for the night secure in the knowledge that the two nearby fords over the Rappahannock were picketed, and that no signs of Federal activity had been seen on the northern bank. The five brigades prepared to join the army's march on June 9 . . . until the sound of gunfire, coming from the nearest ford, roused Stuart and his men with the dawn.

It was a surprise attack—the Yankee cavalry had the audacity to attack Stuart at Brandy Station! Using both fords, Union General Alfred Pleasanton attacked aggressively with two divisions in what would be the largest purely cavalry battle of the war. Although it was touch and go for a while, Stuart's men repulsed the Federals, losing some 500 men while inflicting 900 losses on the 12,000 northerners engaged. Pleasanton's men retired back across the river, but in the action they had learned that Lee's army was on the march.

And they had badly embarrassed General J.E.B. Stuart. There were whispers throughout Virginia that Stuart was more interested in impressing the ladies than he was in military preparedness. The *Richmond Sentinel* boldly admonished: "Vigilance, vigilance, and more vigilance is the lesson taught us by the Brandy surprise!" There is no doubt that these, and even harsher words, stung Stuart to the core, and as the Gettysburg campaign commenced he was determined to restore the glory of his name and reputation.

His first job assignment, however, was relatively mundane. As the long infantry columns moved north through the Shenandoah Valley, to Stuart's horse was entrusted the task of screening the passes in the Blue Ridge Mountains so that the Yankees couldn't strike at the army while it was strung out on the march. He reasoned, as the army moved on, that he could complete this task with but two of his five brigades, so he went to the army commander with an idea for the employment of the other three brigades—with Stuart himself at their head, of course.

He proposed that his riders be allowed to follow Hooker, to harass the Federal army and interfere with its operations. Lee and Longstreet were both agreeable to his plan, with the important requirement that, as soon as Hooker crossed the Potomac, Stuart would do the same and interpose his cavalry between the two armies so that he could cover the flank of the Rebel infantry—and, incidentally, keep Lee apprised of Hooker's movements.

Within the next week, the Army of the Potomac began to move, albeit sluggishly, to follow Lee northward. By June 22, the last of the Federals had abandoned their camps along the Rappahannock, and

Stuart was ready to go after them. He would move fast and travel light, with the only wheeled vehicles being six pieces of horse artillery and their caissons. Lee directed Stuart to move into Maryland and take position on the right of Ewell's corps, which continued to lead the Confederate advance. Longstreet appended a note to the order, adding that Stuart might want to wait until he could follow in the rear of the Army of the Potomac, so that he would be less likely to reveal Rebel intentions. On that same day, some of Stuart's own scouts suggested that Hooker's army was spread out so much that the Rebel cavalry could advance and pass between several of the Union corps.

Stuart's final pre-battle orders from Lee arrived late in the wet, rainy evening of June 23. While continuing to urge his cavalry to keep close to Ewell, even moving into the valley to help screen the army's movement, the army commander left the door of improvisation open a crack with a key phrase: "You will, however, be able to judge whether you can pass around their army without hindrance, doing them all the damage you can, and cross the river east of the mountains." Lee concluded: "The sooner you cross into Maryland, the better."

Stuart made his preparations, and his three veteran brigades moved out at around 1 A.M., June 25. By midday they had encountered the tail end of Hancock's II Corps, the mass of Federal infantry marching stolidly up the roads Stuart himself intended to use. Here he made the decision that would shape the rest of his role in the campaign: instead of turning west, to close on Lee's army, Stuart ordered his men to the southeast, seeking a means around the sprawling Union horde.

The detour extended far through Virginia, and it wasn't until three days later that the Rebel riders were able to cross into Maryland, unopposed, at Rowser's Ford. After a brief rest, Stuart ordered his men northward early on the 28th, intending to join Lee in Pennsylvania. But the direct route went through Frederick, where the Federals were known to be in force, so once again Stuart would have to veer to the east, seeking passage through Rockville and Westminster.

It was in Rockville that the campaign was finally doomed, though the circumstance of that doom seemed like a windfall at the time. Coming upon a major hub of the Union supply chain, Stuart's riders ambushed a Federal wagon train, destroying many wagons in a whooping, rollicking fight. More important, they captured 125 of the nicest, shiniest, newest wagons these men had ever seen. Furthermore, each wagon was being hauled by a team of strong, sleek, well-fed mules, every one of them strapped into a brand-new harness. Commented one of Stuart's colonels: "Such a train we had never seen before and would never see again."

Stuart was determined that this train be returned to Virginia, after it had been taken to Lee, where the splendid wagons could be filled with all the spoils gleaned from south-central Pennsylvania. This meant, however, that his force would move much more slowly than before. Throw in a little time for railroad wrecking, and the expedition didn't reach Westminster until evening of the 29th.

By this time, Lee was fretting very much indeed about his lack of information regarding the Union movements, but Stuart remained blissfully unaware of the fact. The army commander was marching blind, deep into enemy country. To make matters worse, Federal cavalry were reporting on Rebel movements, because the Confederate cavalry was nowhere to be found. In effect, the two most important goals of Stuart's mission—watch the enemy army and screen the friendly army—were not even remotely accomplished.

On the 30th the Rebel cavalry finally moved into Pennsylvania, arriving in the city of Hanover to encounter a force of Union riders. With his men positioned to guard the wagons, not fight, Stuart was forced out of Hanover by a vigorous counterattack. Learning of more enemy horse to the west of the town, Stuart was again forced away from his intended path. At the same time he found newspapers reporting Ewell's spearheads to be in York, north and east of Stuart's current position. So onward the Confederate horsemen rode, spending the night in their saddles, catching such sleep as they could.

They advanced on York on July 1, not knowing that Ewell's advance elements had already been called back to concentrate with the bulk of Lee's army. On that same day, the Army of Northern Virginia and the Army of the Potomac closed in on Gettysburg, with Lee having no idea of how many Union corps he faced, or where they were coming from.

Meanwhile, Stuart—who was due east of Gettysburg—moved north through Dover, still seeking Ewell. When he encountered several thousand Pennsylvania militia in Carlisle, he—naturally—had to teach them a lesson, wasting more hours in a pointless skirmish that resulted merely in his men burning down the Carlisle barracks. That night, he finally learned that Lee's army was engaged to the south, around Gettysburg.

Stuart reported to a clearly disappointed Robert E. Lee at the army commander's headquarters on the afternoon of July 2, when the battle was already two days old. The need for cavalry scouting and screening was well past, though the two men spoke a few words, alone, in a very short time.

History does not record what was said.

Futile Gallantry on
Cemetery Ridge

July 3, 1863: The Third Day at Gettysburg

—

Doug Niles

After two days of savage fighting, the Battle of Gettysburg had been fought to a virtual draw. Lee's valiant Rebels had succeeded in dislodging the stubborn Yankees on the first day of the fight, but his attempt to drive in Meade's left and right flanks on the second day had been repulsed after some of the most brutal fighting of the war. The Federals retained strong positions on Little Round Top and Culp's Hill.

To hold these flank positions so well, Lee reasoned, Meade must have pulled much strength away from his center. It was there, the army commander resolved, that he would strike his great blow on the third day of the battle. He envisioned a success that would split the Army of the Potomac in two, sending the Federals reeling back in confusion, surrendering in droves, and leaving open the road to Washington, D.C., and the path to ultimate victory.

Once again, however, diversion of purpose and misunderstandings among the Confederate high commanders would render any chance of success a very long shot indeed. The trouble began very early in the day, when Ewell's corps resumed the attack against the now thoroughly fortified position of Culp's Hill. Almost immediately his men were met by a sturdy Yankee counterattack, supported by massed artillery on the high ground. Because of the rugged terrain in the rear of the Rebel position, the Confederates could not bring effective artillery to bear, and by 9:30 A.M. were soundly defeated with heavy losses. Not only had they failed to gain ground, but the Yankees had actually reclaimed some of the terrain they had lost the previous day.

To make matters worse—and to illustrate the disorganization in command and control—Ewell received a note at 10:00 A.M. from General Lee, instructing him to delay his attack for several hours until Longstreet could get his men positioned for the main effort of the day. That note, of course, was already overtaken by events.

As for the main thrust, it is hard to imagine an officer in command of an operation with less enthusiasm for the task, and lower hopes for its success, than James Longstreet on the morning of July 3. He began the day with renewed hope for his cherished plan of a defensive battle, and reported to Lee that his scouts reported no Federal troops south of Little Round Top. This meant, Longstreet pressed avidly, that there was still an opportunity for the Rebels to get around Meade's left and take position on some strong ground, compelling the Yankees into the attack.

But Lee would have none of it. He restated his intention of attacking the Union center, Cemetery Ridge, with all of I Corps— some 15,000 men in total. According to Longstreet's own memoirs, the corps commander replied: "General, I have been a soldier all my life, and should know, as well as anyone, what soldiers can do. It is my opinion that no 15,000 men ever arrayed for battle can take that position." But Lee remained confident for, in his mind, the Army of Northern Virginia could accomplish any task he ordered it to do.

Longstreet countered with another objection. His corps had three divisions, Pickett's—newly arrived on the scene—Hood's, and McLaws's. The latter two had been savaged on the fighting of July 2 and, furthermore, their position on the far right of the Rebel line would expose the whole army to an enemy flanking move if they were sent in to the attack. This argument swayed Lee, and he agreed that the two divisions should not attack but instead continue to secure the flank. To make up the strength, Lee decided that Heth's division and half of Pender's would instead join Pickett in the assault. There is no evidence that Lee consulted with either Heth, Pender, or A. P. Hill (their corps commander) in making this change. Surprising as it is, it seems that Lee didn't realize that both of those two divisions had been as badly handled on July 1 as Longstreet's pair were on July 2. They were very far from full strength, and had suffered particularly grievous losses of experienced field officers.

Longstreet continued to object, now claiming that the attack would be shredded by Union artillery. To counter this, Lee consulted a highly regarded artillery officer of his own staff, Colonel Long, who assured the army commander that the Rebel artillery would be able to silence the Union batteries enough to allow the assault. Finally, Longstreet ceased his arguments, though he made it clear that he wished Lee would put someone else in command of an attack he believed to be doomed. With Stonewall Jackson dead, however, there was no other officer Lee could entrust with such an operation, so the die was cast.

The plan was simple and straightforward. The ranks of infantry would wait just beyond the crest on the western side of Seminary Ridge, a little more than a mile from their objective and out of sight of the enemy. The Rebel artillery, under the overall command of Colonel

Porter Alexander, would bombard the Federal positions on Cemetery Ridge long enough to knock many, perhaps even most, of the Union guns out of action. Then the Confederate infantry would charge in full line of battle, advancing through the shallow valley, crossing the Emmitsburg Road, and finally sweeping Meade's army from its commanding high ground.

With the change in order of battle, more than half of the attacking troops came from Hill's corps, though Longstreet would command the attack. It seems that these two proud commanders, who had a testy history with each other dating back to the Peninsula Campaign, did not discuss the dispositions of the men from Pender's and Heth's divisions. Each apparently thought that the other would take charge of specific tactical instructions. As a result, two undersized and inexperienced brigades—Brockenbrough's and Davis's originally, though the July 1 fighting had left them virtually bereft of experienced officers—fell in to form the far left of the Rebel attack.

Lee had a clear idea of how he wanted the attacking brigades organized in the attack, notably with an echelon formation (that is, a trailing unit slightly to one side of the preceding unit) to aid the advance of the flanking units. This intent, however, was never communicated to the brigadiers, many of whom were recently regimental officers promoted to replace casualties sustained earlier in the battle. The charge, in the event, would go in as one long line of battle, with a second long line in support.

Longstreet made one more attempt to dodge the bullet of responsibility for the attack. In a message to Porter Alexander as the artillerist was instructed to open fire, the I Corps commander asked the colonel of artillery to advise Pickett not to attack if it seemed as if the barrage had not done its work. Longstreet then dismounted, went to a shady patch of grass beneath a tree, and to all appearances took a short nap. His rest was interrupted by a note from Alexander, who declined the responsibility of deciding whether the attack should proceed. He further warned Longstreet that it would be too late to make the decision after the barrage, since the fire would use up virtually all of the remaining artillery ammunition.

This illustrated yet another breakdown in communication and understanding. Lee had earlier instructed that, following the barrage, the guns should be advanced in conjunction with the infantry, moving closer to the enemy during the attack and adding their fire to the assault waves. Yet clearly Alexander didn't realize that this was part of the plan, and in fact when the assault began he had very few guns to throw in, due to the exhaustion of nearly all their available ammunition.

It was about 1:15 in the afternoon when Longstreet, who could find no further excuses for delay, finally authorized the bombardment to commence. Quickly the batteries opened fire, until some 150 guns roared across the Pennsylvania countryside. Quickly, too, did the Union batteries open up in equal numbers, blasting their response against the cannons arrayed along Seminary Ridge. For nearly two hours this artillery duel, the largest ever to occur upon the North American continent, raged. Yet while considerable damage was done to the guns of each side, the infantry—Rebels protected by Seminary Ridge, Yankees hunkered down behind stone walls and in shallow rifle pits—suffered little.

It was the Union gunnery chief, Henry Hunt, who came up with an idea to move things along. He suggested, and Meade agreed, that the Yankee batteries begin to withdraw behind the crest of the ridge, giving the impression that the enemy barrage was doing significantly more damage than it actually was. Whether or not the ruse worked, or the Confederates were simply running out of ammunition—which they were—Longstreet took note of the lull and at long last ordered the troops forward.

The attack is still known as Pickett's Charge, of course, though General Pickett commanded but three of the eleven brigades making the attack. Yet he is as emblematic as anybody of the tragic glory embodied by this doomed attack. Dressing as a bit of a dandy, with his long, perfumed hair worn in ringlets, George Pickett had been a division commander for more than a year, but had been denied a chance to attain the glory that had rained down upon so many of his fellows. Now, his opportunity had come!

The Rebel brigades advanced in fine style, flags flying, drums pounding the cadence. They crossed the low crest of Seminary Ridge and started through the shallow valley, a broad expanse of open fields. They had to cross some three-quarters of a mile under fire, and tens of thousands of men in both armies were positioned to watch the spectacle—a sight none of them would ever forget. At first artillery shells ripped holes in the ranks of marching men, but the veteran troops closed the gaps with discipline and élan. As they drew nearer to Cemetery Ridge, the Federal guns—which had been wheeled forward again to confront the attack—blasted away with canisters, lethal sprays of metal balls like blasts from giant shotguns that tore even larger holes in the Rebel lines.

And finally, as the attacking brigades wavered, struggling to cross the rail fences that ran alongside the Emmitsburg Road, the Yankees opened up with musketry, thousands and thousands of rifles spewing lead, flame, and smoke from all along the crest of the ridge. Still the Rebels came on, though they wavered some more. Now the failure to attack in echelon became manifest, as the brigades on the left flank crowded together, struggled until the hail of fire, and finally broke and fell back. There was nothing their young and untried officers could do to stop them.

In the center, Pickett's and Pender's men closed ranks and continued to advance, their objective visible as a little copse of trees on the crest of the ridge. More and more men went down. A Union brigade on the right flank of the charge advanced, faced right, and began pouring a lethal enfilade fire into the lines of Rebels charging past their front. Only now, the lines weren't so well distinguished, and the precise unit formation, marked by those proud battle flags, was all but lost. Still, in the face of a veritable hailstorm of fire, some Confederate officers and men continued to advance. The proud regimental flags clumped together in the center of the attack, their bearers somehow standing in the face of the lethal storm.

It was General Lewis Armistead, a brigade commander, who led a few hundred Rebels to what has long been remembered as the high tide of the Confederacy. Placing his hat on the tip of his sword— though the sword punctured the hat, which fell down to the officer's handgrip—he raced the last dozen yards, crossing a stone wall with some brave Tennesseans and Virginians at his side. He placed his hand on a Yankee gun, and there he fell, mortally wounded.

The fury of the attack had been spent. Grudgingly, angrily, almost in disbelief, the hitherto undefeated soldiers of the Army of Northern Virginia fell back from an enemy position that their valor and numbers could not overcome. Barely half of the men who embarked on this futile attack survived to return to Seminary Ridge. There, Longstreet and Lee tried to rally them, and steadied the lines to prepare for the Union counterattack that all expected.

But the Yankees, too, were fought out. True, there were nearly 20,000 fresh reserves from V and VI corps—proof enough that even if more of Pickett's Charge had crested the ridge, the Rebels would not have survived there long. But the three days of Gettysburg had left both armies drained, shocked, and stunned. The next day, the 4th of July, was a rainy, dreary day during which nothing much happened. Finally, on the 5th, Lee gathered his defeated army and put it on the road back to Virginia.

Meade, for his part, was content to watch him go.

Vainglory: Kilpatrick Orders Farnsworth's Charge

July 3, 1863: Gettysburg

—

Mark Acres

Glory, that harsh, fickle strumpet, drives men to acts of courage and folly, paying them off in the end with fleeting adulation and a silent grave. Her sister, Vainglory, marries some men for life—and makes them murderers. She thus ensnared Brigadier General Judson Kilpatrick, commanding the Third Division of Major General Alfred Pleasanton's Cavalry Reserve, Union Army of the Potomac, at Gettysburg on July 3, 1863.

The grand, doomed infantry assault commonly known as "Pickett's Charge" dominates the story of the third day at Gettysburg. Driven by hubris, desperation, and our lady Glory, the Confederate high command hurled the cream of the Army of Northern Virginia across open ground at the Union position Cemetery Ridge near the center of the Union line. The charge followed the largest artillery bombardment ever to take place on North American soil, a bombardment that proved largely ineffective. Predictably, the Union cannon and muskets slaughtered the approaching Confederates, and after a sharp, desperate struggle at the Angle, the charging Confederates retreated with approximately 50 percent killed, wounded, or missing.

Vainglory, keeping pace with her sister, goaded Kilpatrick into a duplication of Pickett's Charge, only on a small scale, and with cavalry, not infantry. The action occurred after Pickett's Charge had failed and the battle was won by the Union. The ensuing slaughter of Union cavalry was totally in vain. Kilpatrick's order for the needless, reckless charge all but murdered his troopers. As an additional irony, history calls the charge "Farnsworth's Charge," naming it for Brigadier General Elton Farnsworth, who actually led it and died in it. Kilpatrick himself, as a division commander, did not actually participate in the charge.

Born and raised in New Jersey as the fourth child of a former colonel, Kilpatrick went to West Point and graduated in 1861, shortly after the onset of the Civil War. He found himself leading a company of men at the Battle of Big Bethel, where he took canister shot in his thigh and became the first U.S. Army officer wounded in the war. Shortly thereafter he helped raise the 2nd New York Cavalry Regiment. Promoted to lieutenant colonel, he remained a cavalry officer for the remainder of his military career.

Kilpatrick soon distinguished himself as a brash, brazen commander who would hazard his men's lives in pursuit of his own advancement. His fellows considered his camps atrocious—the horses poorly maintained and often run-down, and the men, including Kilpatrick, frequented by prostitutes. Apparently the men had little gratitude to their commander for such companionship; they nicknamed him "Kill-Cavalry" for his habit of ordering reckless, sometimes suicidal charges. But "Kil" was an excellent politician, often using his connections to advance his career. He did have some success on the battlefield, in particular during Stoneman's Raid during the Chancellorsville campaign. Shortly thereafter he performed reasonably well at Brandy Station, and received his brigadier's star on June 13, 1863.

As a new brigadier general Kilpatrick took command of the Third Division of Major General Alfred Pleasanton's Cavalry Corps of the Army of the Potomac. Kilpatrick's command consisted of two brigades. The first, under Farnsworth, could boast five full regiments plus two companies of the 1st Ohio Cavalry Regiment. George Armstrong Custer commanded the second brigade with four Michigan cavalry regiments.

Kilpatrick's division saw action on June 30 against Confederate Major General J.E.B. Stuart at Hanover, Pennsylvania. Stuart was desperately trying to make his way back to the main Confederate army, far to his west. At Hanover he ran into the rear guard of Kilpatrick's division. While the Union men were initially overwhelmed, they quickly sorted themselves out and, in a significant action involving several charges, drove the Rebels from Hanover and demonstrated a rough parity with the troopers in gray. Kilpatrick claimed a major victory, as was his wont whenever he could. He failed to note that he did not pursue Stuart when the latter retreated, and in fact lost contact with Stuart's force completely.

But fate did not favor Kilpatrick at Gettysburg. His division remained out of the big event until the third day of the battle. Then, one of his brigade commanders, George Armstrong Custer, earned a great deal of glory leading a part of the Union cavalry against Stuart as the Confederate tried to cut into the rear of the Union lines. But Custer was detached at the time, operating with Second Division commander Brigadier General David Gregg. There was no glory for "Kil" in Stuart's defeat at Gettysburg.

Instead, Kilpatrick was at the scene of the big battle with little to do, his immediate command reduced to Farnsworth's brigade.

That brigade, too, was short the Ohio men and 2nd Pennsylvania Regiment—they too were with Gregg and Custer. No doubt Kilpatrick welcomed the orders he received sometime on the morning of the third day. Pleasanton directed Kilpatrick to the left flank of the Union Army's line. There he would "press the enemy, threaten him at every point" and strike the enemy "at the first opportunity." In plainer terms, cutting through Pleasanton's flowery, bombastic language, Kilpatrick was to take Farnsworth's brigade and harass the Rebel right flank. In addition, Pleasanton summoned up the reserve brigade of cavalry under Brigadier General Wesley Merritt to augment Kilpatrick's diminished force. Lastly, "Kil" had a total of twelve cannons in two horse artillery batteries, Battery E, 4th U.S. under Lieutenant Samuel Elder, and Battery K, 1st U.S. under Captain William Graham, to support his actions.

The right flank of the Confederate army extended from the Kern House west of the Emmitsburg Road to the base of Big Round Top at the Bushman and Slyder Farms. The flank was held by Evander Law's division (the former division commander, General Hood, had fallen seriously wounded in the previous day's fighting). Most of Law's men were facing east, toward Big Round Top. Only two regiments faced south: the 9th Georgia at the Kern House, and a thin picket and skirmish line of the 1st Texas, stretching across the Bushman and Slyder farm properties.

The men of the 1st Texas found the ground of the Bushman and Slyder Farms ideal for defense. The ground itself was rugged, pitted with hidden holes and dotted with dark rocks thrusting up at all angles from the soft soil. A series of post and rail fences, worm fences, and stone walls cut across the farms in a wild pattern, offering ideal defensive positions with various angles of fire toward any force coming from the south. Even today, visitors to the battlefield find this area a difficult walk; the rugged ground claims many a twisted ankle or knee. Farther west, toward the Emmitsburg Road and the Kern Farm, the ground gradually assumes a more inviting surface.

Upon receipt of Pleasanton's orders, Kilpatrick led Farnsworth and the artillery south of Big Round Top, then, out of view of the Rebel lines, turned west. Eventually, in a wood, the command turned north again and rode slowly forward, coming into view of the Texans facing south on Law's flank. A gray-clad skirmish line at once came forward to feel the cavalry, while two additional regiments reinforced the 9th Georgia on the far end of the right flank. Two batteries of Confederate artillery turned south and opened fire on Kilpatrick's command, driving the line of horses back into the woods.

Kilpatrick responded by sending a Captain Henry C. Parsons with two squadrons from the 1st Vermont Cavalry galloping toward the Texans near the Bushman Farm and in the general direction of annoying Confederate artillery. The sudden onrush of the blue-clad troopers drove in the Texas skirmishers, and Parsons's command was able to shelter from the stepped-up Rebel fire in the Bushman House. Pleased at the bold action and its success, Kilpatrick rode himself to the Bushman Farm, instructing Parsons to hold the position. He then began looking for suitable ground for another, larger charge.

But the ground was clearly unsuitable for any large-scale cavalry action, and now the enemy, fully alerted to the presence of Kilpatrick's troopers, was not likely to neglect any key elements necessary for defending the flank. About 1 P.M. the earth shook and the thunder of more than 130 Rebel guns rent the sky. The Confederates were barraging the Union lines far to the north, preparatory to Pickett, Pettigrew, and Trimble's charge against the Union center. Kilpatrick fumed; it was obvious that a huge infantry assault was in the making, and glory was waiting if he could only find a way to turn the Rebel flank. Alas, his reinforcing brigade under Merritt was not yet on the field, and no suitable ground for a mounted assault had yet presented itself. Farnsworth's brigade could only skirmish with their Confederate foes.

Merritt arrived upon the field at about 3 P.M. Kilpatrick placed the new brigade to Farnsworth's left, facing north, extending the cavalry line as far west as the Emmitsburg Road. Merritt's men dismounted and began skirmishing with what were now three Rebel regiments to their front.

Kilpatrick could only stew in frustrated ambition. No orders came to him, and no "first opportunity" to strike the enemy presented itself.

Finally, "Kil" could stand it no longer. Sometime around 4:30 P.M. he sent Merritt's men forward. The first mounted troopers met with some initial success, driving the Rebel skirmishers and even dislodging the 9th Georgia from the Kern farmhouse. But the two regiments reinforcing the Georgians quickly struck back. Seeing his initial mounted forces repelled, Merritt dismounted his command; the entire brigade went forward on foot over the only ground on that flank that was suited to a mounted charge! Merritt then learned what he should have already known: three full regiments of Confederate infantry significantly outgunned his brigade of dismounted cavalry. Ideally armed and trained for skirmishing and delaying actions, dismounted cavalry were never intended to assault infantry in position. Their failure was a foregone conclusion. The Union troopers did, however, draw Confederate General Law's attention to his far right flank; Law moved to the area to take personal command of the defense.

As Merritt's men were making the initial advance, a courier brought word of the great victory in the Union center. He shouted "we turned the charge," and his stentorian voice rang out the news of "nine acres of prisoners." What was joyous news to the bulk of the Union Army was pure torment to Kil, whose chance for glory was passing away rapidly. While Merritt's men inched forward, Kilpatrick formed Farnsworth's brigade in mounted line of battle. Not willing to let the afternoon pass without striking the foe and covering himself in glory, Kilpatrick first tested the Confederate defenses by ordering the 1st West Virginia Cavalry to charge the midpoint of the Texans' skirmish line.

Galloping as best they could over rocky, broken ground, the West Virginians made a bit of headway before coming upon a strong post and rail fence. Vainly they tried to hack or push the fence down, but the stout obstacle stood. The Texans rushed forward and unleashed a dreadful volley into the troopers. Swirling in the mist of flying lead, hacking at the fence rails in impotent frustration, the West Virginians could accomplish nothing. The charge broke and rode back toward the Union line.

Surely this should have been ample warning for Kilpatrick of the fate that would meet further mounted efforts on this end of his line. But just then he realized that General Law himself had moved to Merritt's front. With the division commander thus "distracted," Kilpatrick saw his moment of "opportunity." He ordered Farnsworth to charge north and then northeast through the rocky, fenced, and stone-walled ground of the Slyder Farm, to break the Rebel flank.

Farnsworth certainly protested this suicidal mission, although stories of a heated argument with both men standing in their stirrups and even a sword drawn are probably apocryphal. But Farnsworth did tell the commander of his 5th New York Regiment, "My God, Hammond, Kil is going to have a cavalry charge. It is too awful to think of." Farnsworth's prediction proved true.

Farnsworth went forward with the 1st Vermont. The 18th Pennsylvania belatedly came forward as well, after a screaming Kilpatrick personally ordered them to charge, but the combination of Rebel fire and the horrid ground quickly repulsed this support for Farnsworth's effort. The 1st Vermont did cover themselves in glory that day. Elements of the regiment under Farnsworth, Parsons, and Major William Wells actually broke through the Confederate line, despite artillery fire, infantry fire, stone walls, and the horrid terrain. More Confederate troops from the 4th and 15th Alabama came down Law's line to join the fray, and the 9th Georgia, with Merritt repulsed, rushed eastward to their support. Farnsworth hacked his way down and along the rear of Law's line, turning back south, and finally circling east after having his horse shot from under him. Remounted, he ignored Rebel calls for surrender. Infantry fire finally dropped Farnsworth; he died shortly after hitting the ground, his body riddled with Confederate bullets.

The rest of his troopers fared little better as the charge dissipated into disorganized groups of mounted men fighting for their lives against the surrounding hordes of Confederate infantry. One Alabama trooper referred to the fight as a "frolic" with the cavalry. In the end, 67 of the Vermonters lay dead on the field with many more captured and wounded.

Kilpatrick would later write in his official report that the Confederate defeat at Gettysburg would have been a complete rout had the infantry on Big Round Top rushed forward as the dying Farnsworth pierced the rear of Law's division. He does not note that there were no orders for them to do so, nor does he report that he made no effort whatsoever to suggest such an action, and sent no word to the infantry that he was going to attack.

Kil's reputation suffered badly after the Farnsworth charge. He would later try to restore it with an ill-fated cavalry raid on Richmond. That failure doomed his hopes of achieving national prominence and someday becoming president of the United States. Instead, he is remembered as the soul mate of Vainglory, as the man who murdered his command in a vain attempt to promote his own career.

Meade Goes Nowhere

July 1863: The Army of the Potomac's Strategic
Odyssey Between Gettysburg and Wilderness

—

William Terdoslavich

Major General George Gordon Meade just won the Battle of Gettysburg.

Now what?

Yes, Meade won a great victory against an overconfident General Robert E. Lee. It was an unimaginative battle of repeated Confederate frontal assaults against Union troops posted on defensible hilltops and ridges. Meade was competent, but not brilliant. He did not follow up his victory by crushing Lee's Army of Northern Virginia.

And this vexed his boss, President Abraham Lincoln. Meade's victory note about "driving the enemy away from our soil" ruffled Lincoln's sensibility. Even though the southern states had seceded from the Union, isn't it all "our soil"? Thus Meade burned a measure of goodwill with the president in the first weeks of his command. This would later grow into doubts and second-guessing as Meade spent the rest of 1863 maneuvering and countermaneuvering against Lee all over central Virginia without triggering a major battle.

What happened?

Or better yet, what did not happen?

Lee Retreats, Meade Advances

July 5, 1863, found two mauled armies staring down each other at Gettysburg. Federal losses were about 23,000, roughly 25 percent of the Army of the Potomac. Confederate losses ranged from 20,000 to 28,000, roughly one-third of Lee's force.

(Casualties represent the total number of troops *not* available due to all losses. At Gettysburg, the Union lost 3,185 killed, 14,529 wounded, and 5,365 missing, while Confederate losses were 3,903 killed, 18,735 wounded, and 5,425 missing. Death rates for the wounded in the Civil War averaged about 14 percent.)

Meade had spent a good part of the battle busting up corps and divisions to fill his line and avert crisis. Those units had to be resorted and reunited with their parent formations. The Army of the Potomac also had to be reinforced and resupplied before pursuing the Army of Northern Virginia. Even though Lee's army was just as banged up as Meade's, it was still Lee who was first off the mark retreating back to Virginia.

By July 7, Lee's columns reached Williamsport, Maryland, in desperate straits. He only had 35,000 men left, given battle losses, desertions, and straggling. A Union raid destroyed Lee's pontoon bridge over the Potomac at Falling Waters, about eight miles to the west of Williamsport. Lee's engineers improvised the construction of a pontoon bridge, cannibalizing the town's buildings for lumber. The alternative was being pushed into the river by Meade's force of 85,000. It would be like the risk taken at Antietam, only with a better chance for Union success. Unlike the slow and indecisive McClellan, Meade never took counsel of his fears. Meade could usually be counted on to make the right decision most of the time and be pretty dogged about getting the job done. If only his subordinates could be as quick or sure!

Come July 12, Meade was within striking distance. Attack? No. His remaining corps commanders counseled caution. (Meade knew he was cursed with a lack of decent corps commanders. All the aggressive ones were killed or wounded at Gettysburg.) Lee used that pause to slip his army across the Potomac on the night of the 13th, sacrificing his rear guard to aggressive Union cavalry probes that came the next day.

Meade was not giving up that easily. He crossed the Potomac farther south and quick-marched his army east of the Blue Ridge Mountains. On the other side, Lee's columns plodded down the Shenandoah Valley. At Manassas Gap on July 22, Meade pushed a corps west to strike Lee's force in the flank. This attack needed the leadership of an aggressive pit bull, but sadly it was Major General William French, a cautious poodle, who commanded. His force only tangled with Lee's rear guard. Meade had hoped to force a battle the next day, but by then Lee was gone.

By late July, the Army of Northern Virginia reached its base at Culpeper Court House, smack on the Orange & Alexandria Railroad, south of the Rappahannock River. Meade's army stayed north of the river, dispersed to cover all crossings.

Lee felt he had failed his cause after Gettysburg, and now Meade was occupying the same lines that Major General John Pope did the year before. Lee tendered his resignation to President Jefferson Davis, who declined to accept it.

Lee Advances, Meade Retreats

The Confederacy faced some serious strategic dilemmas after suffering summer defeats in the east and the west. By September, Jefferson Davis signed off on "the western concentration," a plan that drew reinforcements from other Confederate armies in the field, sending them to General Braxton Bragg's Army of Tennessee. The goal was to defeat the Army of the Cumberland as it advanced out of Chattanooga into Georgia.

Lee had to send the corps of Lieutenant General James Longstreet to aid the effort, leaving the Army of Northern Virginia with 47,000 men split into two corps to face Meade, who had 77,000. Worse, Meade got wind of Longstreet's absence and crossed the Rappahannock in force on September 13, capturing Culpeper while Lee slipped away south across the Rapidan. But Meade's plan to march around Lee came to a halt. Rosecrans was beaten at Chickamauga, and now Meade had to send two corps to reinforce the Army of the Cumberland in Chattanooga.

Meade was aware of Lee's dangerous talent for maneuver. He always kept the Army of the Potomac concentrated, and never took a position where Lee could march around him. The Army of the Potomac managed to stay between Lee and Washington, slowly retreating north toward Manassas. On October 14, Lieutenant General A. P. Hill attacked one of Meade's columns at Bristoe Station, only to see one of his divisions chewed to pieces. Meade entrenched around Centreville, just twenty miles west of Washington, D.C. Lee declined the chance to repeat Pickett's charge. The daring march north had tricked Pope into giving battle the year before, but it didn't work on Meade.

Meade Advances, Lee Retreats . . . Again!

Without a rail line to supply his army, Lee could not tarry long in barren Virginia. He retreated more than forty miles south toward his base—and supplies—all the while tearing up the Orange & Alexandria rail line. Meade followed, his support troops re-laying rail line almost as quickly. By November, Lee was back across the Rappahannock. Only this time, he left a small force to cover a bridgehead north of that river at Kelly's Ford. A surprise attack led by a then unknown brigade commander named Emory Upton captured the bridgehead, bagging two Confederate brigades.

It was now November. The Army of the Potomac crossed the Rappahannock in force . . . *again*! Lee crossed south of the Rapidan . . . *again*! It was now late November, and all this marching around was not leading to a decisive battle . . . *again*!

Meade was not leaving without a fight. He had to do something. Lincoln and the War Department were demanding action. So Meade played the last card up his sleeve. He planned to march east and cross the Rapidan at a pair of fords to get between the two corps of Lee's army and hopefully destroy them one at a time. Speed being of the essence, the wagon trains would be left behind. Each man carried rations for ten days.

The plan looked good on paper, but Meade forgot to factor in extra time to cover the unexpected, in this case the unexpected failure of French's corps to pack enough pontoons to bridge the Rapidan. A day was lost, and things only worsened when French's corps finally crossed and took a turn down the wrong road. Nevertheless, this was a crisis for Lee. He pulled back the corps of Lieutenant General Richard Ewell to Mine Run, a small creek that flows north to the Rapidan. Hurriedly, A. P. Hill's corps advanced to take position beside Ewell. By the time Meade got his mistakes sorted out, his army faced a very strong enemy position.

The victor of Gettysburg was not foolish enough to launch his own version of Pickett's Charge. Taking his last chance, Meade planned to attack with two corps on November 29. One corps would pin Lee's army, while the other would march around Lee's right flank. That morning, Union guns boomed on Meade's right, signaling the pinning attack. But nothing was heard on Meade's left. Riding there, Meade saw his corps commander, Major General Gouverneur Warren, sitting tight. Lee expected the outflanking attack and reinforced his right. The position was too strong to attack or turn, Warren concluded. Meade concurred.

That did not end the "battle" just yet. Lee planned to launch an attack to go around Meade's left. When the move began on December 2, it hit thin air. Meade had "disappeared," pulling his army north of the Rapidan.

Meade and Lee Stare at Each Other

Now that winter gripped Virginia, both armies went into winter quarters—that long pause until spring when troops traded tents for cabins and the lousy weather made it too difficult to campaign. Lee was no longer able to pull off acts of strategic magic that produced victories. When facing timid and incompetent commanders, Lee could get away with dividing his forces in the face of a larger enemy army, marching his corps to a position that threatened it, and fighting at a time and place of his own choosing. But the Union had pretty much run through its sorry stock of mediocre generals, each one getting fired after losing to Lee. Eventually competent Union generals had to rise to the top. Meade was one of them, not brilliant, but good enough.

But good enough for the Army of the Potomac was not good enough for Lincoln. He needed generals who could win battles and destroy armies, for once a Confederate army was destroyed, the land would fall under the control of the United States by default. Meade didn't get this. He still thought in terms of taking Richmond, preferably by way of the Peninsula southeast of the Confederate capital. (It almost worked for the timid Major General George McClellan.) Meade judged the overland route a waste since Lee's Army of Northern Virginia could only strengthen as it retreated toward its base, while the Army of the Potomac only weakened as it detached brigades to protect its supply line.

Meade's relationship with his superiors was further degraded by his attitude. A professional soldier, Meade believed civilians had no place dictating strategy or demanding action. A general's professional judgment should rule. But that made Meade's task of "managing up" more difficult, depriving him of any benefit of the doubt when plans produced barren results. In the end, Meade could not bring Lee to battle, rendering the previous five months of maneuver a complete waste of time. Historians sometimes refer to the closing act of this phase of the war as "the Mine Run Campaign," but the whole thing might as well be called "the Nowhere Campaign."

Disappointed by the lack of victory, Lincoln ordered Major General Ulysses S. Grant to turn over his command in Tennessee to William T. Sherman and come east to take charge of the war, and in turn the Army of the Potomac. And Grant would do what Meade could not—go around Lee's flank and bring him to battle.

In the campaign to come, that would happen again, and again, and again.

The Roof Is on Fire!

1863: New York

—

Paul A. Thomsen

A braham Lincoln is remembered for his sharp mind, cool temper, and steady hand in navigating the nation through the treacherous events of the Civil War. By midwar, even his most ardent supporters, however, admitted that the president was handling far too much for his own good. Lincoln's strategic mind was being subsumed by a veritable sea of complications, personalities, and minutiae in a quest to bring the war to a rapid and decisive conclusion. His generals were consistently failing to seize the initiative and their own men were being slaughtered in the process. The war in the west was also turning into an organ grinder of men and material. Moreover, the strategic situation darkened still further when news reached the president that General Robert E. Lee's Confederate Army was moving to invade the North. Personally, the president's health was also on the decline as his wife's erratic behavior and the sudden demise of his son, Willie, to fever steadily depleted his strength and his sleep was plagued by nightmares. As the Confederacy threw everything they could muster at the Union, in 1863, Lincoln made a terrible political mistake, issuing the ill-timed and poorly executed 1863 Enrollment Act.

Since his entrance into Illinois politics in the 1830s, Abraham Lincoln had distinguished himself as a calculating and cunning figure. Originally a hatchet man for the Whig Party, Lincoln had worked to undermine opposition members' agendas with slanderous accusations, procedural tricks, and newspaper smear campaigns. On June 16, 1858, Abraham Lincoln, now a Republican, decried Stephen Douglas's notions of popular sovereignty, claiming the country's discord over slavery could not long last, just as assuredly as "a house divided against itself cannot stand." Although he failed to win that election, Lincoln's campaigning against Douglas won him a much-needed national fame, which he cultivated for his next electoral run. Hence, in 1860, Lincoln's political savvy and now widely known middle-of-the-road electoral persona propelled him ahead of more seasoned politicians as the most able candidate to reconcile North and South.

Abraham Lincoln was unable to stop the rebel South from re-forming as the Confederate States of America, but, over the next two years, his political skills did manage to save the Union. He saw an advantage to allowing the South to draw first blood and, thereby, solidify the until then fractious North and the divided border states. His earnest understanding of the law and awareness of northern political demographics enabled him to stop the nation's hemorrhaging of seceding states. Likewise, he worked the otherwise politically impossible: simultaneously curtailing civil liberties in tempestuous areas and gathering together a large, initially volunteer-based army to fight the Rebels. Inside the White House, he co-opted vocal opposers to his policies. In the War Department, he neutralized military command by promoting the recalcitrants into dead-end jobs. Abraham Lincoln's self-effacing, humble, and now winning manner also garnered consistent congressional support for hefty spending increases for the war. Moreover, it enabled Congress to overlook damaging political scandals and even brought an otherwise divided party to accept the highly charged Emancipation Proclamation as congressional law. He was definitely born for politics.

As the war progressed, however, Lincoln's proverbial tightrope strained under the weight of his political juggling and threatened to break. For example, by announcing the Emancipation Proclamation after the 1862 narrow Union victory at Antietam, Lincoln both punished the South for rebelling by legislating away their slaves and played to the North's abolitionist demographic by adding an end to slavery as an explicit war goal. The move also provided an additional benefit to enlistments, the recognition of African Americans as a war asset. Finally, this level of legitimacy inspired the creation of several African American units, including the renowned 54th Massachusetts Volunteer Infantry Regiment of the aborted Fort Wagner siege and Olustee battlefield fame.

Still, not everyone was pleased with the president's emancipation maneuver. Many northerners were, in fact, resentful of the president's shifting war objectives. Throughout 1863, support by southern sympathizers living in the North grew among the urban poor in opposition to Lincoln's new mandate. Beyond the period perceptions of race, these individuals were already suffering the loss of well-paying industrial jobs to an influx of cheaper paid runaway slave and free black unskilled laborers. Likewise, the war was already taking many of their loved ones away to fight and possibly die. These delicate feelings were further tweaked with the daily and weekly reporting of the names of the dead on the front pages of local papers. Furthermore, those not already personally invested in the war were frequently confronted with battlefield images in newspaper sketches and photograph exhibitions. For example, Mathew Brady captured both army life and death, including mundane campfires, bloody hospitals, and corpse-strewn battlefields framed in stark black-and-white repose. As a result, many northerners came to see the war as a bipolar event of righteous national vengeance and visceral horror.

With the Confederate Army trying to terrorize the North into abandoning the war in the summer of 1863, Abraham Lincoln, now fatigued and overwhelmed by the duties of wartime governance, mistakenly ignored the pulse of the nation to fixate on the enemy his generals were fighting. To fight the enemy, his nation needed hope, his treasury needed refilling, and his army needed fresh troops. In response, Lincoln ordered his subordinates to initiate the Enrollment Act of 1863, which he saw as having two virtues: 1) countering Lee's attempt at invasion terror by demonstrating the Union's nearly unlimited troop capabilities, which threatened to overwhelm the South, and 2) the replenishment of government coffers with fees from those who could pay the price of a full commutation (which included a deferment until the next lottery). For the president, it seemed like a win-win, but, sadly, Lincoln never considered the ideological conflict brewing within his own northern cities.

On Monday, July 13, 1863, New York City's sudden fall into bedlam over conscription opened a whole new theater of the war for the president far behind Union lines. Now the president was fighting both the Rebel insurgency throughout the South and a fire spreading across his nation's roof in the North. Over the next three days, Irish immigrants, democratic supporters, and Copperheads joined the urban poor in mob rule over Manhattan Island. Some crowds gathered in the streets before the homes of city officials, buildings of city administration, and newspaper publishers, throwing bricks and shouting, "Rich man's war, poor man's fight!" Others looted storefronts and fired houses, orphanages, and places of business. Still others hunted public officials with intent to murder, and attacked and lynched African Americans from nearby lampposts and telegraph wires. In response, the city's wealthy fled north to the Bronx, the city of Brooklyn, or New Jersey, but most of Manhattan's middle and lower classes could not afford to flee and hid, took part in the riots, or attempted to protect their smaller businesses from the rioters. With local police precincts now under siege, Abraham Lincoln, ironically, was forced to wait for Federal troops to forcibly restore order block by block to the now burning city.

Had Abraham Lincoln been cognizant of the anticonscription sentiments permeating the North, he likely would have handled the situation differently. A simple adjusting of the act's imbalance against the poor or a greater public relations effort would have mitigated some of the dissent. Sadly, he did not think to consider either the issue or possible policy alternatives. He was simply tired and distracted by the fight. Even months later, Lincoln's recollection of the incident remained personally defensive.

"It has been used, just before, in establishing our independence," said Lincoln, "and it was also used under the constitution in 1812. Wherein is the peculiar hardship now? . . . Are we degenerate? Has the manhood of our race run out?"

Lincoln's blunder had lasting consequences for Union. According to David Donald and Harold Holzer, the urban insurgency cost millions in property damage and more than one hundred individuals were reported to have lost their lives. Most New York historians, however, believe the number is much larger, as protesters often carried off their own dead and riot victims were believed to have been underreported. Rather than tempt fate again so soon, the New York City draft rioters' actions forced city government to take a pass this time on contributing men to the Federal draft. Instead, the city paid the Federal government more than $300,000 in draft substitutions or commutations to release the city residents from their obligation. The incident was also a propaganda coup for the Confederacy, granting the South leave to talk about liberty. Next, southern agents in New York relished the temporary halt in city wartime industries and likely used the activity as cover to set ablaze a repair dock near the Brooklyn Navy Yard. Furthermore, domestic resistance continued to spread throughout the North against the act. In once case, a riot erupted in Wisconsin. In another, a soldier sent to round up deserters was murdered in Pennsylvania. As a result, in March 1864, the Federal government, having been continuously challenged by more (albeit subdued) protesters, was forced to repeal the commutation provision of the law.

For all his abilities, in 1863 Abraham Lincoln never stopped to consider the brutal effects his attrition strategy was having on the general populace of the North. Union conscription had been intended to resupply the North with fresh bodies and currency, but instead the act nearly razed a vital port city to the ground, withdrew valuable resources from the battlefront, and threatened to undermine the gains made in the war against the rebellious South by creating new pockets of Rebels in the North. It was one of the few times he took his hand off the pulse of the nation and, because of his mistake, a city burned, lives were needlessly lost, and the war became that much harder to fight.

Fight to the Finish at the River of Death

September 19–20, 1963: Battle of Chickamauga

William Terdoslavich

The Army of the Cumberland advanced from Tennessee into Georgia like an unstoppable blue wave. Three times lucky, it was looking to win again.

Major General William Rosecrans, a somewhat mercurial and extroverted commander, did not win the same plaudits and praise that Ulysses S. Grant did, but he was moving in the right direction: south at the enemy's expense.

Little did he know that after kicking the Confederacy out of Tennessee, the South would kick him back, all the way to Chattanooga.

Nasty surprises have a way of doing that.

A Brilliant Maneuver

The road that took the Army of the Cumberland to Chickamauga started at Murfreesboro, Tennessee, where Major General William

Rosecrans won a major battle nine months before by making fewer mistakes than his opponent, General Braxton Bragg, the contentious commander of the Army of Tennessee.

It took six months for Rosecrans to rebuild his army. His telegrams to the war department always asked for more supplies, horses and men. The War Department always replied by demanding action.

On June 26, Rosecrans heeded that order.

Marching his army east, then south, Rosecrans bypassed Bragg's position at Tullahoma. Outflanked, Bragg pulled back his army to Chattanooga, a key rail junction and gateway to Georgia. But Rosecrans's bloodless victory did not improve his standing with the War Department, which took more joy in Union triumphs at Gettysburg and Vicksburg.

It took a peremptory order from "general in chief" Henry Halleck to get Rosecrans moving again in early August. Rosecrans crossed his army over the Tennessee River to the west of Chattanooga, outflanking Bragg again and forcing him to give up the city. Rosecrans believed Bragg would retreat to Rome, Georgia, but Bragg had a different idea. It was the "western concentration," a strategy also advocated by General P.G.T. Beauregard and taken up by Confederate President Jefferson Davis and Secretary of War James Seddon. Extra units would be peeled off from other armies and send to Bragg to double the size of his force, which would then attack the Army of the Cumberland.

Bragg turned to face his enemy in early September, just as Rosecrans began crossing his three widely separated corps through the mountains of northwestern Georgia. If Bragg could pounce on one of these columns with his entire force, he could destroy Rosecrans's forces one piece at a time.

On September 9, Bragg's subordinates failed to spring the trap on a Union division probing east across Chickamauga Creek toward Dug

Gap. It fell back to join Major General George Thomas's corps. On September 12, Bragg again failed to smash the corps of Major General Thomas Crittenden as it moved southeast from Chattanooga. In both instances, good opportunities to destroy Rosecrans's force in detail were blown. Confederate cavalry, in short supply, failed to provide adequate intelligence. Lack of information reinforced the timidity and caution of subordinate commanders, who were tasked with attacking promptly but instead advanced with caution, delay, and poor coordination.

Rosecrans was finally wising up to the consequences of his wishful thinking. To avoid defeat, Rosecrans ordered Major Generals Critten-den and Andrew McCook to march their corps toward Thomas's po-sition at McLemore's Cove, about fifteen miles south of Chattanooga, between Missionary Ridge and Pigeon Mountain.

There was going to be a battle, but not on Bragg's terms.

Over the River and Through the Woods . . .

On the morning of September 19, Thomas dispatched a division to attack a single Confederate brigade that had crossed Chickamauga Creek. Instead, the division blundered into the cavalry corps of Briga-dier General Nathan Bedford Forrest and the corps of Major Gen-eral W.H.T. Walker. Thomas reinforced with a second division when word came back of a bigger fight.

The battle took place in thick, scrubby woods that curtailed visibility and increased chaos. Brigades broke into regiments and regiments into companies. Calls for reinforcements sucked in more troops. Eventually the battle developed into a push against Thomas's lines at Kelly Field, one of the few pieces of open ground in the area. Rosecrans reinforced Thomas's command with two more divisions, and the lines held. The Union still controlled the roads going north to Chattanooga.

That night, Rosecrans and Bragg would plan their mistakes.

Rosecrans met with his corps commanders and chief of staff Brigadier General James Garfield (a future U.S. president). After receiving reports, Rosecrans decided to reinforce his left to protect the road to Chattanooga, a conclusion seconded by Thomas. Orders were drawn to move almost half of Rosecrans's divisions while facing the enemy. This was a risky proposition. If the enemy attacked any unit on the move, the unit would be ill-formed to defend itself, risking disorder, rout, or destruction.

Exhausted from weeks of long days on the march, Thomas rode back from the meeting to his HQ. But he was not tired enough to sleep just yet. He ordered Major General James Negley to move his division to the corps' left flank the next morning. Then he ordered all his front-line troops to erect earthworks to strengthen their positions.

Bragg also had a conference, but not all his commanders met him at the same time. With no chief of staff to translate Bragg's intentions into clear language, many were given vague, verbal orders.

Bragg had five corps to work with, commanded by generals Leonidas Polk, D. H. Hill, Simon Bolivar Buckner, W.H.T. Walker, and the recently arrived James Longstreet. But Bragg put all into disorder by reorganizing his forces into two wings, with Polk on the right (commanding Walker and D. H. Hill) and Longstreet on the left (commanding his own corps and Buckner's). Orders were issued to Polk and Longstreet to renew the attack the next morning.

Tempers Rise with the Sun

Sunrise came at 5:47 A.M. on September 20.

By 6 A.M., Bragg was angry.

He had ordered Polk to begin his attack at sunrise. But Bragg heard no gunfire coming from Polk's sector. Messengers galloped back and forth. Polk finally got his command in gear before Bragg could arrive to chew him out personally. Polk never informed his subordinate, D. H. Hill, to attack at dawn with the divisions of Major Generals John Breckenridge and Patrick Cleburne, so nothing happened. The attack finally came off after Polk prodded D. H. Hill—at 9:30 A.M.

By 11 A.M., Breckenridge made some progress on the Union left, given that his brigades were hitting the recently arrived brigades of Negley's division (which had arrived after marching from Thomas's right earlier that morning.). Thomas sent reinforcements to Negley, so Breckenridge's attack was stopped cold. Cleburne hit the Kelly Field defenses head-on and got nowhere. Cheatham's division from Polk's corps was then committed and repulsed, also suffering heavy casualties. By 11 A.M., Polk threw in his last fresh units, the two divisions of Walker's corps, to support Breckenridge's attack. Turning the Union right at Kelly Field was becoming a hard job.

The morning was just as confusing on the Union side. Never at his best while under pressure, Rosecrans was becoming excitable, just as he had been at Murfreesboro, months before. His temper began to flare.

Recall that Negley's division was ordered to march to Thomas's left early that morning, and tried to move out while its skirmishers were still deployed. Rosecrans chewed out Negley for the error. Rosecrans then ordered Brigadier General Thomas Wood's division to replace Negley in line. Wood misinterpreted the order and deployed his division behind Negley's. When Rosecrans saw this, he blew his top, reaming out Wood in front of his staff. Well charred by Rosecrans's explosion, Wood ordered his brigades to take their place in line, freeing up Negley's division to march to Thomas's left. That was at 9:30 A.M.

Meanwhile, on the Confederate left, Longstreet prepared for attack, thankfully spared Bragg's dysfunctional attention. Unlike Polk, who hastily committed his units piecemeal in unplanned assaults, Longstreet gathered six divisions to hit the Union line in one blow. Three divisions were arrayed left to right on a front of less than a thousand yards, with two more in column behind the center division and a sixth division held in reserve. This force was assembled in thick woods just a few hundred yards away from the Union lines and went unseen.

Rosecrans would unknowingly give Longstreet his golden opportunity. Receiving an unconfirmed report that two divisions in Thomas's center-right were out of position and exposing a flank, Rosecrans ordered Wood to pull his division out of line and reinforce the threatened sector. Garfield was very busy writing orders to coordinate the shifting of two Union divisions from the right to the left, so he could not deal with this problem. Another staff officer was assigned to write the order. He dispatched it without reading it back to Rosecrans to ensure its accuracy.

Wood received the faulty order, but obeyed it promptly rather than face Rosecrans's anger again. At 11 A.M., just as Wood pulled his division out, thus opening a gap in the Union line, Longstreet launched his attack. The divisions of Brigadier Generals Jefferson Davis and Philip Sheridan were on the march when they were caught in the flank by Longstreet's divisions, and were quickly routed after trying to make a stand.

Then Longstreet wheeled his divisions right to roll up the Union flank.

Losses were light.

He was on the verge of destroying a Union army.

And it had only taken forty-five minutes.

Rock Beats Scissors

Rosecrans's HQ was located in a farmhouse not far from the disaster on his right. He could not rally the broken divisions rushing to the safety of the rear. Rosecrans lost his nerve, taking flight with his routed units up the road to Chattanooga, accompanied by McCook and Crittenden. At least he dispatched Garfield to find Thomas, who now faced the crisis alone.

Calm in the face of chaos, Thomas became aware that something had gone wrong to his right. Union troops were fleeing. That could only mean a successful Confederate attack that could sweep up his position, too. Thomas rallied retreating brigades and repositioned unbroken units to form a semicircle, his right wing extended into the wooden rise of Horseshoe Ridge, his left arm bent back to conform with the slopes of Snodgrass Hill. About a half mile east, three more Union divisions were also arrayed in a semicircle, trying to hold their position at Kelly Field. It was 1:15 P.M.

Longstreet sent three divisions to pound Thomas's line, coming within an ace of breaking through. But the unexpected happened. Posted a mile or so north of Thomas's position, Major General Gordon Granger marched to the sound of the guns *without orders*. His timely arrival with two brigades of his reserve corps allowed Thomas to extend his line on Horseshoe Ridge to stop Longstreet's latest thrust.

By 3:30, Garfield had arrived at Thomas HQ, and quickly sent word back to Chattanooga that Thomas was making a stand. With that message, Thomas ascended into legend as "the Rock of Chickamauga." Within the hour, Rosecrans read the message and ordered Thomas to assume command of all units, adding that ammo and supplies were on the way.

The crisis had not passed yet. Polk managed to worm a division to the north of the Union's Kelly Field position. Thomas shifted a division to face the threat, with one brigade dispatched to hit the Confederate division in the flank, rolling it up by 5 P.M. That enemy unit could have cut off Thomas's withdrawal.

Many of Thomas's divisions were battered, bloodied, and very low on ammo. Nightfall would bring an end to the fighting, and under the cover of darkness, Thomas would first withdraw the Kelly Field units, then his forces on Snodgrass Hill and Horseshoe Ridge, and send them north to Chattanooga.

Bragg did not pursue, but eventually took positions in the hills overlooking Chattanooga to begin a siege.

Victory in Defeat, Defeat in Victory

Chickamauga was a rare battle in that the Confederates outnumbered the Union, 66,000 to 58,000. Casualties were frightfully high, about 18,000 for the South (2,312 killed, 14,674 wounded, and 1,468 missing), while 16,000 fell fighting for the North (1,656 killed, 9,749 wounded, and 4,774 missing).

In the wake of defeat, the Lincoln signed off on the creation of a "Division of the Mississippi," giving Major General U. S. Grant overall command of Union forces between the Mississippi River and the Appalachian Mountains. Grant removed Rosecrans, Crittenden, and McCook from their respective posts, giving Thomas command of the Army of the Cumberland.

The Army of Tennessee went into another self-destructive round of command rebellion, with Polk, Breckenridge, Buckner, and Cleburne all agitating President Jefferson Davis to relieve Bragg. Even Longstreet concurred. Davis kept Bragg, not removing him from command until after his later defeat at Chattanooga.

But the real loser proved to be the spirit of the Confederate Army. "[It] seems that the élan of the southern soldier was never seen after Chickamauga," wrote D. H. Hill, several decades after war's end. "He fought stoutly to the last . . . with the sullenness of despair and without the enthusiasm of hope."

Chickamauga proved to be an empty victory for the South, as Bragg failed to either destroy the Army of the Cumberland or retake Chattanooga.

For the Union, it was not a defeat, just an inconvenient setback.

Götterdämmerung in Tennessee

Hood's 1864 Campaign

—

Roland Green

The roots of military catastrophes often go deep into the past. One might argue that the disastrous Confederate campaign in Tennessee in 1864 started with the decision of a Kentucky family named Hood to send their son John Bell to West Point. He barely graduated, and when the Civil War started, he went with his adopted state of Texas.

Commanding a brigade of Texans who were natural heads-down fighters like him, Hood distinguished himself early in the war. By 1864 he was a lieutenant general commanding a corps in the Confederate Army of Tennessee. He would also, in any modern army, have been in a veterans' hospital, after having one arm crippled at Gettysburg and a leg shot off at Chickamauga. How much laudanum (liquid opium) he took to fight chronic pain remains a mystery; a reasonable guess is that it was occasionally enough to cloud his judgment.

Certainly his handling of his corps was less skilled than his work at the brigade and division level. Certainly also he showed ethical flaws in writing to Confederate President Jefferson Davis, impugning the competence of his army commander, Joseph Johnston.

This might not have made such a difference, except that Davis did not like Johnston, blaming him for the fall of Vicksburg the year before. It also did not help that Johnston had retreated eighty miles in the face of William Tecumseh Sherman's advance on Atlanta. Atlanta was a transportation nexus and an industrial center that the South could not afford to lose. It was also a symbol of southern resistance. If Grant remained bogged down in front of Petersburg and Sherman got bogged down in front of Atlanta, it might swing the November elections in the North against the Republican administration.

A more aggressive strategy seemed worth a try. So Hood tried it, as soon as he replaced Johnston. He lost 20,000 men in three battles, without driving Sherman away. Then Sherman swung almost his whole army around to the south, cutting the last railroad into Atlanta. To save his army, Hood had to abandon the city.

That should have been the end of Hood and possibly the war. However, Hood was able to revert to a delaying strategy, raiding Sherman's long railroad supply line back to Tennessee. He never quite broke it. Sherman's repair crews were too good. But Sherman had to keep a large part of his army guarding his tunnels and bridges against Confederate raiders, reducing the strength he could bring to a decisive battle that would crush Hood once and for all.

This impasse put pressure on both parties. Sherman could not advance any farther as long as Hood's army was intact and mobile. Hood was in the same situation, and it is possible that it also offended his sensibilities not to be able to lay Sherman's scalp at the feet of Sally Preston, a flirtatious Charleston belle to whom he believed himself betrothed.

Jefferson Davis may have increased the pressure on Hood by

speaking publicly of planting the Confederate flag on the banks of the Ohio River. He may have also increased Union knowledge of Confederate plans, not a good move, either.

So history saw the spectacle of two large armies trying to get at each other by marching in opposite directions. On November 15, Sherman burned Atlanta and took his stripped-down army off toward Savannah, planning on living off the rich and untouched agricultural heart of Georgia. Hood sidestepped to northern Alabama to be connected by rail to a food-producing area, loaded his wagons, and headed north.

This was a risky undertaking on Sherman's part and outright folly on Hood's. Sherman's army had to keep moving or starve, and it was weak in artillery and cavalry. Hood would have done better to maneuver on Sherman's flank (either one would have offered good foraging) and cut off Sherman's detachments with cavalry. (That cavalry would have been under Nathan Bedford Forrest, about whose qualities nothing more need be said.)

But Hood was reluctant to retrace his steps to Georgia, and it was a long way. What he did instead was plunge north with an army of 38,000 men (all arms), the largest Confederate force left outside Virginia. He was plunging north, dependent on supplies brought forward by half-starved draft animals or foraged from a fought-over countryside. He even spun dreams of recruiting 20,000 men from Tennessee, although by this point in the war it is likely that every male Tennessean willing to bear arms for the Confederacy was already in a gray or butternut uniform.

Hood did believe in moving fast, however, and this military virtue nearly paid big dividends. When he marched south, Sherman had left his senior subordinate, George Thomas, to quite literally hold the fort in Nashville. Properly reinforced, Thomas would have an unbeatable edge in numbers. However, right now those potential reinforcements were scattered all over the upper Midwest. If Hood was lucky, he could defeat Thomas in detail.

After crossing into Tennessee on November 21, Hood marched straight for Nashville. On November 29, he reached Spring Hill, about thirty miles south of the city. So, very nearly, did two detached corps of Union veterans under John M. Schofield. If Hood could force Schofield to fight his way through superior numbers, the defeating of Thomas in detail might well begin.

It still isn't entirely clear what went wrong for the Confederates. They had marched fast and far, most were hungry, some were already barefoot, and their leaders seem to have been stricken with complacency. (Certainly Hood was—he went to bed early, possibly full of laudanum, and resisted all warnings of Union movement.)

Those warnings were not hallucinations. Having sent his artillery and supply train on ahead, Schofield and his subordinates slipped nearly 20,000 men within four hundred yards of the Confederate pickets.

When Hood woke up, he was apoplectic. Schofield's army was digging in at the town of Franklin nine miles to the north, using some old earthworks and busily creating more.

Hood's tactics that day had all the subtlety of a bull charging a matador. Never mind that one whole corps of infantry, most of the artillery, and all of Forrest's cavalry were not yet up. He would attack the enemy now, where he was—and test the courage of the men he blamed for Atlanta and Spring Hill through being too cowardly to press home a charge.

That accusation may have been bluster, both then and later. But made under circumstances that guaranteed it would be remembered until the end of time, it was a mistake.

It was late afternoon of an unseasonably warm Indian summer day when Hood launched two corps of infantry straight at Schofield's line. They made a splendid spectacle, 18,000 men in immaculate formation, battle flags waving, the fading light still enough to make swords and musket barrels gleam a grander spectacle than Pickett's Charge at Gettysburg, and just as certainly doomed.

The attack was in the best (or worst) "hi-diddle diddle, right up the middle" tradition, over more than a mile of open ground that offered neither cover nor concealment. The Confederate corps on the right got some help from a Union tactical error in deploying a heavy picket line ahead of the entrenchment. The pickets had to get back to their own lines before the artillery could open fire. Friend and foe tumbled into the trenches, some of the most intense hand-to-hand fighting of the war erupted, and for a few minutes it looked as if Hood's tactical madness might pay off.

However, a Union brigade taking a break behind the lines thought it had been ordered to counterattack. They did this so effectively that they halted any Confederate breakthrough, and earned a brevet major generalship for their commander, who had initially tried to stop them.

On the Confederate left, the Union artillery had a clear field of fire, and the Confederates took punishment all the way to the Union lines. Here they also suffered their single most serious loss—Irish-born division commander Patrick Cleburne, a splendid leader and fighter, who might have commanded a corps except that he favored freeing and arming the slaves . . .

Within two hours the assault had irrevocably failed. The Confederate problem now was to get their men who were trapped before the Union trenches back through the killing zone behind them to friendly lines. Doing this kept the fighting going for three more hours, until well after dark, and it only died down after the Union Army started withdrawing over the newly repaired bridges across the Harpeth River to their rear.

The Battle of Franklin need never have been fought. Schofield had planned no more than a rearguard action, to allow a safe crossing of the Harpeth. What he got was one of the decisive victories of the war, in which he inflicted 7,500 casualties (including six dead generals) while losing only a third that many.

What Hood *should* have received was a strongly worded order to commit seppuku, or at least to resign his command and retire to his estates. He had not only fought the battle, he had fought it as an old-fashioned frontal assault, when by 1864 any reasonably sophisticated ten-year-old knew that was no way to run a battle.

So Schofield's weary men hurried north to join the defenders of Nashville and catch up on their sleep, while those Confederates still fit to fight slogged after them, in weather that rapidly grew worse. Schofield's men enjoyed the amenities of a well-supplied, dug-in army; Hood's men shivered in hastily dug field fortifications, staring across their enemy's positions at the Tennessee State Capitol.

Some of them had other things to stare at. Hood sent Forrest's cavalry and a brigade of infantry off to Murfreesboro, thirty miles west. "Why?" the reader may well ask. "As a diversion" is the answer. A threat to Murfreesboro (on the railroad) was supposed to force the Union Army to send help to the garrison of the town.

It did no such thing. The Union garrison in Murfreesboro squatted down behind their defenses. The Union commander in Nashville watched Hood's army sit outside the city like a stoned groundhog, all the while fashioning his army into an effective club.

That Union commander was George Thomas, nicknamed "Old Slow Trot" because of his riding style. This did not accurately describe his mental processes; he was probably the best tactician of the war on either side. But many people confused his methodical approach with slowness, and as he was also a Virginian who had remained loyal to the Union, there were long-standing suspicions about his motives.

In any case, Thomas was methodically going about solving his problems. He had to organize a motley crew of replacements into combat units. He had to equip thousands of dismounted cavalrymen with horses, for pursuit of a beaten enemy. (To this end, he confiscated Vice President–elect Andrew Johnson's carriage horses.) Finally, he had to convince the high command that he was not George McClellan, unwilling to fight at all.

The worst offender in the high command back east was, of all people, the normally unflappable Ulysses S. Grant. He and Thomas were not friends, but during the first half of December, Thomas might have been pardoned for wondering if Grant was a worse enemy than John Bell Hood.

Grant's hectoring telegrams arose from a rare attack of nerves. With the war so nearly won, he was afraid that Hood, a wild card if ever one wore uniform, could cause major problems. Suppose he got away from Nashville because Thomas was too slow? He could march north to the Ohio, as Jefferson Davis had foretold. Or he might march east, to join up with Lee, giving the Gray Fox the strength to break out of Petersburg and move south to crush Sherman.

With all due respect to Ulysses S. Grant, he was giving himself nightmares. Hood had neither the food, the clothing, nor the draft animals to march north, and not enough ammunition to fight when he got there. The same limits applied to marching across a winter-bound Virginia, not to mention that the Army of the Potomac fighting close to its main bases could have tackled both Lee and Hood at once. If Hood did the sensible thing and went back the way he had come, he was admitting defeat, and could be rounded up in the spring.

The one thing Thomas's skill could not control was the weather. In the second week in December, it turned bitterly cold and the ground was a glaze of ice, too slippery for horses to move. Rather than undertake to teach the cavalry mounts to ski, Thomas held up any movement until the ground thawed.

Grant had a conniption. He had actually prepared a telegram relieving Thomas of command, and was in Washington preparing to go to Tennessee, when the telegraph line went down. The telegraph officer pocketed Grant's telegram and crossed his fingers.

When the line came back up, the first thing to come through was a day-old telegram from Thomas, indicating that the weather was improving and he would attack tomorrow. An hour and a half later, another telegram came through, announcing a successful attack on the 15th and promising another on the 16th.

Thomas was true to his word. On the 15th he had spent part of the day twirling his club, because the Confederate groundhog was hidden in a pea-soup fog. Then he brought the club down hard, holding the Confederate right with a strong diversionary attack while pressing back their left. On the 16th Thomas repeated the same tactical combination, and broke through the system of mutually supporting redoubts on the Confederate left. (Hood was too short of artillery ammunition to make that arrangement work.)

This time there were groundhog parts scattered all over the hills around Nashville. Out of 55,000 men, Thomas lost no more than 3,000. Hood lost 6,000 out of 25,000 on the battlefield, and eventually more than that to exposure and desertion as Thomas sent his remounted cavalry in pursuit. Hood might have lost everything if on the 17th Nathan Bedford Forrest and a brigade of infantry hadn't fought an effective rearguard action.

It was the end of the war in the West, as both armies got tired of fighting the weather while trying to fight each other. It was also the end of Hood's career, as he had compounded all of his previous offenses by not giving a full and accurate report of the campaign. It was also the end of his betrothal to Sally Preston, although he later married and fathered eleven children before dying of yellow fever in 1879.

His soldiers had long since composed the best epitaph for their general's career:

So now I'm marching southward.
My heart is full of woe.
I'm going back to Georgia
To see my Uncle Joe.
You may talk about your Beauregard
And sing of General Lee.
But the gallant Hood of Texas
Played Hell in Tennessee.

Jubal Early's Pile of Mistakes

1864: The Shenandoah Valley

Roland Green

The Shenandoah Valley runs approximately 130 miles from Lexington, Virginia, to where its namesake river flows into the Potomac at Harpers Ferry. It is one of the most beautiful scenic areas in the eastern United States.

In 1864 it was a military asset, not a tourist attraction. It offered a protected way from northeast to southwest or vice versa. A Union army marching up the valley could sever the important Virginia Central Railroad, capture the salt works at Saltville, menace Charlottesville, and devastate a rich agricultural area conveniently close to Richmond and the Army of Northern Virginia. Conversely, a Confederate army marching down the valley could feed itself, cross the Potomac, and strike north into Pennsylvania, northeast into Maryland, or southeast to Washington, D.C.

In 1864, General Ulysses S. Grant was determined to prevent any Confederate initiatives, and perhaps take one of his own. Unfortunately, he sent a boy to do several men's jobs.

In May, a small Union army marched up the valley. Its commander was Franz Sigel, a hero to German Americans but even more inept than the usual Civil War political general. The Confederates mangled him at New Market, with some help from the cadets of the Virginia Military Institute.

Sigel was eased out. His successor, David Hunter, assembled a larger force, won a small victory, and burned Lexington (including VMI). Then, hearing rumors that Longstreet was on the way with his whole corps, Hunter fled over the Allegheny Mountains into West Virginia.

This left nothing in the valley except the hilly terrain and the crumbling roads to slow a Confederate march to the Potomac—and beyond. Jubal Early from the Army of Northern Virginia promptly marched down it with I Corps, what was left of Stonewall Jackson's old command.

By all accounts, Early was a close relative of Oscar the Grouch, but he was a capable infantry general. His 15,000 men were about as good as the Confederacy still had—which is to say, about as good as any fighters who have ever marched on American soil.

On July 5, Early crossed the Potomac at Harpers Ferry, his men feeling vengeful over Hunter's destruction of VMI and civilian property in the valley, and turned toward Washington. On July 9 they encountered an improvised Union mini-army at Monocacy Junction, just east of Frederick, Maryland. The Union commander, Lew Wallace, is better known as a historical novelist than as a combat leader, but he had one good day then, and held up Early's advance for twenty-four hours.

By this time everybody in Washington except Abraham Lincoln was pushing the panic button. Washington was one of the most strongly fortified cities on earth, but most of its garrison troops were fighting in the trenches around Petersburg. Fortunately Grant understood the crisis the Union faced, and was sending his crack VI Corps and also XIX Corps, newly arrived from the Deep South.

On the morning of July 11, Early was in sight of the U.S. Capitol dome, with still undermanned earthworks the only thing between him and it. However, his men had marched fast and far, in hot weather over dusty roads, and fought a battle on the way. He decided to give them a day off.

Mistake! That day cost Early his last chance of attacking Washington and inflicting a major blow to Union prestige at a critical time. Grant's Overland Campaign had been a bloodbath, Sherman was still slow-waltzing toward Atlanta, and it was an election year. The Lincoln administration could hardly survive even a temporary loss of its capital, not to mention the loss of supplies and the prospect of having to virtually evacuate Virginia.

But 15,000 fresh Union veterans arrived that afternoon. By next morning the Battle of Washington was canceled before it had begun. Abraham Lincoln got a good look at an infantry skirmish from the parapets of Fort Stevens, nearly giving his handlers heart attacks, but that was about all the excitement until the two Union corps moved out on the trail of the retreating Early.

It was high summer, so the pursuit was hot in several senses of the term. Early was able to keep his distance, and in fact for a while the Union didn't know which side of the Potomac he was on. He used the fog of war to send two cavalry brigades raiding north, another mistake that suggests Early was not the best combined-arms general in the Confederacy. One brigade burned Chambersburg, Pennsylvania, but Union troopers destroyed that brigade in West Virginia in August. The other rode off to liberate the Confederate POWs at Point Lookout, Maryland, but the Union authorities reinforced the guard and this cavalry brigade took weeks to rejoin Early.

At this point, Grant and Lincoln agreed to deal firmly with Early's hubris. The reaction was led by Philip Sheridan, formerly chief of the Army of the Potomac's Cavalry Corps, now commanding a new Department of the Shenandoah. This large military department, or command, had been created by combining the forces of four previous departments in the area. He had orders from Grant to "put himself south of the enemy and follow him to the death" and to so waste the valley that "crows flying over it for the balance of the season will have to carry their own provisions."

He also had Lincoln's promise to back him to the limit. There would be no political interference.

So Sheridan went to the Shenandoah Valley, into which Early had long since retreated. The new Army of the Shenandoah started off with about 43,000 men, in three infantry corps (VI, XIX, and Hunter's old troops, now the VIII Corps) and three divisions of cavalry. This outnumbered Early by nearly two to one, even though Lee had sent Early what he said bluntly were the last reinforcements he could spare.

Although nearly as short-tempered as Early, Sheridan was a better combined-arms general. He spent most of the month of August getting his army organized while advancing cautiously south. Honors were about even in the skirmishing, leading Early to believe that Sheridan was another timid Union valley commander riding for a fall.

So optimistic did this error make Early that he divided his army to carry out several missions. He soon learned that Sheridan had outflanked him, just in time to concentrate and fight near Winchester on September 19. This first major battle of Sheridan's campaign was a close-run thing, as two of his corps attacked along diverging lines, to be nearly defeated in detail. But the Union infantry eventually held, the Union cavalry hurried Early's retreat with a classic cavalry charge, and Winchester changed hands for the last time during the war.

The Confederates retreated to a line of high ground called Fisher's Hill. On September 22, Sheridan came up with them, holding on to their noses with two corps and kicking them in the pants with the other. Flanked out of position, the Confederates retreated farther south, with the Union cavalry again discouraging loitering.

By now Sheridan was detaching troops to guard his supply lines from Confederate partisans, from John S. Mosby's elite light cavalry to angry farmers with shotguns and plow horses. The bushwhacking and retaliation were turning the war ugly.

Sheridan's next move turned it uglier. He withdrew northward while his cavalry destroyed everything that might help the Confederate army—not only food and fodder, but livestock (killed or driven off), barns, mills, stables, bridges, ad nauseam. Union troopers found it distasteful. Confederates found it a horror.

Early found it a dilemma. He could no longer forage a valley that Sheridan was stripping bare. Bring in supplies—in rickety wagons pulled by half-starved draft teams? Leave the valley altogether—and give Sheridan a clean shot at the Virginia Central, Saltville, and possibly Lee's western flank? Or attack?

A counsel of desperation, but "desperation" was a good one-word summary of the Confederate situation in the fall of 1864. Besides, John B. Gordon, Early's ablest subordinate, had discovered by a personal reconnaissance that a path led across a wooded ridge and down a small canyon to within four hundred yards of the Union position on Cedar Creek. If a flanking force could move along that path . . .

Gordon got the job. On the night of October 18, he took two divisions along the path, moving in single file and stripped of everything that would make a noise. In the predawn twilight (made murkier by fog) Gordon's men stormed into the camp of VIII Corps and routed it in a matter of minutes.

The fugitives crashed into the camp of XIX Corps while the men were barely awake, and the Confederates followed, screaming the

Rebel yell like fiends from the Pit. XIX Corps gave ground in more order than VII Corps, but still abandoned tents, guns, hot breakfasts, and a steady leakage of fugitives.

By now it was daylight, and Early's whole army was up, prodding at a VI Corps making a fairly orderly withdrawal, with its rear and flanks screened by two cavalry divisions. That force was almost equal to Early's whole strength.

Early and Gordon fought a postwar battle of the memoirs. Early claimed that attacks were made on the VI Corps, but that too many men had left his ranks to forage breakfast and loot in the Union camps. Gordon claimed that one more attack would have finished VI Corps and Sheridan's army, but that VI Corps "would not go unless we drive it from the field."

Early's window of opportunity was rapidly closing, because in Winchester (fifteen miles away, not twenty as it says in the poem "Sheridan's Ride") Sheridan had heard the predawn gunfire and grown suspicious. After breakfast he saddled up and rode south. When he started meeting fugitives, teamsters and ambulances, and the odd rider, he grew angry and went from there to furious.

So began "the most notable example of personal battlefield leadership in the war" (James M. McPherson). Sheridan rode at a trot, a canter, and only sometimes a gallop, but he left a trail of dust and blue air every mile of the way. Sometimes he swore at the fugitives for being cowards; sometimes he cajoled them with promises of having their own camps back by nightfall. Almost always the fugitives turned around and started back for the battlefield.

Sheridan spent the early afternoon getting his army reorganized, which cost Early his last opportunity to salvage something from the day before Sheridan slammed the window shut on Confederate fingers. A hasty withdrawal might have got away Early's guns, wounded, prisoners, and even some useful loot from the Union camps.

Instead Early was still on the field when Sheridan's revitalized men finished tying their last bootlace and rolled forward like an avalanche. The Confederates fought gamely but were overwhelmed by weight of numbers. Gordon himself had to ride his horse off a low cliff to escape.

At every Confederate attempt to rally, Sheridan would ride up to urge his men on, or the cavalry would swing around a flank and start the rout again. The Union infantry did have their camps back by nightfall, when they rested on their arms and left the pursuit to the cavalry. The blue troopers pressed the chase, finally burning a bridge in the Confederate rear and forcing Early to abandon his guns, wagons, and wounded.

Although he had actually inflicted more casualties than he suffered, Early had lost one thing that no surgeon could heal—his army's fighting spirit.

Early's chain of mistakes finished the serious fighting in the Shenandoah Valley. Early finished his days as founder of the Southern Historical Society and the cult of Robert E. Lee.

Sheridan finished his as the commanding general of the United States Army.

Throwing a Mule Shoe

May 1864: Battle of Spotsylvania

—

William Terdoslavich

The Yankees did not fall back like they always did before. Two days of bitter fighting in the dense woods of the Wilderness left Robert E. Lee's Army of Northern Virginia in possession of the battlefield—technically a victory. But the Army of the Potomac, under the strategic control of Lieutenant General Ulysses S. Grant, had just sent two corps past Lee's right flank. Hurriedly, Lee pulled his troops south, trying to keep his army between Grant and Richmond.

In previous years, the Army of the Potomac would be under the command of someone more foolish or cautious. Lee could get away with dividing his forces, turn a flank, and strike the Army of the Potomac hard where its commander least expected. That was not going to work with Grant, who maintained constant contact and always looked to turn Lee's flank.

For the next week, the advancing Union forces breathed down the necks of the retreating Confederates, looking to catch some careless division or corps out of place and smash it. Lee took great care to make sure this never happened. When the Army of Northern Virginia stopped near Spotsylvania Court House, the infantry whipped out their tin mess cups and bayonets and began to dig. In a few hours, they raised a knee-high dirt wall. But by the end of the day, that position would be a six-foot earthen wall fronted by a ditch, lined with a tangle of sharpened tree branches pointing out, topped with logs, and interspersed with loopholes and firing positions. One man behind an earthwork was equal to three in open ground assaulting him.

And so the line ran straight from west to east, except in one place where some high ground caused the Confederate line to bump out northward toward the Union Army. That was how the Mule Shoe came to be. Every southern soldier from corps commander down to private thought the position was poor because it could be fired on from three sides. Lee wasn't wild about it, either, but he let it stand.

It was Grant who would not let it stand in the way.

Grant's Plan, Upton's Gamble

The Civil War was undergoing a tactical change. Armies were now digging in to defend their ground. A frontal assault against a prepared position usually got a lot of soldiers killed. In the past, these trenches were "accidental," like the sunken road at Antietam, or the railroad cut at Second Bull Run. It was trench warfare, only in 1864 instead of 1914.

If the prepared position was a difficult nut to crack, then get a better nutcracker. For the Union, that was Colonel Emory Upton. He saw a simple solution: advance across the shortest stretch of open ground at the double-quick. Do not pause to fire. Rush the dirt walls. Penetrate the enemy perimeter and fan out. Follow-on troops will widen the breach. Eventually the enemy will be overwhelmed and the position taken.

Upton had demonstrated these tactics by taking Lee's bridgehead across the Rappahannock the previous fall, capturing two brigades. His reputation did not escape notice afterward. So when Grant gave the job of capturing the Mule Shoe to corps commander Major General Horatio Wright, he turned to Upton to work his magic again. Twelve regiments were picked to form the assault force and divided into an advance guard, a follow-on force, and a reserve, altogether numbering 5,000 men.

Upton did his own reconnaissance, identifying a stretch of forest that sprang eastward to the western edge of the Mule Shoe, about halfway up its length. The woods would cover his force while it staged. It was only two hundred yards from the objective. He then made sure all twelve regimental commanders looked at the ground, and made sure they all understood the plan. The attack was set for May 10.

Wright also acquired the division of Brigadier General Gershom Mott to assault the northern edge of the Mule Shoe at the same time. The defenders were expected to crumble if they got hit from two sides in a converging attack. But Mott's start line was more than 1,200 yards away. Worse, Mott received a contradictory order from the Army of the Potomac's commander, Major General George Gordon Meade, to tie in Wright's corps with the corps of Major General Ambrose Burnside, which was operating to the east of Wright's position, as well as to attack the Mule Shoe.

Sloppy staff work was making Mott's mission impossible. Wright ordered Mott to begin his attack on the Mule Shoe at 5 that evening. New orders came from Grant and Meade pushing back Upton's attack from 5 to 6 P.M., but that order never reached Mott. So Mott attacked on time, with just two brigades, his striking power reduced to just 1,500 men. His troops weaved through a forest, slogged waist-deep through a bog, blew away a Confederate picket line, and finally advanced into open ground, where southern infantry and artillery then began using the Union troops for target practice. The attack went nowhere fast. As bodies piled up faster, Mott pulled his troops out.

Now Upton got his forces ready for attack, still slated for 6 P.M. Three Union batteries began pounding the Mule Shoe. At 6:35, Upton began his rush job, leading his brigade in the first wave. Rifle fire took down men left and right, but the column maintained its push, rushing through obstacles right up to the parapet, hitting the first of three trench lines manned by the brigade of Brigadier General George Doles. Upton's lead regiments rushed the Confederate guns before they could rake the breakthrough with case shot. Union follow-on forces were close behind.

The Confederates would not take this like sitting ducks. Lieutenant General Richard Ewell, whose corps controlled the Mule Shoe, rushed his brigades to counterattack northward into Upton's force. Upton's follow-on regiments were now coming into play, trying to roll up the Confederate positions inside the Mule Shoe.

Ewell finally got his counterattack going, with four brigades striking Upton's force from the southern base of the Mule Shoe while the two brigades pressed Upton's force from the north. The Union regiments fell back to the breach, taking cover on the outside of the parapet. Now was the time for Upton to commit his reserve force of three regiments, but he was shocked to find they were in the thick of the action already. Now the men were all mixed up. Upton could no longer tell any regiment where to go or what to do.

It was now nightfall. Wright was alarmed. He asked Grant for advice, and the reply was simply to pour in more men to hold the ground. But the corps commander saw Upton's attack faltering against increasing enemy reinforcements. He sent one regiment out to cover Upton's retreat. By 7:30 P.M. it was over. Upton was rewarded with brigadier's stars on the spot, but fully one-fifth of his attacking force was dead, dying, wounded, or missing. The Confederates may have lost several hundred more, but the killing stroke that was supposed to break Lee's position failed. The Battle of Spotsylvania would go on.

Two Days Later . . .

Grant's stubborn nature was now getting the better of him. If he could not go around Lee, he would go through him, and now that meant striking the Mule Shoe with greater force.

So on a rainy, muddy May 12 the attack was renewed, with Hancock's corps striking the position from the north and Burnside's corps hitting it from the east. The attack would begin at dawn.

Ewell was expecting an attack . . . again. Union troops staging at their start lines could be very noisy indeed, even when they tried to keep quiet. By this time Lee had removed his artillery from the Mule Shoe to begin consolidating the Confederate line. Now Ewell wanted his guns back, but they were not handy when Hancock's men rushed the earthworks en masse. It took only thirty minutes to break into the Mule Shoe. Ewell rushed six brigades north again to counterattack. With no guns in place, this would be a straight-up fight, infantry only. By 7 A.M., the Confederate counterattack had Hancock's men pinned to the edge of the Mule Shoe. By 10 A.M., the bodies were beginning to pile up on both sides as brigades slugged it out at close range. The swift stroke was again becoming a bloodbath.

A supporting attack by Wright's corps went nowhere that morning, merely adding to the body count. Now Grant was going to commit Major General Gouverneur Warren's corps to attack a western sector of Lee's line to relieve the pressure on Hancock and Wright. But Warren and his division commanders saw little hope of success assaulting a prepared position, so they sat. When Meade found out, he blew his stack and made the attack order peremptory—Warren had to obey it promptly and without discretion. The attack was stopped cold, with the Union suffering massive casualties.

By 2 P.M., the edge of the Mule Shoe was renamed "the Bloody Angle." Two Union corps pressed the perimeter while one Confederate corps desperately defended the ramparts. The notoriously tardy Burnside finally made his attack in midafternoon against a portion of line covered by Lieutenant General Jubal Early's corps at the base of the Mule Shoe, but the attack was quickly undone by a flanking attack by two Confederate brigades. Burnside retreated.

By nightfall, Grant canceled plans to renew the attack. Union troops held their ground. Confederate units were pulled out after midnight to new positions prepared across the southern base of the Mule Shoe.

At sunrise on May 13, Grant advanced his forces into an abandoned position filled with mud, blood, and the dead. He paid for that hollow victory with the loss of 9,000 men. Lee may have lost between 5,000 and 8,000 men that same day, defending a position not worth keeping. Much of the loss was concentrated in Ewell's corps. It started the campaign at the Battle of the Wilderness with 17,000 men, but had only 6,000 left after surviving the Bloody Angle. One of Ewell's divisions suffered 75 percent losses over the week, mustering only 1,500 once the fighting stopped.

Overall, the Battle of Spotsylvania had run from May 8 to 21. Union losses amounted to about 18,000 total—2,735 killed, 13,416 wounded, and 2,258 missing. The hectic pace of marching and fighting did not leave the Confederacy with much time to devote to paperwork, so losses went unrecorded. Estimates run to about 13,000 casualties.

No battle would be won in a single, daring stroke. No war could be won in a single day's fight. Wilderness and Spotsylvania were merely back-to-back battles, and the losses suffered there were only the beginning as Grant moved south.

Worse was yet to come.

Grant Smashes Against the New Era of War

June 3–12, 1864: The Battle of Cold Harbor

—

Doug Niles

On March 9, 1864, President Lincoln made his final alteration to the command structure of the Union Army. While General George Meade had defeated Lee at Gettysburg, the president grew increasingly dissatisfied with the Army of the Potomac's lack of aggressive campaigning in the nine months following that epic and decisive engagement. As the winter merged into 1864 with no sign of significant progress, Lincoln decided that yet another change in the command was warranted.

As a result, General Ulysses S. Grant was finally promoted to a new rank of lieutenant general, the first such in the United States Army since George Washington (though the Confederacy had several commanders of that rank). Grant was given command responsibility for all the Union armies. While he would be responsible for campaigns including areas west of the Mississippi, throughout Tennessee,

Georgia, and the long southern coastline, Grant soon joined the Army of the Potomac, where he would remain for the duration of the war. He delegated William T. Sherman as commander of operations west of the Appalachians, while he would take charge of the theater to the east. Meade would remain as the army's commander, but his superior, Grant, would be in direct consultation with him on more or less a daily basis for the remaining thirteen months of the war.

And those would be thirteen very bloody months, indeed. Both Grant and Sherman understood that the objective now must be the destruction of the two significant Rebel armies remaining. Sherman's objective would be Joseph Johnston's Army of Tennessee, currently in northern Georgia, while Grant and the Army of the Potomac would pursue the elusive, wily Robert E. Lee and the Army of Northern Virginia. For perhaps the first time, Lincoln resolved to really keep his hands off military operations, writing Grant to say: "The particulars of your plan I neither know nor seek to know. . . . I wish not to obtrude any constraints or restraints upon you."

Grant took these words to heart. He joined the Army of the Potomac in the camps north of the Rapidan and Rappahannock Rivers, where it had been since its desultory pursuit of Lee following the previous summer's Battle of Gettysburg. In April 1864, the huge army began to stir. At the same time, Grant issued orders for a coordinated movement to support his operations against Lee, ordering General Franz Sigel to move down the Shenandoah Valley; General Benjamin Franklin Butler was directed to advance from Fort Monroe, on the Virginia coast, toward Richmond.

Meade brought his army south over the Rapidan, with some 105,000 men, and marched into the Wilderness, covering much of the same ground where the Battle of Chancellorsville had been fought a year earlier. It was Grant's intention to march fast enough that he would be out of the tangled mass of new forest and trackless brush before Lee (with about 61,000 men) could react, so that the two armies could clash on an open battlefield.

But Bobby Lee was not one to let the Yankees, even under command of a new general, steal a march on him. He got his tired, footsore, but still tough force onto the march and drew up across Grant's path. The advance in defensive tactics from previous campaigns was demonstrated immediately in the two-day Battle of the Wilderness (May 5 to 6), wherein the Rebels hastily erected entrenchments of dirt and logs and fought from behind these fortifications. Despite stubborn and courageous attacks, the Federals could not dislodge their foes. May 7 was spent pulling the wounded from the now-burning brushland and regrouping for the next operation. The Union killed, wounded, and missing totaled some 17,500, while Rebel losses were estimated at around 12,000. (Accurate records of Confederate losses during these campaigns did not survive the war.)

The veterans of the Army of the Potomac no doubt had a "here we go again" feeling about this setback, but this time they were frankly astonished when, after the army muddled through the rest of the Wilderness, it turned south. This simple, forthright proof of action had a tremendous salutary effect, and the soldiers cheered and hollered when Grant rode past them, convinced that, finally, they were on the right track.

With Lee's army in an impregnable position, Grant simply backed away from the fight and moved east, passing around Lee's right flank and continuing south toward Richmond—not so much because he wanted to capture the city, as because he knew Lee would have to fight to stop him from doing so. His goal remained the destruction of the Army of Northern Virginia, and he hoped to attain that objective this summer.

The next opportunity to do so came at Spotsylvania, where, once again, Lee had rushed to interpose his units in Grant's path—and once again those Rebel soldiers scrambled to throw up an impressive array of defensive works while the Yankees gathered their strength for an attack. After several days of piecemeal battles (May 8 to 11), Grant had enough troops on hand for a major push. By this time Lee's field-works had become truly extensive, and in a series of bloody attacks the Federals poked and prodded and achieved some breakthroughs. The fulcrum of the battle was a massive triangular redoubt known as the Bloody Angle, and Lee was able to shift his reserves skillfully enough that, again, the Yankees could not achieve victory. The Battle of Spot-sylvania lasted some ten days and inflicted some 18,000 Union casual-ties (about 3,000 killed) compared to about 12,000 Rebel (1,500 dead).

Thus two of the war's bloodiest battles occurred between the same armies, within the same two-week period. This was unprecedented, as, after every previous major engagement, the two armies had sepa-rated for a time, resting and refitting. Yet once again, Grant didn't back away to reinforce, recover, or regroup. Instead he repeated his maneuver, disengaging from the enemy fieldworks, moving east and then south to get around Lee's right flank.

As a side note to the infantry clashes, Union cavalry strength, com-mand, and performance continued to improve. Grant had brought General Philip Sheridan with him from the west, and with Sheri-dan in command the Federal horse were unleashed on a devastating raid. On May 11 Sheridan's 10,000 riders encountered Jeb Stuart and some 4,500 of his legendary troopers. In the Battle of Yellow Tavern the Rebel cavalry was defeated, and Stuart himself slain—a loss that struck Lee terribly. "I can scarcely think of him without weeping," said the commander of the Army of Northern Virginia.

Even so, the disconsolate Lee recognized the familiar dance step in Grant's advance and moved his army southward yet again to take up a strong position on the North Anna River. He arrived here on May 22, one day before the Yankee vanguard. Grant sent a reconnaissance in force against the position but decided it was too strong to assault, and once again did his side step around the Rebel right flank.

This time the Pamunkey River was in the way, and the Federals needed two days to cross the swampy bottomlands. This crossing gave Lee time to react, and even though he realized he was getting dangerously close to the Confederate capital he had little choice but to counter Grant's move. So he moved south and created a fortified position near Mechanicsville, along Totopotomoy Creek. Again Grant concluded that the position was too strong to take with a frontal attack, so with a careful study of the map, he directed Meade to order his army one more step southward, sending cavalry ahead to occupy the strategic crossroads of Cold Harbor—another one of those insignificant country stations that assume their place in the history books because many thousands of opposing men try to claim the place at the same time.

Cold Harbor was about the last place on the map where Grant could perform his now almost routine maneuver. South of the crossroads the ground dropped into the swampy, tangled bottomlands of the Chickahominy River, where McClellan's army had encountered so much trouble during the Peninsula Campaign of 1862. Beyond the Chickahominy was the wide, deep James River, a significant barrier to further operations in that direction.

Sheridan's cavalry arrived at Cold Harbor on May 31, hours before Lee's men, and the Yankee troopers bravely held on against Rebel cavalrymen. Then, on June 1, they stood firm against Confederate infantry until Federal infantry came up to stiffen the line. Both sides poured troops into the position over the night of June 1 to 2, but with Rebel troops barely arriving on the scene they did not have time to construct the fieldworks that had thwarted every previous attack in what was coming to be known as the Overland Campaign.

Grant ordered an attack for early on June 2, but now one of his most reliable corps commanders, General Hancock of II Corps, let him down. Hancock, who had fought heroically before, during, and after Gettysburg, was beginning to show the stress of a long and unforgiving war. Suffering from fatigue and the continued aftereffects of a painful, nearly fatal wound in his thigh, he was not the commander that he had been a year before—nor was his corps the elite fighting unit of Cemetery Ridge. In the advance, II Corps became lost among the tangled, poorly defined roads and did not reach their positions until the night of June 2. As a consequence, Grant delayed his attack for twenty-four hours, ordering it to commence in the early morning of June 3.

It probably goes without saying that Lee's veterans put that extra day to very good use, digging trenches, felling trees, clearing fields of fire, placing batteries, and gathering supplies for the coming fight. The position was naturally strong, with the left flank anchored on Totopotomoy Creek, the right on the Chickahominy River, and the whole position on a low, gently curving ridge. A newspaper reporter described the position thus: "intricate, zigzagged lines within lines, lines protecting flanks of lines, lines built to enfilade opposing lines, works within works and works without works." Capping the challenge, the Union attackers would have to wade through a swamp before they even reached the ground where they could commence their charge, and all of their advance would be exposed to Rebel fire.

It seems clear that the men in the ranks knew what was coming, even if their commanders didn't. They grimly anticipated heavy losses. For the first time during the war, thousands of soldiers who were going into the attack took the time to write down their names and home addresses, sewing these grim labels to the backs or the insides of their uniforms so that, when they were killed, their relatives could at least be notified as to their fate.

The offensive was targeted against Lee's right flank. Three corps were ordered to make the attack side by side, with Hancock's on the left, Wright's in the center, and Smith's on the right. Grant and Meade assumed that their corps commanders would order careful reconnaissance of the ground, but they did not specifically direct this and none of the corps commanders thought to do it on his own. In any event, the Rebels had posted swarms of skirmishers ahead of their defensive works, so any attempt to gather information would likely have been unsuccessful.

At dawn, the three corps, some 50,000 assault troops, moved forward through a thick, dreary mist. They slogged across the swamps, many men having to wade through waist- or even shoulder-deep water. Then they struggled onto the barely dry ground before the Rebel works, and faced as withering a storm of fire as any troops in the world ever faced before the turn of the twentieth century. The Yankees pressed forward with courage, and some of Hancock's men even captured the initial line of works—only to be plastered point-blank by Confederate guns that enfiladed the captured trenches and turned them into a killing ground.

Within half an hour the thrust of the attack was broken, and survivors huddled on the ground with the dead. However, instead of withdrawing—and being without orders to do so—the Federal soldiers began to dig in on the ground they had captured at such cost. Lacking entrenching tools, they used cups and bayonets to entrench, and even employed the bodies of slain comrades as parts of their desperate breastworks. By midday, hearing from the corps commanders that the attack was hopeless, Grant gave permission to halt the attacks, but this was only acknowledging the reality that had been established many hours earlier.

Union losses on this day were some 7,000 men, about a third of them slain. Most of the men fell during the first hour of the battle. Rebel casualties numbered 1,000 to 2,000. The Battle of Cold Harbor would continue for nine more days, until June 12, but the combat in those days bore little resemblance to what we have come to think of as "battles of the American Civil War." The troops on both sides hunkered down in deep trenches, while sharpshooters—men despised by both sides—took careful aim and killed any man who showed his head. There was no maneuver, no coordinated attacking—there was just hunger, and killing, and dying.

In many ways, Cold Harbor marked the end of a way of making war that had been around since the advent of portable, reasonably accurate firearms. While the tactics of Antietam, Shiloh, and Gettysburg showed traits that would have been recognizable to Frederick the Great or Napoleon, the men who fought and died at Cold Harbor provided only a grim foreshadowing of the massive killing grounds of Verdun and the Somme.

Grant recognized the mistake of his attack at Cold Harbor, writing in his memoirs: "I have always regretted that the last assault at Cold Harbor was ever made. . . . At Cold Harbor no advantage whatever was gained to compensate for the heavy loss we sustained." Grant being Grant, he wasn't finished, of course. Soon he would astonish Lee by moving south of the James River across a pontoon bridge nearly half a mile long. He would lay siege to Petersburg, and slowly throttle the Army of Northern Virginia with a steadily more elaborate ring of trenches. Eventually Lee would be forced to flee, and his valiant but tattered army brought to bay at Appomattox.

But from Cold Harbor on, the whole face of the war had evolved into a new kind of monstrous horror, a horror that would shadow the face of battle for many decades to come.

Butler Gets Lost in the Bermuda Hundred

May 6–20, 1864: The Battles of the Bermuda Hundred Campaign

—

Doug Niles

If there was to be a "poster boy" for the political generals that plagued the high commands of both sides during the American Civil War, Benjamin Franklin Butler deserves serious consideration for the, er, honor. He was a successful Massachusetts lawyer, and held the rank of brigadier general in that state's militia. It should be noted that this rank was gained in great part due to his extensive political connections, as Butler had virtually no actual military experience before the war.

Although he rose to prominence in Democratic Party politics, he would become a key supporter of Abraham Lincoln during Honest Abe's first term as president. His abolitionist credentials were impeccable, and by 1864 Butler's political support in Massachusetts was judged so crucial to Lincoln's reelection chances that Butler would retain his field commands during the war even as his performance proved almost completely unsuccessful.

In May 1861, Butler was one of three major generals of volunteers appointed by President Lincoln. By virtue of being listed after John Dix and Nathaniel Banks, Butler was thus third in seniority among these appointees. (Dix was judged too old for field service, while Banks would go on to a career every bit as lackluster as Butler's.) Butler's first assignment was to take command at Fort Monroe, in Virginia. In his first venture into operations, his small force was soundly defeated by an even smaller force of Rebels at the Battle of Big Bethel.

More notably, while he commanded the Federal zone in Virginia he refused to return to their owners escaped slaves who had made it into the Union position. His stance regarding these "contrabands" would eventually become standard policy, and it won him growing respect from the politically influential abolitionists in the North.

A year later, Butler was sent to New Orleans to take command of that city, which had been captured by the Union Navy. He proved to be a decent administrator and the city was an orderly place under his leadership. Still, he advocated harsh treatment of those he deemed disloyal, declaring that any woman showing disrespect for a Federal officer should be treated as a prostitute—a dire insult in the prideful South. He ordered the execution of a citizen who tore down the U.S. flag from the U.S. Mint in New Orleans, and earned the sobriquet "Beast Butler." He was so unpopular among the Rebels that Confederate President Jefferson Davis declared him a "felon," fated for hanging if he could be captured by southern agents.

Late in 1863 he returned to Fort Monroe. Here he proposed an operation against Richmond itself and, just after the new year, he was given permission to try. The Army of the Potomac, some distance to the north, demonstrated along the Rapidan River, holding the attention of Robert E. Lee, while Butler moved out with a smaller force from Monroe. He moved up the James peninsula at a fairly brisk pace, until his leading elements encountered a broken bridge just a few miles from the Rebel capital. After a few days of pondering the bridge, wondering what to do, Butler called off his operation and retired to Fort Monroe.

It was just a few months later that General Ulysses S. Grant arrived to take command of all the Union armies, including Butler's. While Grant, Meade, and the Army of the Potomac would make the main effort against Lee, the commanding general had in mind plans for other generals with far-flung commands, including Banks on the coast of the Gulf of Mexico, Franz Sigel in the Shenandoah Valley, and of course Butler on the James peninsula. Abe Lincoln reacted to Grant's plan with a typically colorful phrase: "Those who aren't skinning the hog can hold a leg."

But none of the political generals proved very adept at leg holding. Butler, in particular, was provided with a splendid opportunity to earn some of that military glory that he had so long coveted. Knowing that the Richmond defenses were very poorly held, and desiring that such Rebel troops as were there would stay rather than reinforce Lee, Grant ordered Butler to advance against the rail lines linking the capital city to Petersburg, an important transportation hub some twenty-five miles to the south.

Embarking on naval transports, Butler took his troops—now designated as the Army of the James, numbering some 33,000—up the James River and landed at a little fishing village known as the Bermuda Hundred. While Grant was skeptical of Butler's military capabilities, he knew he could not remove the political general from command, not when the hotly contested presidential election of 1864 was far from decided. He tried to support his subordinate by supplying him with experienced corps commanders, but Butler's vanity would not allow anyone but himself to make key operational decisions.

The Army of the James arrived at Bermuda Hundred on May 5, the same day Grant moved the Army of the Potomac into the Wilderness to commence the Overland Campaign. Butler's men moved out to cut the railroad line, and met with some initial success, pushing the Rebels back to Swift Creek and for a brief time driving the enemy off the front. Instead of exploiting the opening, however, Butler contented himself with destroying some railroad tracks. In the meantime, the Rebels regrouped, as they had a way of doing.

Some 18,000 men were mustered for the Richmond/Petersburg defense under the command of P.G.T. Beauregard. These troops included every available male from boys to old men. They were poorly equipped and trained. But they were willing to attack, and in a series of engagements they drove the Army of the James back to the Bermuda Hundred. Here Butler knew that he had a strong position, protected on three sides by a wide loop of the James River and on the fourth by his fieldworks.

However, the Rebels had the same advantage and constructed an equally impressive line of fieldworks, called the Howlett Line, that would prove impervious to any of Butler's desultory attacks. In effect, he had marched his army into a prisoner-of-war camp and pulled the gate shut behind himself. As a result of Butler's ineptness, Beauregard was able to send about half his men to reinforce the Army of Northern Virginia. Butler, in the meantime, languished behind his fortifications until Grant finally sent some ships to collect him and his troops, which were employed during the siege of Petersburg.

Later in the year Butler was sent to North Carolina, where he refused to attack the objective, Fort Fisher, assigned to him by Grant because he viewed it as impregnable. The election being over, Grant ordered Butler removed from field command—but this was a fight

Butler was ready to wage. He went before the congressional commit-
tee on the conduct of the war, supported by witnesses and vast sheaths
of documents attempting to prove his position that Fort Fisher was
impervious to attack.

Unfortunately—and embarrassingly—for this political general,
the fort was captured by another general even as the hearings were
going on, an act that proved a fitting and appropriate coda for Benjamin Franklin Butler's military career.

Throw Courage into a Hole

*July 30, 1864: The Battle of the
Crater, Siege of Petersburg*

—

William Terdoslavich

The Battle of the Crater stands as a monument to incompetence. Never have so few screwed up so much for so many. A shortcut to win the war found its grave in a raw hole, lined with the bodies of soldiers who paid with their lives for the mistakes of their generals.

In war, the general leads and the soldier bleeds. That requires a compact between the two. The soldier will risk his life obeying an order in battle, but the general must back that order with a good plan and the leadership that ensures good execution. Victory justifies the sacrifice the soldier makes.

At the Crater, the generals did not lead, but the soldiers bled anyway.

I Have a Good Idea

From the beginning of May to the end of June 1864, the Army of the Potomac was either fighting every day or marching every night, sometimes both in the same twenty-four hours. Battles were fought against General Robert E. Lee's Army of Northern Virginia at the Wilderness, Spotsylvania Court House, North Anna, Totopotomoy, and Cold Harbor. The War Department tallied about 40,000 casualties—6,586 killed, 26,047 wounded, and 6,626 missing. In early June, Lieutenant General Ulysses S. Grant crossed his army over the James River and began marching on Petersburg, Virginia, hoping to cut the rail lines that fed the Confederate capital of Richmond to the north.

Grant's movement was an added problem for Confederate General P.G.T. Beauregard, whose scant forces had already bottled up a secondary attack by Major General Ben Butler, whose "Army of the James" was trying to take the back-door route to Richmond. With some reinforcements from Lee, Beauregard extended his line south to cover Petersburg, defending it for a week against Grant's persistent attacks. With both armies entrenched, the struggle was beginning to resemble World War I, long before that war ever happened. Frontal assault was the quickest way to lose.

And so it was in late June that Lieutenant Colonel Henry Pleasants, commander of the 48th Pennsylvania, had a good idea. Before the war, Pleasants worked as an engineer managing a tunnel project. Now he commanded a regiment made up of former coal miners from Schuylkill County, Pennsylvania. Why not dig a tunnel to reach underneath the Confederate line, pack the end full of gunpowder, and blow it up? The Union Army could push through the gap, take Petersburg, cut the rail line supplying Richmond and Lee's army, and maybe win the war in 1864.

Pleasants put his thoughts to paper and sent the missive to his division commander, Brigadier General Robert Potter, who in turn relayed the note to his corps commander, Major General Ambrose Burnside. Within a few days, both men met with Burnside, who signed off on the project. In turn, Burnside told Major General George Gordon Meade, who exercised tactical control of the Army of the Potomac. (Strategic direction belonged to Grant, who commanded from "the tent next door" to Meade's.)

Aside from Meade's surly consent, the project got zero support from army command. Pleasants's men started digging the tunnel from his regiment's position, just 130 yards east of the Confederate earthworks. Used cracker boxes were fashioned into handbarrows to haul out dirt, which was disposed in a nearby ravine. Pick handles were shortened to make the tools useful in tight spaces. An abandoned sawmill behind Union lines was put back into service to cut roof timbers for the five-foot-high tunnel. Requisitions for special gear to triangulate the tunnel's course went unanswered. Burnside managed to scrounge a theodolite from a friend in Washington, D.C., to make do.

It took four weeks for the ex-miners to dig down twenty feet, then west for another 510 feet, terminating under a Confederate redoubt. Then a lateral gallery seventy-five-feet long was dug out, crossing the T on the end of the tunnel. Eight chambers were cut into the gallery to accommodate 320 kegs of gunpowder, each keg weighing twenty-five pounds. Pleasants asked for 560 kegs, but Meade cut the requisition. No reason was given.

Planning for Success

By July 26, Burnside outlined his plan of attack. The mine would be exploded at dawn, with a division ready to rush through the newly blown breach. Engineers would be posted at the head of each attacking column to clear obstructions. Attacks would be made elsewhere against the Confederate line to pin forces that could be shifted to cover the breach.

Burnside tasked his corps' fourth division, under the command of Brigadier General Edward Ferrero, to train for the attack. Ferrero's division was made up of freed slaves but had never fought before. He drilled his men to advance in narrow columns, then to fan out left and right once past the expected crater.

Now things began to go wrong.

On July 29, just twelve hours before the attack, Meade ordered Burnside to use a different division. Meade reasoned that an unseasoned division would not be able to execute the mission. If the unit took heavy losses, it would look like white generals using black troops for cannon fodder. Worse, the Confederate Army did not take "colored troops" prisoner. But the black troops were the only ones who were trained to exploit the breach.

Now it was Burnside's turn to make a mistake.

He had three other divisions to choose from, commanded by Brigadier Generals Potter, Orlando Willcox, and James Ledlie. Did Burnside choose a lead unit? No. He had his three remaining division commanders draw straws! Ledlie, who commanded the weakest division, drew the short straw.

No, this story is not made up. This really happened.

Ledlie had already failed to lead in battle when Petersburg was first assaulted in mid-June, staying in the rear to get drunk while his staff covered up this failure from Burnside. Now Ledlie was given his specific orders by Burnside—advance his division through the breach and take a hill four hundred yards behind the Confederate front line. The remaining three divisions in Burnside's corps would follow, while a reserve corps waited to the rear, ready to add its weight to the attack.

Achieving Failure

After midnight, Ledlie's division and the rest of Burnside's corps were ready. At 3:15 A.M., Pleasants lit the fuse. Thirty minutes ticked by. Nothing happened. The fuse might be lit. Or it might not. Did it go out?

At 4 A.M., Pleasants ordered Sergeant Henry Reese, a former mine boss, and Lieutenant Jacob Douty to go into the tunnel and find out what went wrong—and hopefully not get blown up unexpectedly. The two men found the fuse had gone out at a splicing point. They respliced the fuse, lit it, and got the hell out of the tunnel very quickly.

At 4:45 A.M., four tons of gunpowder exploded in the mine's gallery. Earthworks, men, and cannon were sent skyward in a slow, roaring blast, followed by a cloud of smoke and dust. Clods of dirt, stones, bodies, and wrecked cannon fell back to earth. The explosion vaporized the Confederate position, killing about 300 men. Once bloodied by battle, an ordinary crater became a proper noun. "The Crater" measured 60 feet wide, 170 feet long, and 30 feet deep. All who saw its violent birth were shocked and awed.

The troops in Ledlie's division finally regained enough composure to move forward without command. At that moment, 110 Union guns and 55 mortars opened fire to support the attack. Burnside's inattention to detail was showing results. He had neglected to order anyone to clear paths for the attackers through the abatis (felled trees with sharpened branches pointing outward). Soldiers going over the tops of their trenches had to work their way through the tangle before they could rush the breach.

And where was Ledlie? Huddled in a bunker, getting drunk. Without a leader, his division could not fight as a single unit. Reaching the crater twenty minutes after the explosion, Ledlie's men marched into the Crater. And they could not easily march up its steep slopes to get out.

Willcox's and Potter's divisions marched toward the breach. Each general was ordered to march around the hole, but still more men marched into the Crater to shelter from the increasing Confederate gunfire coming from a ravine to the west and the objective hill. Cannon fire now poured in from the flanks.

By 7 A.M., Ferrero's division of black troops marched forward, ordered to take the hill behind the Crater. Ferrero peeled off from the assault and joined Ledlie in his bunker. (Intoxication is the better part of valor?) Another leaderless division was going into the fight as an unclenched hand instead of a fist. Three black regiments made it past the Crater to attack the small ravine halfway to the objective hill, which the Confederates were using as an improvised trench. The Union troops could not carry the position and fell back, pursued by an angry enemy that was not going to take any of them prisoners.

At 9:30 A.M., Meade ordered Burnside to pull his units out. Soldiers in the middle of a battle can't disengage easily, facing attacks by Major General William Mahone's division at 11 A.M. and again at noon. Union fire slackened as men ran out of ammunition. Many tried to retreat, some being gunned down as they fled, while those that remained in the Crater were shot like fish in a barrel. The Crater had turned from a shelter into a trap.

Bury the Dead, Bury the Blame

By 1 P.M., it was all over. The Crater was littered with Union dead, some with smashed faces from being clubbed to death by Confederate musket butts. Union casualties were close to 3,000 (504 killed, 1,881 wounded, and 1,413 missing), with one-third of them coming from Ferrero's division, thanks to the Confederate policy of not taking black troops prisoner. Confederate losses numbered about 1,500. (An incomplete return showed 361 dead, 727 wounded, and 403 missing, with losses from other units unaccounted.)

Grant's disappointment was palpable. "A stupendous failure . . . all due to the inefficiency on the part of the corps commander and the incompetency of the division commander who was sent to lead the assault." Grant had a right to be bitter. In 1862, incompetence in command could be explained by inexperience. But by 1864, defeat should have weeded out all the deadbeats from command.

Removals were in order. Ledlie went on sick leave and was never given a command again. Ferrero was transferred to Butler's two-corps "Army of the James." Burnside would later be relieved of corps command, his reputation further tarnished by an army court of inquiry. It's a wonder he was not relieved earlier for his failures at Antietam, Fredericksburg, and Spotsylvania. Meade and Grant stayed in their respective commands. No one faced a court-martial.

Meanwhile, the Civil War went on for another nine months.

The generals continued to lead.

The soldiers continued to bleed.

The South's Last Stand
on the Gulf

August 1864: Mobile Bay, Alabama

—

John Helfers

By 1864, the Anaconda plan was working better in some areas than in others. Grant's brilliant campaign to take the Mississippi River in the west had cut the Confederacy in two, preventing supplies from reaching the beleaguered states east of the river. The blockade in the Gulf of Mexico and Atlantic Ocean was less successful, as fast cargo ships and Confederate raiders ran the Union gauntlet with apparent ease. The CSS *Florida* was a particular thorn in the Federal navy's side; the ship slipped past the blockade into Mobile Bay in December 1862, where it received a heroes' welcome. In January 1863, it left port and evaded the enemy fleet again. But by August 1864, the Union Navy was ready to stop the traffic in and out of Mobile Bay once and for all.

With Vicksburg and the entire Mississippi River securely in Union hands, Rear Admiral David G. Farragut could now pursue one of his original goals for the West Gulf Blockading Squadron: capture Mobile Bay. Thirty-three miles long and twenty-three miles wide where it flowed out into the Gulf, the critically important bay was the South's last active large port in the eastern half of the country. Anything that could be transported by sea came in and out of it, so one would think it would surely have been heavily defended to keep it out of the Union's hands.

The Confederates certainly seemed to think they had matters well in hand. On land, three forts protected the harbor, under the command of Brigadier General Richard L. Page. Fort Morgan was the largest, containing forty-six cannons, twelve of them rifled, and a garrison of 600 men. On Dauphin Island, across from Fort Morgan in the channel, was Fort Gaines, which held twenty-six guns and another 600 men. Finally, on the western side of the bay was Fort Powell, containing eighteen guns and about 140 men. All three forts had tactical problems, however; none was protected from the rear, and none of the guns in Forts Powell and Gaines could traverse the bay.

The Rebels' naval force was also small, but determined. In addition to three small side-wheel gunboats, the CSS *Selma*, the *Morgan*, and the *Gaines*, they also had the *Tennessee*, an ironclad ram. The flagship of the small fleet, the *Tennessee* was commanded by Admiral Franklin Buchanan, with its guns prepared by Commander Catesby ap Roger Jones; both of them had commanded the CSS *Virginia* at separate times during her famous duel with the USS *Monitor* in 1862.

Finally, the entrance to the channel had also been mined with sixty-seven torpedoes set by the Confederate Torpedo Bureau, a department of the Confederate Secret Service tasked with developing and placing munitions. The minefield was clearly marked, both as a warning to friendly vessels and to try to force enemy ships to steer closer to Fort Morgan's guns as they attempted to enter the bay.

The Union fleet had sheer numbers on its side. Among the eighteen ships were seven wooden vessels (the *Hartford, Brooklyn, Richmond, Oneida, Kennebec, Itasca,* and *Galena*) that fired traditional broadsides from the cannons mounted in the sides of their hulls. Three ships, the *Octorara, Metacomet,* and *Port Royal,* were double-enders, built with a bow and rudder at each end especially for river duty. Finally, the Union had four ironclads; the *Manhattan* and the *Tecumseh* were improved versions of the prototype *Monitor,* while the *Chickasaw* and the *Winnebago* were river monitors with twin turrets.

Like the Vicksburg assault, this operation would also be a joint mission between the Union Army and the Union Navy. Major General Edward Richard Sprigg Canby estimated that 5,000 men would be enough to take Fort Morgan, but before the attack could commence, Grant called all available men up to Virginia, where the fighting was entering a critical phase. Left with only 2,000 men, Canby modified his strategy, planning to take Dauphin Island and thereby control the lower bay and provide communication between the fleet in the bay and the blockade in the gulf. They wouldn't be able to take the city of Mobile, but they would be able to stop shipping into and out of the waterway.

Early on the morning of August 5, with the tide running into the bay and a southwestern wind that would carry cannon smoke into the eyes of the soldiers at Fort Morgan, Farragut gave the signal to begin the attack. The wooden Union ships were lashed together in pairs; if the engines of one were damaged, the other could still maneuver them out of the fight. The fleet approached in two columns, with the *Tecumseh* leading, followed by the *Manhattan, Winnebago,* and *Chickasaw.*

The second column was headed by the USS *Brooklyn,* with its "cow catcher" mine remover, which would detonate any mine before it could hit the hull, and four chase guns, small cannons used to destroy enemy sails and rigging, pointing forward, lashed to the *Oc-*

torara. Following were *Hartford* and *Metacomet*, *Richmond* and *Port Royal*, *Lackawanna* and *Seminole*, *Monongahela* and *Kennebec*, *Ossipee* and *Itasca*, and *Oneida* and *Galena*.

At the first shot fired by the *Tecumseh* at 6:47 A.M., the forts returned fire and the battle was joined. Except for the lead ship *Brooklyn*, the rest of the second column could not fire at the Rebel ships and instead had to concentrate on the forts.

Minutes after the fighting began, Commander Tunis A. M. Craven sailed the *Tecumseh* toward the *Tennessee*, apparently intending to engage her. Either forgetting or disregarding the orders to avoid the mines in the channel, he sailed his ship directly into the field. A mine detonated under the ironclad's hull, and the ship sank within three minutes. Rescue boats recovered only 21 of her 114 crew members, with Commander Craven going down with his ship, so he could never explain what he had been thinking.

On the *Brooklyn*, Captain James Alden was confused by conflicting orders, which said to stay both on the left side of the monitors and to the right of the minefield, effectively preventing him from going anywhere. Halting his ship, he signaled Admiral Farragut for orders. The rear admiral, who had been lashed into the rigging to get a better view of the battle, ordered Captain Percival Drayton to sail around the stopped ironclad and into the minefield with the immortal order, "Damn the torpedoes. Four bells, Mr. Drayton." Despite the lethal effectiveness they'd had on the *Tecumseh*, Farragut gambled that the rest of the explosives, which had been in the channel for several months, had been submerged too long to still be active. His bold action paid off, and the rest of the column passed through the mines without incident.

Now Farragut ordered his fast gunboats to take on the three Confederate gunboats. The *Metacomet* subdued the *Selma*; the *Gaines*, breached by cannon shot at the waterline, was beached by her crew before she could sink. The *Morgan* retreated behind the guns of Fort Morgan; she would sneak through the Union lines and escape the following night.

With only the *Tennessee* left, Buchanan went on the offensive. He would have rammed the Union ships as they passed, but his ironclad was too slow. Nevertheless, he intended to take out as many enemy vessels as he could. But hampered by his ship's slow speed, and facing multiple vessels, he became the prey instead of the attacker. Several Union ships rammed the *Tennessee* during the seemingly lopsided fight, but each time the attacker took more damage than its target. The same results happened with each volley of fire between the Federal fleet and the Confederate ironclad—the Union's shots bounced off the enemy ship, while the *Tennessee*'s volleys caused significant but not fatal damage. The harm would have been more severe except for the poor-quality powder in the Rebel ironclad's guns, which often failed to ignite when the cannon was fired.

But even protected as she was, the *Tennessee* took significant damage by the time the monitors *Chickasaw* and *Manhattan* arrived. With her smokestack destroyed and several of her gunport shutters jammed, the ironclad was in no condition to take on two fresh ships. The first volley from the *Manhattan*'s fifteen-inch guns hit the *Tennessee*'s ram, bending the iron shield and smashing its oak backing, sending splinters into the crew compartment. Several were injured, including Admiral Buchanan. Unable to keep fighting, Commander James D. Johnston requested orders from Buchanan and received permission to surrender the vessel three hours after the first shot had been fired.

With the Confederate ships out of the way, Farragut moved to capture the forts on the bay. When troops landed to take Fort Powell, they found the soldiers had spiked the guns and waded to the mainland. The garrison at Fort Gaines held out a little while longer, but

Colonel Anderson, realizing the futility of his position, opened communications with Farragut and surrendered his fort on August 8.

The Union soldiers then besieged Fort Morgan by establishing parallel lines on the island that could be moved ever closer to the fort, supported by shelling from mortars and the ships offshore, including the repaired *Tennessee*. On August 22, Fort Morgan was subjected to a daylong bombardment, forcing Brigadier General Page to flood his powder stores to prevent accidental detonation. After part of his fort caught fire, he spiked or destroyed his guns and surrendered early on the morning of August 23. The last open southern port on the Gulf of Mexico was now closed.

The battle was fairly bloody by Civil War naval standards; the Union fleet lost 150 men and had 170 wounded, but the Confederate ships only suffered 12 dead and 19 wounded. The armies of both sides fared much better, due to little hand-to-hand fighting, with 1 dead and 7 wounded on the Union side, and only slightly more on that of the Rebels.

Because the city of Mobile wasn't taken, the victory didn't receive as much attention as it might have until the last days of the war, when, in conjunction with the fall of Atlanta, it was seen as one of the final blows against the Confederacy. Mobile itself lasted until 1865, when it fell to another combined Army-Navy attack.

The Confederate defenses at Mobile Bay suffered from the same limitations that plagued the South all through the war—lack of men and lack of materials. Outnumbered and outgunned by a ratio of four to one, the Rebels relied on the untrustworthy mines (which, if they had done their job on the rest of the fleet as effectively as they did on the *Tecumseh*, would have given this article quite a different ending) to thin the fleet's ranks, and when that didn't happen, tried to repel the invaders as best they could, but to no avail. The forts had little effect on the battle (which makes sense, since once the two fleets joined, the forts could hardly fire in the battle for risk of hitting their own people). And there is no doubt that the superior naval technology of the North played a vital role in defeating the bay's defenses. But when it comes down to it, by the time the Battle of Mobile Bay occurred, the Confederacy was already on its way to defeat. It is suspected that many of the men in the forts and on the ships defending the bay already knew this, which accounted for their already low morale and lackluster performance. Even with Admiral Buchanan's spirited defense in the *Tennessee*, by the time the Union fleet steamed into Mobile Bay, it, like the rest of the South, was only waiting to fall.

Horsing Around: The (F)utility of the Cavalry Raid

1861–1865: All Theaters

—

William Terdoslavich

It started out as a good idea that worked.

It ended as a waste of time.

The deep cavalry raid was a Confederate specialty. Just send a thousand troopers hundreds of miles into the Union rear, burn a few rail bridges and supply depots, and watch the Union chase their shadows. Meanwhile, the Union Army at the front takes no action because its supply line has been cut.

And worse, each cavalry raid made the Union look stupid.

Accounts of cavalry raids read like good adventure stories. Raiders were always outnumbered and had to keep moving, lest they be destroyed. They had to be aggressive and crafty. Their leaders were often colorful, dashing, and brave.

Trooper and leaders alike contributed to the Confederate cavalry advantage that lasted much of the war. Over half of the old army's cavalry officers opted for service in the CSA and understood cavalry's raiding capability. Many troopers were farm boys born to the saddle and could easily perform this mission.

Right up to the end of the war, raiders usually won their battles. They just could not win the war. Why?

Smart and Fast Beats Dumb and Slow

The true long-range cavalry raid was born in the western theater, where the Union had to march its armies over long distances through rough country, dependent on railroads for supply.

Theory was turned into practice in July 1862, when Major General Don Carlos Buell advanced his army toward Chattanooga, a vital rail center. Confederate generals John Hunt Morgan in Kentucky and Nathan Bedford Forrest in middle Tennessee both launched cavalry raids that cut the rail line supplying Buell. At first, Buell tried to patch the situation by sending two divisions back to protect the railroad. That robbed his advance of some force. But the full-blown Confederate invasion of Kentucky compelled his withdrawal north, saving Chattanooga for the South as Kentucky needed to be saved for the North.

Later in 1862, Major General U. S. Grant was massing his forces for an overland march south from Memphis, Tennessee, to Vicksburg, Mississippi. It was going to be a conventional march, supported by a series of supply bases. Major General Earl Van Dorn led a cavalry raid that burned out the Union depot at Holly Springs, Mississippi, putting Grant out of supply. Temporarily, Grant's forces "lived off the land" as it marched back to Memphis. He finally solved the raiding problem in early 1863 by shifting his supply line to the Mississippi River. No cavalry raid could ever stop a steamboat.

Major General William Rosecrans took the next hit. He had spent the fall of 1862 building a mountain of supplies at Nashville to propel his army's advance to Murfreesboro. Confederate raiding cut his rail line several times, but it became irrelevant as the water level of the Cumberland River rose, thus permitting supply deliveries by steamboat. As Rosecrans fought the Battle of Stones River, Confederate Brigadier General Joseph Wheeler's troopers mauled several Union wagon trains coming down from Nashville. Union cavalry couldn't protect these convoys for beans. But Rosecrans did not retreat, having enough supplies on hand to fight and hold his own in a sloppy battle.

A raid could just as easily distract an enemy commander as it could immobilize him. In 1863, Union Brigadier General Benjamin Grierson conducted a raid that ran from Tennessee through Mississippi to Louisiana. He didn't destroy anything irreplaceable, but Confederate Lieutenant General John Pemberton had to dispatch a few brigades to guard his railroads, ignoring Grant's maneuver that put a Union army south of Vicksburg.

Equally duped was Major General Ambrose Burnside. In July 1863, Morgan led about 380 troopers on an eighteen-day romp from Louisville, Kentucky, through southern Indiana to Salineville in eastern Ohio, where he finally surrendered. This checked the planned advance on Knoxville, Tennessee, which required an uncut supply line and quiet rear sector to ease the cautious Burnside's worries.

But raiding also had its downsides. An army that sends its horse soldiers off on a deep raid was usually blind to the movements of the enemy. This happened to General Braxton Bragg, whose Army of Tennessee was turned out of its positions at Tullahoma and Chattanooga by the Army of the Cumberland's well-executed flank marches. Each movement went unseen because Morgan, Wheeler, and Forrest were off raiding. Likewise, Major General Joseph Hooker blinded his own command, the Army of the Potomac, by sending his cavalry off to cut the lone railroad supplying General Robert E. Lee's Army of Northern Virginia. The raid failed anyway, but worse, Hooker's forces lacked cavalry reconnaissance as they crossed the Rapidan River and marched into the heavy woods surrounding Chancellorsville. Lee retained his cavalry and eventually figured where to aim his decisive counterattack.

Iron Horse vs. Horse Soldier

The Union learned the hard way how to neuter enemy cavalry raids by relying on rivers as supply lines. But rivers don't run everywhere. Rail lines do, usually crossing areas populated by Confederate sympathizers who could aid raiders, or worse, through barren, mountainous areas where there was little for an out-of-supply army to forage.

To protect a rail line, a Union department (area of operations) might devote up to one-third of its manpower to guard wooden rail bridges and supply depots, both equally flammable. These postings robbed the army at the front of much-needed manpower, and the resulting point garrisons were often captured or defeated by enemy raiders.

The Union partially solved the problem by using freedmen to garrison the rail lines. Each former slave who enlisted in the army removed one slave from the Confederacy's plantation economy. Another partial solution was to apply the Union's massive industrial and manpower advantages to simply replace raiding losses. After a while, Union engineers got very good at replacing railroad trestles, reducing cut supply lines to mere inconveniences. Blockhouses also made point garrisons harder to eliminate. But these measures did not render raiding useless.

It would take a change of thinking to finally kill the effectiveness of the cavalry raid. That was Grant's specialty.

Grant's army had to make do without supply lines following the setback at Holly Springs. But he practiced the concept by having Major General William T. Sherman march his divisions east from Jackson to Meridian, Mississippi, and back, all the while scrounging foodstuffs from surrounding farms and plantations.

Thus was born the doctrine of the infantry raid. For if a Union army did not need a supply base, then the Confederate cavalry raid against it became useless.

Why Ride When You Can Walk?

A Union army unshackled from its supply line had total freedom of movement, supplying itself at the expense of the populace along its line of march. This also robbed the Confederacy of supplies needed to feed its own armies. Rail lines were meaningless—tear them out. That robbed the Confederacy of any ability to shift troops from one theater to another. Confederate cavalry raiders could loot and burn all they wanted—their actions had no effect whatsoever against an army that did not need a supply depot to advance.

Cavalry raids never numbered more than 1,000 to 2,000 troopers, had to keep moving in order to avoid capture or destruction, and never had a lot of time to destroy much. They were always fleeting annoyances compared to an infantry raid. Any army with tens of thousands of soldiers could protect itself and have the manpower to tear up hundreds of miles of track, burn out thousands of farms, and free tens of thousands of slaves. Worse, by inflicting material suffering on the local people, a Union infantry raid proved that the Confederacy could not protect its citizens, which thus killed the political will to support the war.

The main agent of destruction was Sherman. Unable to protect his rail line from Atlanta to Chattanooga against the predations of Lieutenant General John B. Hood's forces, Sherman abandoned the rail line and Hood, marching a pair of Union armies to Savannah in late 1864. His "March to the Sea" consumed all forage in a sixty-mile-wide corridor that paralleled his line of march. Sherman would later advance his armies north through the Carolinas, meeting no serious resistance until fighting a final minor battle at Bentonville, North Carolina.

Grant also launched smaller infantry and cavalry raids that ripped through Alabama and Mississippi, wiping out the Confederacy's ability to move forces between the eastern and western theaters, as well as destroying secondary industrial sites. A similar raid led by Major General Philip Sheridan wiped out farm production in Virginia's Shenandoah Valley, thus depriving Lee's army of supplies.

All this time, Confederate cavalrymen raided as far west as Memphis. But it didn't make a difference. Anything they destroyed was replaced, and the raid removed Confederate cavalry from even challenging Union forces on the move.

As Grant kept Lee's army pinned in Virginia, his raiders slowly destroyed the ability of the Confederacy to supply and reinforce its diminishing armies. The infantry raid proved to be a decisive factor contributing to the end of the war. By April 1865, the Confederate States of America had nothing left to fuel its war effort, and in turn lost its bloody struggle for independence by default.

"Useless, Useless"

1865: Washington, D.C.

—

Paul A. Thomsen

By late 1864, victory was rapidly slipping from the grasp of the rebellious South. The Confederate States of America's economy was plummeting. Stockpiled resources were running low and there was no hope of gaining new supplies in the near future. Army desertion was on the rise. Home-front morale was ebbing. In the field, the Confederate Army continued to fight the enemy against overwhelming odds, but, with each passing day, their victories were becoming fewer and their limited pool of soldiers was, likewise, dwindling. For many, it seemed the conflict was rapidly devolving into a lost cause, but John Wilkes Booth refused to give up his southern supremacist dream. In fact, the Maryland-born actor-turned-spy mistakenly believed that his simple plan to capture or kill the president of the United States would single-handedly vanquish the enemies of the South.

Born in 1838 into a famous acting family, John Wilkes Booth grew to adulthood traveling the country, studying stagecraft, and perform-

ing to packed houses. As a spur to be and want the best, he was constantly followed by a seemingly endless supply of star-seekers, women,
and well-wishers. In the late 1850s, Booth, however, became deeply
enamored with southern proslavery ideals of the virtues of farm work
and African American paternalism. For example, when abolitionist
John Brown was sent to the gallows for attempting to incite a slave
uprising, Booth defied standing orders against the presence of civilian
bystanders at the execution. He "borrowed" a friend's military uniform and stood at attention before the gallows so he could later brag
that "I helped to hang John Brown, and while I live, I shall think with
joy upon the day. . . ."

Shortly after the Civil War began, Booth offered his professional
talents of guile, creativity, and subterfuge to the Confederate States of
America. Booth's formal profession also offered ample cover for otherwise highly visible missions in exotic ports throughout the North,
Canada, and the border states. In some port cities, he managed to
finesse the shipment of much-needed supplies past Union blockades
for his Confederate friends. In others, he made connections with
northern-living Confederate sympathizers, called Copperheads in the
Union press. In still others, he met with members of the Confederate
Secret Service (CSS), who were working to undermine the North's
ability to make war.

Still, a superspy Booth clearly was not. While his celebrity allowed
him freedom of movement, Booth's wartime comings and goings
frequently attracted the attention of status seekers, starstruck pass-
ersby, and a veritable cavalcade of female suitors. Likewise, Booth's
own adopted cover story as investor in the nascent nineteenth-century
Pennsylvania oil industry did little to dissuade attention. As a result,
by mid-war, the actor was little more than peripheral support to the
Confederacy.

In 1864, a confluence of events did, however, manage to bring the actor center stage in the fight to revive the South's declining fortune. While John Wilkes Booth was visited with associates along the Atlantic coast, a few of his friends in the CSS were in the process of reviewing President Lincoln's security detail. Once their preliminary analysis was completed, the CSS presented Confederate President Davis with a plan, which, they promised, would change the course of the war. Lincoln, the agents noted, rarely traveled with more than one guard along his favorite path between the White House and his summer residence, the Old Soldiers' Home near Washington. Only a few armed men, they claimed, would be needed to capture and convey the man to Richmond. Once safely behind Confederate lines, he would then be ransomed for a number of prisoners or, possibly, be used to force a final negotiated peace between the two regions.

While Jefferson Davis found the notion of abduction morally distasteful and promptly tabled the plan, surviving CSS documents and eyewitness accounts show Booth was rather taken with the clandestine design. First, Booth was in contact with several CSS cell leaders who contributed to the initial plan. Second, before the plot was tabled by Davis, Booth was frustrated with the war, his dwindling personal fortune, and his minor role in the conflict. Afterward Booth seized upon the idea with renewed vigor. Third, Booth was both a chance-taker and eager to see the South reclaim its flagging political and military dominance. On his own, the actor gathered intelligence, revised the plan, put a team together, and gambled that he could trap Lincoln on a small backwoods roadway at midday. Fourth, if Lincoln resisted capture or attempted to escape, Booth told his comrades that he was perfectly willing to shoot the president. Finally, although Lincoln had failed to appear on Booth's chosen day, the actor's coconspirators later confirmed that Booth continued to obsess over the plan for the next several months.

In early 1865, as the southern cause grew more desperate and the

Confederacy fell to pieces before his eyes, Booth came to see the plan as more than a tactical exercise. In his illogical mind, the plot became *the* solution to the South's salvation. Like the capture of a king in chess, Booth's capture of the president would instantly grant victory to the Confederacy. With this idea in mind, around April, Booth once again pulled together a plan and doled out orders to his circle of southern sympathizers. Before they could move from the discussion stage to planning and action, however, Booth received news that Richmond had been burned to the ground, that Jefferson Davis was in flight and that on April 9, 1865, General Robert E. Lee's Confederate Army surrendered. Hence Booth realized there was no longer a Confederacy to which his conspirators could take Lincoln for ransoming.

With the spy at this point gripped in a deep depression, the now-misshapen plot should have ended there, but a random occurrence soon presented John Wilkes Booth with another chance. On April 12, Booth happened upon the White House grounds just as Abraham Lincoln was delivering an impromptu speech about his plans for African American suffrage. According to eyewitnesses, Booth listened for a moment to the president's words, then, growing noticeably angry, reached for his breast pocket, but suddenly stopped himself, remembering that he had left his Derringer at the Surratt Boarding House. Booth then swore an oath to his associates, saying, "That means nigger citizenship. . . . Now, by God, I will put him through." He just needed to figure out where and when the plan would be set in motion.

On the morning of April 14, Booth learned from a worker at Ford's Theatre that the president would be attending that night's performance of *Our American Cousin*.

The plan was set in motion. Once more, he gathered together a circle of coconspirators, briefed them on his intent to kill Lincoln that night, and doled out assignments for the others to simultaneously kill Vice President Andrew Johnson and Secretary of State William Seward. The new iteration of the plan, he said, would paralyze the northern government. It would allow time for word to leak out about his perceived glorious deed. It would bring the now-scattering Confederate Army back together. Above all, it would, he thought, achieve a final southern victory over the Union.

John Wilkes Booth was persistent and the plan had the virtue of being novel, but the actor-turned-assassin was hopelessly delusional and surrounded by incompetents. While Booth walked unmolested into the president's box at Ford's Theatre that night and put a round metal ball through Abraham Lincoln's skull, Lewis Payne forced his way into William Seward's house and found the secretary of state bandaged and lying in bed, trying to recover from a recent carriage accident. Although Payne found his target to be bedridden, the would-be assassin was unable to land more than a few superficial cuts against the now alert and defensive Seward. Not thinking to pull back the linen to verify that his knife's many cuts and thrusts had mortally wounded Seward, Payne reportedly considered the bloody mass of sheets and the now motionless Seward having passed out beneath them sufficient testament that he had assassinated the president's right-hand man and fled the scene of the crime . . . with Seward still very much alive. The other coconspirators fared little better, losing their nerve and fleeing into the night. Although the actor had succeeded in his task, Booth's dreams of a swift decapitation strike and a foundering northern government had failed to materialize.

Yet the actor's analysis had been, in part, correct. Booth did finally kill Lincoln and the president's demise did paralyze the Federal government for a few minutes, but the benefits of his achieved plan didn't measure up to Booth's expectations. After riding on a broken ankle and hiding out for several days in woodland and swamps, Booth discovered the initial signs that he had grossly miscalculated the effects of the plan on the South. Instead of rising to fight again, his noble Confederate soldiers considered the murder to have been a cowardly act and went home. Instead of reigniting southern pride, the citizenry very quickly backed away from the spectacle in mixed sorrow for the nation and fear of what the North might do to them in acts of reprisal. As a result, instead of being seen as a noble hero, Booth had become the cowardly, cold-blooded murderer of an honorable man who had now given the last full measure of his devotion to the ideological conflict.

Booth's miscalculated actions also robbed the South of her primary supporter for an easy reconciliation, Abraham Lincoln. Where the president had acted generously on behalf of the defeated southern populace (offering pardons for Confederates as early as 1863 and reinforcing his general's light-handed treatment of captured men), the same could not be said for the administration officials and military personnel Lincoln had long kept in check. For example, Secretary of War Stanton was merciless in his pursuit and prosecution of the Booth conspirators. After the murder, Stanton closed off the city, detained hundreds of civilians, and sent out roving military units with orders to take any steps necessary to capture those involved. When most of Booth's accomplices and associates were arrested, Stanton saw that they were given speedy military trials, brutal sentences, and the swiftest executions he could devise. Of the several individuals directly involved in Booth's plots, only John Surratt, a Booth confidant who had helped facilitate past attempts, and who was an active agent of the Confederate Secret Service and had been traveling at the time of the assassination, was spared the gallows.

Likewise, the Radical Republicans, once held in check by Lincoln's masterful manipulation, were now free to systematically dismantle the South that Booth had defended. First, they funded the Union's military occupation of the South. Second, they freed the slaves. Third, they enfranchised the former slaves as full citizens. Fourth, they provided assistance to the new citizens in the forms of programs aimed at teaching the individuals how to read and write, how to review land contracts, and how to negotiate business. Fifth, they assisted in efforts to undermine the southern planter aristocracy, punish former Confederate officials, and crush any glimmer of southern dissension of northern rule. Finally, the Radicals supported the raising of several former slaves to governmental offices.

To add further insult to injury, Andrew Johnson, a fellow native son of the South and by the assassination now president, further despoiled Booth's utopian vision of a South governed by southern hands. In lieu of prison time, the new president publicly shamed the Confederate veterans, mandating that southerners who had been a part of the rebellion petition him for clemency and swear loyalty oaths. Likewise, his resentment of the rich both terrified the southern land gentry and promoted the previously minuscule influence of middle-class Caucasians to widespread action across the South. In fact, it would take the work of several Ku Klux Klan generations and a new breed of plantation owners to recapture even a small vestige of Booth's southern cause, the civil oppression of African Americans.

On April 26, 1865, John Wilkes Booth was cornered in a Virginia barn by Union forces. Unwilling to surrender, the soldiers set fire to the barn to force the fugitive into their hands. Booth rose to flee and was shot in the back by a Union soldier. With Booth's fourth cervical vertebrae now shattered, the assassin fell, paralyzed, through the barn doors and hit the ground.

John Wilkes Booth was pulled away from the now raging fire to lie for a handful of hours on a nearby porch, struggling to breathe and dipping in and out of consciousness. In his final moments, he dictated a message to his mother, saying, "Tell my mother I died for my country; I did what I thought best." Finally, he asked one of the soldiers to raise his hands to his face. As if acknowledging the utter folly of his machinations, Booth was reported to have spoken the words, "Useless. Useless," and then died.

In his wake, John Wilkes Booth left behind a fulfilled plan and a futile dream. The bitter results of his miscalculations the South and the American nation would have to endure.

Four Great Mistakes
and Their Matrices

1861–1865: Thoughts on the American Civil War

Dennis Showalter

Determining and analyzing the four greatest mistakes of the American Civil War involves confronting a compound plethora of choices—especially for an amateur on the subject whose academic focus is on the other side of the Atlantic. As John Keegan asserts in his recent *The American Civil War: A Military History*, the conflict may have been necessary, but was not unavoidable. It erupted like a series of wildfires, in an environment where neither combatant had made anything like consequent preparations, across a country whose founding principles emphasized peace and fraternity.

That meant the Civil War would be in every sense a war of improvisations. Improvisations cost blood and resources. Their consequences were further exacerbated by a geography offering no decisive objectives to either side. Armies were the only targets promising decision—and that in turn structured the Civil War as a series of battles, still among the fiercest ever waged.

It is correspondingly reasonable, then, to seek the Civil War's decisive mistakes in its military aspects. Those mistakes were in turn structured by the ad hoc nature of the combatants. Both Union and Confederate armies had high learning curves—but they started at near zero in every aspect of effectiveness but enthusiasm. Leadership at all levels on both sides, retrospective mythmaking to the contrary, was characterized more by character and personality than talent or experience. The result was improvisation compounded: a continuing emphasis on solving immediate problems, with tomorrow expected to take care of itself.

The mistakes occasioned by this synergy of factors challenge enumeration and classification. They have, however, a common defining feature. They were not intentional. Military history—academic, professional, and popular—is the home of hindsight. In retrospect the mistakes of armies and generals are so pitilessly highlighted that it is easy to overlook the fact that in war, no one shows up to lose. The military mistakes of the Civil War in particular seemed like good ideas at the time—or at least the most promising alternatives. To support that position this essay offers a case study from each of the recognized levels of war making: policy, strategy, operations, and tactics.

At the policy level, the mistake with the most significant consequences involved Confederate President Jefferson Davis sustaining Braxton Bragg in command of the Army of Tennessee long after his sell-by date. That issue is by no means closed. Among the Civil War's major combatants (a category that excludes the trans-Mississippi), the Army of Tennessee suffered the most from inadequate training, inadequate command from regiment to corps, and logistical insufficiency. Its hinterland was far less developed than the midwestern states supporting its immediate Union rivals. In staff terms Bragg can legitimately be described as doing everything possible to improve discipline and administration. As a field commander he arguably emerges as no worse, and marginally better than the generals he faced.

Without denying the negative effects of his dyspeptic, contentious personality and his ability to nurse grudges to the point of official misrepresentation of facts, Bragg's efforts to mold at least a semimodern army from the backcountry volunteers and levies he commanded were more commendable and more successful than generally conceded at the time or understood later.

THE NEGATIVE ELEMENT OF THAT PROCESS INVOLVED THE INCREASING, systematic alienation of the Army of Tennessee's senior command structure. These men too were under a generally overlooked set of pressures. As a group they embodied the Peter Principle: struggling to cope with responsibilities at the upper limits of their existing abilities. As a rule they managed. But learning to command a corps or a division on the job, without the more developed supporting structures of the eastern theater, was the kind of strain that helps explain such compensating behaviors as alcohol abuse—or hypersensitivity. For a toxic mixture of personal and professional reasons, a reciprocal synergy emerged: from disliking Bragg and questioning his abilities to loathing him and denying his abilities. The pattern is hardly unusual in modern war. The Army of Tennessee could not afford it. Winning even marginal victories in Civil War battles involved minimizing the fog of war and friction of battle. Institutionally the Army of Tennessee was a case study in both.

There is where Davis comes in. His reasons for sustaining Bragg and his reasons for not making convincing examples, if not a clean sweep, among the dissenters were essentially the same: finding replacements likely to do any better. It was that problem, rather than indecisiveness or misguided loyalty to friends, that led the Confederate president to carry water on both shoulders from the summer of 1862 until the compound disasters in front of Chattanooga in the summer of 1863 caused him to act. In a typical Civil War improvisation, Davis appointed—actually reappointed—someone he neither liked nor trusted, Joseph E. Johnston, to a command whose fortunes he was unable to reverse.

From the beginning this was a problem with no good solution. The Army of Tennessee's situation demanded, if not a band of brothers, then at least a corps of comrades, able to cooperate to maximize opportunities against an increasingly powerful adversary. By the time Davis acted, no outsider, not even Lee himself, was likely to restore equilibrium, let alone harmony. The least bad alternative probably involved replacing Bragg with the steadiest pair of hands available from within the army, accepting the risks, and hoping for the best. Hope can in fact be a policy. It is seldom a winning one. The Confederacy could not afford to wait, like Charles Dickens's Mr. Micawber, for something to turn up.

A DEFINING EXAMPLE OF ERROR AT THE STRATEGIC LEVEL INVOLVES Abraham Lincoln's failure to support George McClellan's campaign against Richmond in 1862. Ethan Rafuse has recently and perceptively challenged conventional wisdom by arguing that McClellan designed the Army of the Potomac to implement his concept of limiting the war in space and time by winning a victory so overwhelming that no illusions of southern independence could survive. Tactical and technological factors combined with geography to make a Napoleonic-style "overland campaign" in northern Virginia a task as unprofitable as it was daunting. Two years later, U. S. Grant hammered the Army of the Potomac to near pulp before implementing a variant of McClellan's proposed approach.

McClellan argued for using Virginia's rivers to support a set piece: a campaign of sieges and positions built around Union sea power, engineering skill, and artillery superiority. Properly implemented, it would not only capture Richmond but also cripple the field forces defending it. Objections jump out of the evidence—especially McClellan's often demonstrated shortcomings as a battle captain. Would an additional corps, would wholehearted support from an administration that in fact saw an overland line as the shortest distance between decisive points, have mattered? It requires no mastery of counterfactuals to make a case that, even without the president's growing reluctance to leave Washington uncovered, even this measured eighteenth-century-style operation would have exceeded McClellan's capacity to execute. Perhaps. But McClellan's strategy reflected the North's culture of efficiency, discipline, and management: a businesslike approach to war. It played to Union rather than Confederate strengths: top-down leadership and a deductive approach as opposed to inductive inspiration. Nor was the opposing force as yet the Army of Northern Virginia in anything but name. Lee was not Marse Robert, but then sometimes called Granny Lee and the King of Spades. Lee and Jackson had not yet honed the six-month partnership that made them icons of maneuver war. Even a poorly swung hammer can drive a nail—if the hammer is heavy enough.

As much to the point, the Army of the Potomac was not yet "imprinted" with the often remarked sense of inferiority to "our masters the rebels," as author Michael Adams described the situation.

Even if a bulked-up methodical campaign did not capture Richmond, mounted against a stronger force Lee's counterattacks might well have mauled the Army of Northern Virginia badly enough to imprint it in reverse: giving it a respect for the Yankees strong enough to avert the formation of the near insouciant confidence that informed it until almost the end of the war.

Lincoln's concern for Washington's security may have been exaggerated. It was not imaginary. Neither was his growing concern for McClellan's wider ambitions unjustified. Nor, finally, does it denigrate Lincoln's eventual development as a strategic thinker and a judge of generals to describe both as works in progress in the spring of 1862. Nevertheless, it can be reasonably suggested that Lincoln's refusal to back McClellan's strategic plan at policy levels, combined with his growing belief that McClellan should fight precisely the kind of battle he was least able to fight, led to a strategic mistake no less significant because it seemed a good idea at the time.

At the Civil War's operational level a clear winner in the mistakes sweepstakes is the Franklin/Nashville campaign of 1864. Usually considered from tactical perspectives (the blindfold slaughterhouse at Franklin, the final destruction of the Army of Tennessee at Nashville) or command contexts (the decisions of John Bell Hood and the denigration and ultimate vindication of George Thomas), Franklin/Nashville also invites discussion in terms of a mistaken application of operational art.

To begin with, it must be understood that "operational art" is not even a neologism when applied to the Civil War. Even in Prussia, often considered the concept's home, "operations" was barely emerging at midcentury in its now understood form as a bridge—or an O-ring—between strategy and tactics. As developed by Hood, Franklin/Nashville became a strategic plan. But a synergy of calculable, if not predictable, factors forced it downward to the operational level of theater war under circumstances where the Confederacy's last chance was no chance at all.

The Atlanta campaign of 1864 was a study in learning curves. W. T. Sherman defeated Joe Johnston at his own game, consistently outmaneuvering him tactically until Johnston found himself in front of Atlanta with no maneuvering room left. His replacement John Bell Hood sought to break Sherman's grip on the city by a series of desperate attacks against superior numbers, usually with the advantage of field entrenchments. Their outcomes were predictable. Unable to defend the vital rail and industrial center, Hood abandoned it.

Hood—and Davis—understood that the Army of Tennessee, lacking the strength to respond directly to Sherman's movements, must do something to recapture the initiative. That "something" began tactically, as a proposed army-scale raid against Sherman's communications, drawing Sherman in pursuit. It rapidly metastasized, acquiring a strategic dimension by becoming a full-blown invasion of Union-occupied Tennessee. The offensive's objective was relieving the hard-pressed Army of Northern Virginia by drawing troops from Grant's front.

Hood lacked neither skill nor intelligence. Contrary to the belief of some even today, he was not consistently addled by painkillers for the arm lost at Gettysburg and the leg at Chickamauga. Nor was he contemptuous of the Army of Tennessee's fighting power compared to its Virginia counterpart. He knew he was betting a long shot depending on shock, speed, and surprise. But operational surprise was lost when Sherman, instead of pursuing, divided his own ample army and sent half—the half he considered dispensable—north as a blocking force. Speed was lost operationally because the distances involved were too great for a poorly supplied foot-marching army to outpace a well-fed and clothed one able to make use of railroads. That left shock. And Hood's equation of shock with speed meant that at Franklin he left his artillery behind his infantry, seeking to compensate tactically for an operational dilemma.

The butchery resulting from pitting spirit against spirit plus fire-power plus entrenchments in front of Franklin left Hood out on a limb. Able to lunge forward to Nashville, he could neither advance nor retreat from there—only construct entrenchments his army was too weak to hold once Thomas prepared the massive (might one say

"McClellanesque"?) counterstroke that shattered the Army of Tennessee beyond reconstruction and left Lee strategically isolated.

Operational art cannot exist in a vacuum. It either meshes with strategy or devolves to tactics. The German experience in two world wars indicates the likely outcome of the latter process. The Army of Tennessee was like short money in a table-stakes poker game—a wasted asset unless played. But John Bell Hood fatally overbet his hand.

The Civil War's defining tactical-level mistake again fell on the Confederate side. It was Lee's attack on the third day of Gettysburg. That event has been so thoroughly dissected there is no need to set its physical stage—or, indeed, to spend much time exploring Lee's motives. The conclusion that the attack was a high but acceptable risk in context is reasonable. Neither in the Army of Northern Virginia nor in the Confederacy as a whole was confidence in Lee significantly diminished in its aftermath. When myth is stripped away and memory factored in, Pickett's Charge was, in Carol Reardon's words, "after all, simply an infantry assault that failed."

But was it? Two factors combine to justify defining the attack of July 3 as a crucial tactical mistake with wide-reaching consequences. First, it was a charge to nowhere. A breakthrough along Cemetery Ridge was by itself unlikely to produce a decisive victory. Meade still had the fresh VI Corps in reserve. Lee had nothing behind Longstreet's force to develop a sector victory, much less turn it into a rout. In that context the third day at Gettysburg invites interpretation as a precursor of Franklin.

More significant, Lee was staking moral as well as physical assets on July 3. After two years of war, the focal point of the Confederacy had become the Army of Northern Virginia—for the North, arguably even more than the South. Its comprehensively reported mastery over its immediate opponent generated a mystique and an aura that could not be duplicated. As the survivors of Pickett's Charge fell back to shouts of "Fredericksburg! Fredericksburg!" the casualties they left behind marked the beginning of an end of the Army of the Potomac's collective inferiority complex. The shortcomings remained, and would be bloodily highlighted throughout 1864. But after the first searing fights in the Wilderness, when Grant turned south toward Spotsylvania instead of taking the road to Washington, the decision was cheered by men who knew they would pay its price. Pickett's Charge had sown the seeds of belief that the Rebs after all could be beaten in a stand-up fight—whatever they might believe or say.

Moral factors in war are easily overestimated: as the song says, "a cannonball don't pay no mind." But neither can they be underestimated. The mistakes discussed above were not only material but psychological. They reflected undeveloped understanding of the new nature of war in the mid–nineteenth century, which in turn reflected the Civil War's improvised nature. And in a long war to the knife, a war defined by its battles, they had a disproportionate impact.

BOOKS BY
BILL FAWCETT

HOW TO LOSE WWII
Bad Mistakes of the Good War
ISBN 978-0-06-180731-2 (paperback)

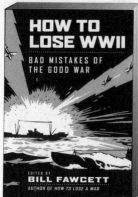

Going back to the subject of Fawcett's bestselling collection, *How to Lose a Battle, How to Lose WWII* is an engrossing and fact-filled collection that sheds light on the biggest, and dumbest, screw ups of the Great War.

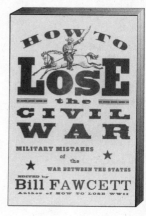

HOW TO LOSE THE CIVIL WAR
Military Mistakes of the War Between the States
ISBN 978-0-06-180727-5 (paperback)

Written in a tongue-in-cheek style, *How to Lose the Civil War* chronicles the thrilling history of the conflict between the Union and the Confederacy, with its high stakes, colorful characters, and the many disastrous decisions made by both sides.

HOW TO LOSE A WAR
More Foolish Plans and Great Military Blunders
ISBN 978-0-06-135844-9 (paperback)

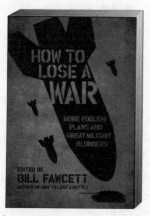

From the ancient Crusades to the modern age of chemical warfare, history is littered with horribly bad military ideas, and each military defeat is fascinating to dissect.

HOW TO LOSE A BATTLE
Foolish Plans and Great Military Blunders
ISBN 978-0-06-076024-3 (paperback)

Whether a result of lack of planning, miscalculation, a leader's ego, or spy infiltration, this compendium chronicles the worst military defeats and looks at what caused each battlefield blunder.

IT LOOKED GOOD ON PAPER
Bizarre Inventions, Design Disasters & Engineering Follies
ISBN 978-0-06-135843-2 (paperback)

This book is a collection of flawed plans, half-baked ideas, and downright ridiculous machines that, with the best and most optimistic intentions, men have constructed throughout history.

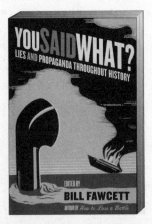

YOU SAID WHAT?
Lies and Propaganda Throughout History
ISBN 978-0-06-113050-2 (paperback)

From the dawn of man to the War on Terror, Fawcett chronicles the vast history of frauds, deceptions, propaganda, and trickery from governments, corporations, historians, and everyone in between.